A Lifestyle Worth Living...

A Powerful How To Guide for a Happy, Healthy and Purposeful Life

By C.A. Human

GenerationAwareness.org

Please be advised for legality purposes nothing within this book should be viewed as a substitute for pertinent medical care. Check with a trusted physician for medical clearance before beginning any exercise program including the one is this book.

First published by Dog Ear Publishing
4010 W. 86th Street, Ste H
Indianapolis, IN 46268
www.dogearpublishing.net

ISBN: 978-160844-163-1

This book is printed on acid-free paper.

Printed in the United States of America
1 60844 163 6

Special Thanks

Cover Design and Logo by E. I.

David Michael Photography @ www.dmichael.biz

Chris & Michael Goff Owners of Anytime Fitness Bonita Springs Florida

Cindy Leleux "Lu Lu" Yoga Instructor @ www.liveforyoga.com

To schedule special workshops, host events, book signings, corporate events & more please contact us at info@generationawareness.org with your requests.

Why did I write this book?

Have you ever been stressed out about money, your health, your weight, your relationships or your job? Have you ever just been fed up with your life and how it's **NOT** turning out the way you thought it would? I'm with you, I understand completely and I've been there myself!

Before you move on to the next book on the shelf or surf to the next website **READ THIS PAGE.** Imagine what it would be like if you could live a happier, healthier more care free life. Picture yourself waking up each morning with no stress or anxiety about anything but just excitement and enthusiasm for the day ahead of you.

This could truly be you!

As you read this book and absorb this information and follow the easy steps along the way you will feel a sense of calmness, joy and empowerment.

The initial reason that I wrote this book was to help my clients and students take action to get better results in their daily lives. Now I'd like to help you experience this unique formula that will catapult you into a higher, healthier and more purposeful state of consciousness.

Who this book is written for

As you read each word in this book you will quickly realize that this book was made for you! The truth is that it doesn't matter if you are a baby boomer, a teenager, a son or daughter, mother or father, grandparent, uncle or aunt, rich or poor. We all share these common problems and can benefit from the solutions that this book offers.

This book crosses all generations, has no nationality, race, culture or any other stigmatisms that come with most books. This book was written to help everyone understand the basic principles of building a better way of life. Imagine having an exclusive reference guide to keep you centered and grounded, that's what this book will become for you.

How to use this book

Have you ever read a book that really inspired you but after time the words and thoughts slowly faded away and you fell back into the same old rut in your life?

Although many self help books have wonderful words of wisdom that flow from the pages, after a few days, weeks and months we lose direction and insight and the inspiration quickly fades away.

For all of these reasons I have designed this book as an exclusive interactive book/workbook. When you purchase this book online or offline, you will be granted a "Free Trial Membership" to www.GenerationAwareness.Org which is the social network that gives you the option to create a profile to answer and journal all of the exercises within the book.

So if you want to go solo and complete the book yourself or use the website or create your own group at home, this will give you the capability to do so. This social network will also give you the ability to share as much or as little of your answers, comments, journaling, discussions and anything else that involves your experience with the book and your life that you wish.

This book and www.GenerationAwareness.Org was not only designed to help you just talk and interact with people but more so for you to share your answers to some of life's important questions with generations of the future and the past. Imagine the day that your grandchildren or someone else's child finds your information that you've put out there for the world to see which inspires them to take action and live a better life. This is evolution at its best! The lessons in this book will provide such valuable information and allow you to take a better look at your life today. The answers you provide, journaling that you document and lessons that you share, will help not just you but everyone that you share it with.

Dedications & Acknowledgments

I would like to dedicate this book to my beautiful wife, my wonderful children, my momason, papason and all of my brothers, sisters and the many friends and family that have helped me become who I am at this moment.

I feel that it is absolutely important to acknowledge all of those who have been inspirational to my purpose and journey in life today. These are the masters and mentors of the world.

Thank you

Albert Einstein, Carl Jung, William James, Andrew Carnegie, Napoleon Hill, Dr. Steven Hawkings, Earl Nightingale, Dr. Emmet Fox, Dali Lama, Mahatma Gandhi, James Redfield, Dr. Wayne Dyer, Deepka Chopra, Albert Clayton Gaulden, Dr. T. Colin Campbell, Dr. Thomas Campbell II

Eckert Tolle, Dr. Stephen Covey, Zig Ziglar, Bob Proctor, Jim Rohn, Oprah Winfrey, Brian Tracy, Anthony Robbins, Kenneth Blanchard, Donald Walsch, Les Brown, Ram Dass, Jeff Primack and anyone else I may have missed.

Most importantly, all of my gratitude to my Creator and His sons and daughters that have and continue to walk the path of truth towards true enlightenment and freedom, personally and collectively.

IF I COULD CHANGE THE WORLD

If I could change the world, what would I do?

If I could make a difference in not just one life,
but two.

If I could help others slow their pace.

If I could take the frown from just a few peoples face.

If I could help people see the true beauty and
meaning of their lives.

If I could teach them how to eliminate stress in life
and give them hope and encouragement in stride.

If I could do these wonderful things for humankind
then let it first be in the example of mine.

C.A. Human

Contents

MIND

Chapter 1   KNOWLEDGE 1

Chapter 2   ATTITUDE *"A starting point to awareness"*........8

Chapter 3   SEEING THE BIG PICTURE 15

Chapter 4   LEARNING A HIGHER AWARENESS.................21

Chapter 5   THE MASTER OF EMOTIONS.........................33

BODY

Chapter 6   WE ARE CREATORS..48

SUNSHINE

Chapter 7   AIR...54

Chapter 8   WATER 61

Chapter 9   NUTRITION 66

Chapter 10   EXERCISE..111

Chapter 11   FLEXIBILITY 208

Chapter 12   RECOVERY 229

Chapter 13   TOUCH 232

Chapter 14   BELONGING 237

Chapter 15   BALANCE 241

SOUL

Chapter 16   **SPIRITUAL ENERGY** **243**

Chapter 17   **TAKING THE VOO DOO OUT OF MEDITATION** **251**

Final Chapter   **HARMONY IN LIFE** **277**

"The most important part of your life!"

Dear Friend,

Hi, my name is C.A. Human and I am the author of this book. I would like to open with the following knowledge to all: I am not, nor do I claim to be, a guru, swami, scientist, prophet, activist or anything of that description. I am just a young man that loves to think, help, and share with others my take on things. In this book I would like to share with you my personal journey on understanding and living a healthy lifestyle. Although by trade I am a full time Emergency Professional, for most of my adult life I have been a Lifestyle Trainer and Coach. I enjoy educating and helping others become better mentally, physically and spiritually in their daily lives. With this passion, I have trained professionals of all scopes and in all calibers of life which in return has intrigued and allowed me several years of studying, researching and reinterpreting many of the things that you are about to read. I would like to make it clear that it is not my intention to convince anyone that what I say is the only way to live healthy; but rather, to share with you some interesting perspectives that may change your perception to this journey we know as life and our processes thereof. It has always been my objective to find simplicity from deep-rooted teachings and turn them into common sense points of view. I will not impress or mystify you with fancy words or sayings, however, I will be allowing you to step into my shoes for a while so that hopefully I can teach you some wonderful concepts that I have created for myself and others that allow many to live an extremely happy and healthy lifestyle. I will teach you my ideas of a lifestyle free of much worry, stress and anxiety, a lifestyle of understanding and control of your mental health. I will also educate you as to the misconceptions of good physical health in our world today and provide you with a straight path to good physical health. I will also provide you with several tools that will give you the power to find happiness in the life that you live today.

The following information in this book is what I believe to be some of the most important lessons in the existence of humankind. With this in mind, please take time to read this book more than once, as a matter of fact, I challenge you to read it several times. Read the chapters one at a time and complete the exercises in order. After you've completed each chapter, TAKE TIME TO STOP! Find a quiet place to ponder the message or lesson and how you relate to it. Take notes of your thoughts. Record your thoughts and evaluate your life with these concepts. Mold your life around these valuable lessons in this book and make it a conscious part of your everyday life. Educate others as to the thoughts and experiences that you have gained along the way. Strike up conversation among friends and family and listen with sincere interest at others views and allow your beliefs to become ingrained into your life through your intentions and the actions that inspire you. If just a few sections of this book become a part of you, like it has with many, then I guarantee you will be well on your way to living the most rewarding life you could ever possibly imagine.

Sincerely,

C.A. Human

MIND
Chapter 1

Knowledge

All human beings, in all walks of life, continue in all cases to do one thing. Learn! Whether learning to walk for the first time, learning to ride a bike or learning to read our first book. This is the greatest power of humankind, the <u>complete ability to grow in knowledge</u>. Although some choose to learn much less than others, there are great exceptions like you! Like most others you may be at a standstill or a cross road in your life; looking to better yourself in some fashion and for that I commend and congratulate you. You are an A+ student of life. You are one of the few that has actually become disciplined and determined enough to educate yourself for your own personal growth in your life. That is why I give you an A+ in *willingness*.

However we decide to grade ourselves in life, whether A+ or D-students, one thing is for sure; we are all students of life. Why? Because everything we do in our lives keeps us constantly learning day in and day out.

Within this learning process there are two things that all your learning experiences are based on: GOOD and BAD! Your likes your dislikes, what you fear, what you love and or enjoy. What gives you pleasure or pain? From each of these experiences, either joyous or painful, an opportunity to learn ALWAYS ARRIVES.

During my own intense study in the improvement of my life, I have stumbled upon one of the most fascinating understandings of human life. Our lives are based on three factors within every second of our existence. In some cultures this is called the yin, the yang and the chi. Yin are those things in life that hurt, disappoint, discourage, and create anger, frustration, worry or any other negative thought or action for one's self or towards another. Yang is the opposite; joy, happiness, goodness, relief, comfort, or any other positive thought or action for one's self or towards another. Chi is defined as circulating life force energy. In Chinese philosophy, it is thought to be inherent of all things; the balance of negative and positive that perpetuate life and all that exist. Simply put, the positive and negative experiences are what create a balance and perfect the scale of life. Now I understand that most would consider a self-help book to tell you that everything must be positive, positive, positive. However I will share with you a thought, if everything was perfect in this world and everyone was just fine and dandy then what in the world would we compare ourselves too? Therefore, it is through knowledge and understanding that will allow us to release ourselves from the concept that any negative experience is bad and realize it's just the balancing act in the learning experience of a better more rewarding life.

THOUGHT + ACTION = EXPERIENCE
The equation above is really the easiest way to understand the way that we live our lives. With each thought that is registered in our minds it is <u>our awareness</u> of each thought and the translation that creates action.
(+ or -) THOUGHT + AWARENESS + ACTION = LEARNING EXPERIENCE
As the old saying goes, **<u>life is what you make it.</u>** Whether complex or simple, stressful or carefree, beautiful with every living breath or as miserable with every dying breath. However you're living your life at this moment, you must understand and believe that there is a way towards improving your life to live happily, healthy in life, day by day throughout this human experience.

Having a fulfilling and happy life has nothing to do with fate, luck or chance, but more importantly with understanding and living with the common laws of nature. One of the most basic laws of nature is the law of equality and balance. As some may see it, The Rule of Cause and Effect! For every action there is a reaction! This rule of life or nature is one that's been taught over and over again by many great people that have lived on this earth. From Albert Einstein's theory of relativity, to Jesus Christ's lesson of doing to others as you would have them do unto you. So to make it as simple as possible, it goes like this: for every thought that you take action to, there is an equal or greater reaction that will inevitably come back to you. *What comes around goes around!* So it is extremely important to always remember that our rewards and accomplishments in life always match our work and disciplines in life, whether for others or ourselves. It is our job to serve not just others, but first and most importantly our selves. This is the most confusing part of life for most to understand. In saying this, a common question many times will arise as to why me, before anyone else. Isn't that a selfish way to live?

With that question in mind let me ask you if you've heard the saying that "<u>you have to truly love yourself before you can love anyone</u>

else". This is the same lesson applied. The lesson is that by taking care of yourself in all aspects of life: emotionally, mentally, and, believe it or not, physically, you will be able to build a life of integrity, truth and honesty. This is the foundation that most people don't realize you should build your life around. This will give you such a radiance of light and energy in the person that you become, that you will be a real and truthful example of the person that everyone strives to be. Example is the key word; you will be pure enlightenment to everyone that crosses your path. Within this person that you will become, you will see that being true to yourself is all about being true and honest with everyone that you come into contact with. Now to get to the truth that matters, the type of truth I want to discuss is the most valuable of the word.

I'm sure you're asking: "What do you mean by this?" Inner truth is best described as taking on the responsibility of everything we are made of. Our most valuable tool that links us between spirit and body is our mind. With these, we develop unique abilities and talents for many things. The other tool that we have to work with is time, better known as our lifetime. Both, our minds and time are our most valuable possessions in this human experience on earth. How we invest our time into our minds and body determines the value of our life. The only real wealth we have in life is really determined by our everlasting commitment to this truth in ourselves.

Everything that we are and will become in life is based on your consistent ability to take advantage of every moment in life, to be true to our full potential and take every opportunity to grow your mind in every aspect of your life. By making the commitment to do this, you will learn to master your spiritual, mental and physical realm.

Make the effort to follow these three steps:

1st Educate yourself every day to be of better service
 whether in business, family or your own personal self.
            (Expand your mind in every aspect.)

2nd Learn and be aware of how you can be of service
 to everyone you meet.
            (Always find ways to give to others.)

3rd See your life as a treasure map: understand the value of the **X** and the potential that there is in using this comparison to life. Know that the real joy of life is not just the treasure where X marks the spot, but the journey and adventure of finding and sharing the lessons or treasures of life. **Remember that life is not about how much you have or know, but about what you become in striving to be the best you can be. Vision, belief, positive thought and imagination, breeds a higher purpose**!

Ask yourself how you can improve your life today.

Life does not need to be complicated or stressful. If you're worried about something in your life you're looking at it from the wrong end or perspective. You should be looking for ways to improve your life. Again, remember that every negative thought or action by rule of nature triggers a negative consequence. The same principle is even more so true with positive thoughts or actions triggering an abundance of growth and joy in our lives. Knowing and living this truth gives you a massive advantage in life: honesty and truth. Be true to you. Be accountable for what we have; our minds, our abilities and time to grow and improve our lives; nothing more, nothing less. It's our choice what we decide to do with our lives, know one else's. Invest in your mind's intelligence and receive an abundance of wealth in your everyday life. Making the best of our minds will give us the best opportunities. Take the time to do what you need to do, what you feel you should do to improve your learning skills in life.

Truly happy people in life understand the law of cause and effect. Don't sell yourself short by not using your time talent or abilities. Remember, when we fail to give the best of ourselves, we're hurting no one but ourselves.

This Life plan that you are embarking on through the organization of this book is the structure that I believe will help you on this challenge or journey that we call life. Your life, whether young or old, is by your own design, no one else. You are at this point in your life because of the choices and decisions that you have made. You are here today reading this book, this chapter, this page, **this word**, because of your choice, your attitude, your awareness, your commitments, your beliefs, your decisions and most importantly, the action that you have or have not taken in response to all of the individual thoughts of your mind, intentions that you set, and intuitive awareness that you have followed either blindly or consciously. This is your life, right here, right now.

Answer these questions to yourself:

<u>Do you take responsibility for where you are at in your life today?</u>

<u>In what areas of life do you want to improve? Relationships, family, work, finances, inner self, health, maybe all of these! Explain.</u>

<u>How do you feel about yourself as a person, HONESTLY?</u>

What do you love about you? Why?

What do you dislike? Why?

Do you want to change or improve your life? How?

I hope with these questions asked, you can see a little clearer picture of your life today. My objective with these questions is to give you a greater realization of what you feel you need to improve in your life.

In the following chapters, I will always provide you with questions and definitions that I'll ask you to put in your own words. Remember again that writing/recording/logging all of your thoughts and answering the questions throughout the book will help you not only develop and improve your lifestyle, but is one of the key principles of this program which will give you the opportunity to review your thoughts and grow as a person. (Please, truly make the effort to complete all of the exercises in the book, from beginning to end.)

The true power of life

In conclusion of this chapter, I leave you with these common sense thoughts that when completely understood and truly comprehended should make you the happiest person on the face of the planet.

Understanding the law of nature, where bad, evil, negative, hurtful thoughts are conjured. Actions of pain, destruction, torment and pure hate are unleashed. This downward cycle of life can only be broken by one thing – **Conscious Awareness!**

Whether in the form of selfless giving, true compassion, understanding and most importantly, forgiveness, Conscious Awareness is the most powerful most positive gift ever given to mankind and perpetuates everything in our existence as a species. This higher consciousness that I'm referring to is the balance or the chi to us as human beings. This experience allows us to be in alignment with our higher self; the spiritual and eternal being that lives forever in which everything lives or exists in all realms of our life and spiritual journey. The purest interpretation of this power is the word **LOVE**. Please don't confuse this interpretation of the word with the stereotype of hippies running around naked in a field somewhere but rather a higher frequency of energy that resonates from our spiritual intellect into our human mind and experiences.

Therefore, know your self-worth. Love everyone and everything, beginning with you. Know that you have the power not just to change your life, but all of mankind. Know that with positive conscious awareness, in everything you think and act upon, your compassion and love for life, for yourself and others will ripple through this universe effecting, helping and blessing everyone and everything in its path on more levels than you could ever imagine.

Chapter 2

Attitude

A starting point to awareness

William James, the father of American physiology, said that the greatest discovery of his generation was that "Human beings could alter their lives by altering their attitudes of mind." To truly understand that, you must acknowledge that no one is stuck in or with an attitude. Our attitudes are our first and most important conscious choice, which reflect every result whether good or bad in life. You see, the attitude that you have towards your own self always determines the attitude that we have towards others and is most times a reflection or subconscious view of the world in many instances. This will radiate to the world and everyone around us. Negative people with bad or poor attitudes tend to lead miserable lives. This tends to become a habitual pattern for these people and makes them and others around them ineffective at living a healthy life. In most cases, a pessimistic attitude repels people in the opposite direction. Have you ever met someone whom you just can't stand to be around? You know, the co-worker always complaining about their job, or the family member always finding fault with others in the family. Maybe a stranger in the elevator complaining about the weather or as you read this; do you see yourself on the other side? Do you attract people that are negative or complain all the time? Do you attract positive people?

Attitude is the absolute reflection of an individual person. Our attitude determines our moods, feelings and the action that we take in response to these thoughts. Our attitudes, in return, control our success and failure in life. Again, this is the basic law of cause and effect. A poor attitude toward someone or something is bound or destined for failure. Whereas a positive or good attitude towards someone or something is the design for determination, objective learning and success in many ways.

To sum it up, our environment is the result of our attitude.

If your environment is polluted with pessimistic or negative attitudes then fight back. <u>Remember, positive attitudes are contagious and tend to rub off on the people around you, which in return helps you and them live a much happier more uplifting life. However, beware of negative attitudes for in the same instance, negative attitudes can rub off as well.</u>

Our attitudes are the determining factor of how we choose to view every conscious and unconscious thought in our mind. Remembering this will be the absolute determining factor of how you choose to live your life.

With this in mind, ask yourself the question, how is my attitude most of the time? Why?

Attitude in the physical

Attitude is often taken into the physical form of our bodies as well. Often you will see people with extremely bad attitudes tend to have horrible posture, whether developing slumped shoulders, hunched backs, hyper extended neck positions or even a permanent discontent look or frowning face. This is very common, to see in people who consistently become disappointed or upset for some reason. Whether rolling their eyes as to seem bothered, or annoyed or making a gesture or noise of disgust. These gestures or postural deviations are carried with most of us throughout adolescence and clear up to adulthood.

These postural deviations are nothing more than reactions to negative thought patterns. In all cases these negative attitudes affect our bodies in one way or another. Believe it or not, attitude affects our lives in every single aspect: physically, spiritually and mentally.

Questions to ask yourself!

How is my posture most of the time?

Do I let others drain me with pessimisms or negative attitudes?

How am I physically affected?

Do I have certain gestures when I don't agree with others?

Do I allow other people's attitudes to rub off on me?

Positive thinking is the key to developing a much more fulfilling life. When you develop more of a conscious effort to always find the good in every situation, then the battle is won before it is fought. With a positive mental attitude you will automatically walk with a bounce in your step. You will notice a change in your physiology and posture as well as the positive outcomes of your surroundings consistently. **For the real truth in a positive attitude is that you can never lose. A person that views life in this manner always sees adversities as learning experiences and valuable lessons in the walk of life. They don't let things get them down, nor do they let life's challenges whip them. This common knowledge is certainly one of the master keys to a successful life.**

Criticism

To truly master a positive attitude a person must understand the absolute negative power of criticism. The definition of a critic is one who judges or finds fault with someone or something. We are all guilty of this pollution of life. Whether talking about your neighbor, brother or the movie you saw last week. No matter how you look at it; criticism is poison. It is not our place to judge others but to learn to observe ourselves in all situations in life. Criticism has truly become one of the worst habits of human beings in today's societies. This negative influence, thinking that man has the right to judge one another for any reason is absolutely wrong! This negative (or toxic) pollution has killed millions and millions of men, women and children, because of the color of their skin or their race, background or religious beliefs. It scares people's spirits and destroys people's lives, changes multitudes or nations into a hateful jealous rage.

Criticism is an evil seed that when planted into a person's conscious and unconscious beliefs, grows like a relentless weed that stealthily sprouts vines of hate until it chokes the life out of everyone in its path. Criticism ruins friendships and relationships, destroys businesses, paralyzes work environments and murders families.

I hope that these words of wisdom bring you to a greater understanding of the destructive power of something as simple as a pessimistic opinion.

With all of this in mind, I urge you to be very conscious of your opinions towards anyone or anything.

Remember Positive breeds Positive!
Negative breeds negative!
Which do you choose to live by?

Criticism Exercise

Task 1, Here is a great lesson in criticism. Pick a day out of the week to completely fast from criticism. Use this page below to write a 1 to 2 paragraph commitment statement to yourself in the morning. State your commitment for the day to observe and listen while fasting from criticism. Place this note in your pocket and read it throughout the day to remind you of your commitment. This will take a tremendous effort on your part. Be aware and make no comments of a negative nature. If you must voice your opinion, voice it with nothing but praise or up lifting words. (If you slip with a pessimistic thought or comment, correct yourself immediately and keep on going.)

My commitment not to criticize today
Write your paragraph below and place it in your pocket today.

Tasks 2, Study others attitudes in relation to their criticisms.

Task 3, Finish the day by writing your thoughts and what you've learned from this experience. Keep this information and share it with others.

This will enforce your thoughts to yourself so that you can live a healthy life with minimal criticism.

"A day without criticizing."

Today I've learned:

Author,

In summary of this lesson, remember that your attitude is everything. Your attitude will determine your happiness and contentment in life. Your attitude is your power to how you interpret and live your life. No one can take this power from you. You are the master of your own domain of thoughts that will determine the outcome of your life.

Therefore avoid negative influences or people that will challenge your spirit. If cornered by this plague of pessimisms, fight back with every ounce of goodness that you breathe. In doing this you will become a silent teacher of all the beautiful and glorious opportunities of life. You will make your life a shining example for others to follow. You will become an expert listener and find that you are an invaluable solutions expert to adversities of life. You will help people break down walls of negative outlooks on their lives. Most importantly, you will be servicing and helping every one placed in your path while living and learning one of the most rewarding lessons of life: the power of positive thinking.

Did you know: that if you take the word "ATTITUDE" using the alphabet A representing one, B representing two and so on. Attitude adds up to 100. Maybe this is for a reason; to let us know that our attitude represents 100% of our life.

A B C D E   F G H   I   J   K   L
1 2 3 4 5   6 7 8   9 10 11   12
     M   N   O   P   Q   R   S   T   U   V   W
13 14 15 16 17 18 19 20 21 22 23
                      X   Y   Z
                     24 25 26

ATTITUDE

1 + 20 + 20 + 9 + 20 + 21 + 4 + 5 =**100%**

Thanks for teaching me this Mom!

Chapter 3

Seeing the Big Picture

In many ways, you are constantly making decisions in life, which will affect you, however, most decisions are trivial. Whether it's what type of toothpaste you'll buy or how you'll have your eggs made for breakfast. All of these less important decisions are part of a master-mind plan that you are deciding on day in and day out. They all affect your life and the future that exist for you. Unfortunately, most of our human existence is never really thought through. It's as if most of us were walking through all of the years of our lives aimlessly drifting as empty sailboats wondering where ever the breeze of life might blow us.

Most people are raised as a child through adolescence with one or two parents providing, sheltering, feeding and supporting most of our needs. We proceed through the chains of societies common knowledge, from preschool to grade school on to high school and if fortunate enough to a university of our choice. We fly away from the nest. We fall in and out of love a few times. We have a few great moments in life and a few tragic setbacks as well. We follow our parents or friend's leads as to our beliefs in religion, politics and so on. We find a steady 9 to 5 job that like clockwork pays the bills. As five o'clock roles around we jump into our automobile that most of us really can't afford, and drive home just in time to give a nice long stretch of relief as we head to the refrigerator to see what we can stuff our face with, which is normally some type of unhealthy snack to get you through until dinner is ready. After or during dinner, we sit in front of the television entranced between surfing the channels or on our computers surfing the World Wide Web. We do this until we become so mentally exhausted that we just can't take it anymore. After which we retire to our bed tossing and turning all night until the sun rises and it's time to do it all over again.

If you can relate to even one part of this common lifestyle that I've just described, then I suggest that it's time you "SNAP OUT OF IT!" Don't put this book down until you are finished and complete every one of the mental physical and spiritual exercises in this book. (This discipline will change your life!)

Unfortunately, millions of people are victimized by a minimal exis-tence that our society in this day and age molds us to become. We are not living a life playing follow the leader, but rather a life playing fol-low the follower, walking through our daily lives as robotic drones, enslaved to a life of uncertainty and boredom in many cases. We forget the value of our purpose in lives and the liberty and freedom that comes with it. As you read this chapter ask yourself which are you? Are you a leader in your life or are you just going with the flow of the blind masses of people in this smeared world.

Although many people are lost in this rut or lifestyle, one thing is true; most people really don't know what they want in life. Most of us live our life day by day, never understanding our true potential of happiness as human beings. Adapting to our environmental surroundings so that we can keep up a certain level of ego-driven social acceptance. We become professional thieves in robbing ourselves of one of our most valuable positions and understandings. We never bother to ask ourselves the questions that really matter, a question of true meaningful purpose and the tools that it takes to live it. (This book is one of many!)

Life Purpose

The word 'purpose' in the dictionary is described as: something that one intends to get or do; or the object for which something exists or is done with intention and planning.

Here's my interpretation of this word. I believe that purpose is an idea of completeness, a goal, mission, or dream that is intrinsically desired to the point of true ambition and intention. Whether we keep a purpose in view with conscious persistence is the question to our happiness in life. In all, a purpose is a dream or passion that has carefully been thought through and studied until it has become a master plan that is put into action.

How we develop our purpose is one of the keys to our happiness and fulfillment in life. So finding your life purpose may start with questions like: Why do you feel you are here? There are so many answers to this question, but what is it that really sticks out in your mind, what answer, when carefully thought out, gives you a powerful sense of good for everyone around you and in your world at this moment in time? One of the best ways to view this most important question is to step out of your shoes for a while and truly ponder it. View your life from different perspectives and see what it is that makes you totally joyous and happy!

The questions on the following pages will help you immensely find the answer to this awesome question.

<u>Understanding your purpose</u>
Take your time and Answer the following questions completely.

What are the most valuable feelings or accomplishments that you've had in your life?

What moments in your life have been the most rewarding to you?

What do you love?

Are you a teacher or a provider in your life? Maybe both! Explain.

What is the most important thing to you in your life?

Now that you've answered these questions, I'm sure that you are well on your way to understanding your true purpose in life. I know from experience the more you think about this, the more defining your purpose of life will become. As each one of us grows through this life journey we become what we consistently contemplate and think about.

If we live in fear (negative thoughts) of something long enough, then eventually we will draw this to us, and it will be manifested in our lives.

If we believe and have never ending faith in something and stay persistent with and mold our thoughts to a specific purpose in this life experience, then the rewards manifested will be limitless. The next few questions below are going to take you a little bit of time to complete. If you don't feel that you can answer these questions completely at this time then relax. Take a day or two to think this through. Remember, as you evolve your purpose may shift or mold and take different avenues. This may be a better position in your career or a completely different career. In many people that begin to experience this greater awareness of life's purpose there is suddenly change that comes in many forms. Maybe they pick up their roots and travel to other lands or begin a new business adventure that allows them to wake up each morning and live their life purpose. In any direction that you decide to venture and accept as your life purpose, be prepared to experience more enjoyment and enthusiasm than ever before. You can trust yourself that by doing this you will grow in more ways then you could ever imagine.

What's my Purpose in life?
Answer these questions in detail

Do I have a clear direction as to what I truly want out of my life or am I just going with the flow? Explain!

What motivates me with what I truly desire out of life?

In answering these questions with integrity, you will find your strength in life, the power to rise above the masses of followers and take charge of your life. No one's life can be mastered until we decide to become dedicated, committed, focused and determined with never-ending discipline as to our true purpose of life. Remember, with a true understanding of purpose and direction you have a master goal to strive for in life. This is a turning point in your life now. Take these written thoughts and begin taking action!

Make this a time to go within yourself and find true meaning to your life. Remember that to go within means to really take some time out just for you. Go for a long walk, find a quiet spot to sit and think clearly and consciously. Do some serious soul searching. Find out who you are and how you feel. Develop a mission for your life and hold on with all of your might. **Don't pass this opportunity to get to really know you!** I challenge you to truly take the time to do this, write these thoughts out and live by this. With a true life purpose, your life will never be the same.

Mission Statement Exercise: Review all of the answers that you have written in this and previous lessons and develop a mission statement for your life. Redefine your mission to be as precisely defined as possible. Write this statement on the worksheet page that follows and keep it with you where ever you go during the day. Stick it in your pocket and review it daily. Better yet, if you have a business card place this on the back so people can see your mission statement and commitment to yourself in life. Also leave a space to place your signature of commitment to yourself and everyone you share this with. This is a powerful tool that makes a difference in your life whether business or personal. Not only will this remind and help you to be a great example but this will shine to everyone that crosses your path and let them know what you stand for and what you're all about: happiness, health, love, compassion and all the goodness within you as a person. Memorize this statement and live by it. Repeat it every day, and every time you question anything in your life. Give yourself a precise dedicated purpose to your life. Narrow it down to be exactly what you believe, and who you will become. Do this and you will be well on your way toward a lifestyle worth living.

Mission Statement
For My Life

Signature:

Chapter 4
Learning a higher awareness

As we've covered in previous chapters, life is certainly what you make it. In understanding the laws of nature and the power of a positive attitude, why is it that all of us at one time or another develop so much stress in our life? Is it because we're trying to be more than we can possibly be, that we're taking on too much of life's adversities? If life is what we make it, then why do we make this stress in our lives?

You may be looking for some hidden secret or mystery, however here's the real truth. Whether you want to believe this or not, your life and the stress, complications, awkward positions, failing moments, downfalls and all the misery thereof, is formed from your negatively mastered creations. That's right, "your creation!" You see, most people's stress in life is nothing more than misunderstandings, miscommunications, self doubts, self pity, anger, rage, lack of control or organization and so on. All of these problems or worries in life normally stem from one thing: lack of effective communication with ones true self. This is the real reason that people create misery in their own lives. So, when you really think it through, in simple terms, the only *one* that can stress you out is *you*! You have been given the most powerful tool of all existence, your own free mind, which didn't cost you a penny! With this, we can create everything that you see on this earth. Just think of everything that exists today, because of the human mind. Some scientist's say that the average human brain only uses about 5 percent of it's worth, can you believe that? Imagine most of us have 95% of our minds that are untapped, untrained or virgin plains of unlimited and infinite potential. Then why is it that we feel overwhelmed with all of the pressures of life? Why is it that some of us let our worries consume us to the point of physical or mental sickness? It's been mentioned before in scientific studies at Harvard University that most of our internal thoughts or what we can call "self talk" consists of about 77% negative thoughts. *(This is when we do most of our rationalizations and try to understand our thoughts and actions.)* Zig Ziglar points out in his book "How to be A Winner", that coincidently psychosomatic (meaning self-conjured) illnesses in life are also the equivalent of 77%. If we could take the time to develop our minds to understand this and work through this, to train and develop this infinite potential of our minds, we would never have a miserable day in our lives again. Given, some days may involve more problems to solve than others. However, understanding ourselves is the key to understanding that simplicity in life is the answer to our successes and ultimately our freedom as a human being. In the earlier chapter on attitude I explained to you that your attitude is your choice. Your state of mind against any opposition in life is controlled by your choice of thought. For example, if someone does something to make you angry. Do you **react** by getting upset or mad at the situation or person or if someone purposely says something to hurt your feelings? Does this make you sad or depressed? In most cases the average person will react without thinking it through.

When you visualize yourself in any of these situations, you will quickly find out your level of awareness.

*Are you a knee jerk reaction type of person or as my father used to call it, do you suffer from "foot in the mouth syndrome?"

*Are you a hide and sulk type of person that runs away from the situation to continue working yourself up to the point of tears or increased self-conjured fear?

*Are you a grin and bear it individual with a "whatever" passive type of attitude that attempts to push or suppress your feelings and emotions for fear of what people think of you directly and indirectly.

*Are you a maniacal or sinister person that retreats using the incident as stored ammunition allowing dissolution thought patterns to fester and waiting for the right or unexpected time to attack with revenge?
(Also known as being passive/aggressive)

Answer these questions

Which do you use most?

Why?

What is your STATE of mind?

The word STATE is another meaning for condition. What is the condition of your mind, or for better words, how have you conditioned your mind to react? **To understand your state of mind and be able to control your mental attitude at every given moment is one of the most challenging but powerful lessons to be learned in life.** For some this may seem impossible, however practice makes permanent! As mentioned before, your conscious effort to understand your state of mind and reasoning makes the battle already half won. The challenge is in persistence and discipline, remembering to be aware; to look above every situation in life that presents itself with your higher consciousness, and to become a consistent observer.

Emotions

Understanding the concept of awareness and making the habit to consistently use this super human resource that we have in our life is one of the most important keys of understanding the freedom that all of us have within us already. Developing and understanding this truth is a major key in preventing ourselves from worries and stress in life.

With a greater awareness that every limitation you've had in life or every situation you have or will experience, is your creation - you will develop a mode of thought which may be seen as a higher level of maturity and/or understanding. This way of thinking and communication with one's self pulls you to the forefront of consciously aware thinkers, taking you out of the blind masses and transforming you into a take-charge leader in yours and others lives.

Remember, you've created your own limitations, whether consciously or unconsciously, through your own interpretations of yours and others experiences, comments, expressions or feelings. In other words, you have created an emotional representation that limits you from believing that you can accomplish what you truly desire, based on a compilation of your own perceptions of yours and others experienced emotions.

Being able to step back from a situation or problem in your life provides you with an open and objective point of view or standpoint. This will give you a large advantage at each and every struggle or situation that comes up. Knowing that we have the ability to control our emotions, whether good or bad, gives us the ability to choose our views in life and the lessons that we chose to learn.

Understanding that we can control the flow of our emotions gives us the ability to turn the emotions of our minds into conscious reality. How we evaluate our present moment is our state of emotions. We have a choice to decide how we interpret our adversities in life and how to react or respond in which ever manner we choose. The ability to take full control of how we perceive every thought or emotion thrown at us; how we ingest everything with all of our senses; how we have the ability to step back and evaluate every detail of all our confrontations in life, and then be able to reason, and develop our own interpretations and then take action accordingly to receive the best conclusion or results thereof is what you are looking to achieve – greater awareness in dealing with your emotions.

The power of emotions

Remembering that your state of mind is a condition that you've created mentally and physically, the mind receives thoughts, which are evaluated and interpreted into your human experience, which are in return your state of emotions. However, notice that with any state of emotion your body responds as well. When a person takes a particular emotion, this emotion will physiologically be manifested in the actions of their body. For example, if a person takes on an emotional state of sadness, according to the intensity of emotions the physical actions or reactions, he could become very introverted as to shy away from people, to cry or sulk, or to quiet themselves. Even their body language will change. You may notice crossed arms, folded legs, slouched shoulders, lowered head diverted eye contact as just a few of the physiological elements of a sad individual. What if a person becomes enraged with anger! What would you notice? Rather than backing or shying away, they may stand closer than usual as to overwhelm a person's comfort zone. Their physical gestures may be a pointed finger, clinched fist or jaw with a solid eye contact.   Most all emotions are expressed physically in one way or another. These physiological expressions are a neurological response that can be controlled as well. These **reactions** of the body are a short cut to training yourself and taking control of your emotional states. Do the following exercises and log your responses.

Emotions Exercise
Task 1
Anger: First, Find a quiet spot where you will not be disturbed. Think of something either in the present or past that really made you angry, mad, upset, and frustrated. Find this thought and dwell on it.
Think about it for just a few moments.
* Set or stand as you were standing at that moment in time.
* Feel the way you felt at that time.
* Breathe the way you were breathing at that moment.
* Act the way you were acting at that time.
* Remember where you were and how you really felt.
Take yourself into that moment of anger.

How did you feel?

What were you thinking at the time?

What reaction do you feel like taking at this moment?

Log your thoughts:

Happiness: Again, in the same quiet spot you've been in before, think of something that made you totally joyous and happy - a special memory in your life that you can never forget. Close your eyes and take yourself back to that moment in time.
* *Think about it for just a few moments.*
* *Set or stand as you were standing at that moment in time.*
* *Feel the way you felt at that time.*
* *Breathe the way you were breathing at that moment.*
* *Act the way you were acting at that time.*
* *Remember where you were and how you really felt.*
* *Take yourself into that moment of Happiness.*

How did you feel?

What were you thinking at the time?

What reaction do you feel like taking at this moment?

Log your thoughts:

By consciously re-enacting those moments in your life, whether angry or happy, you can bring those states of emotion right back to the present. You can literally create a mental state of consciousness that will be reflected in the physical realm. This is a very powerful tool to comprehend in life. This lets you see that you do have control over your life and how you want to live it. You do have the choice to be aware of everything you choose to be conscious of. You do have the ability to evaluate and change any decision that enters your life. If you want to be sad, be sad. If you want to be angry, be angry. If you want to be happy, be happy. These are your emotions, with cognitive awareness, you control them. You control the dimmer switch as to the intensity of each. You have the remote control and it's called your conscious mind. Use it daily and as consistently as possible.

Understand that our mindful observation is one of the key principles to being in control of our lives. Learning to observe our thoughts in relation to our attitudes, our emotions, and habitual states (conditioned thought processes) of our minds is critical to good mental and physical health in life. Learning to observe our self communication will help us to practice better communication with others in all situations good or bad in life and lead to better coping skills and less dysfunction.

When we can begin to practice this higher state of conscious thinking, we will begin to become aware of who and what we truly are; a spectacular, wonderful, happy, fulfilled and mindful being that just happens to be going through a human experience.

Answer the following questions below

<u>What emotion do you take on most predominantly?</u>

<u>Do you sometimes feel stuck in a particular emotion?　What is that emotion?</u>

<u>How do you feel?</u> *<u>(One Word)</u>*
Why?

<u>What emotions feel best to you?</u>

<u>How do they make you feel?</u>

Do you feel confident enough after reading this chapter to make a commitment to changing your emotional states?

<u>Commitment to my Awareness</u>

I, _____, am consciously committed to developing complete awareness of my emotional states of mind. I hereby obligate myself to effectively communicate with myself and others and to develop a state of awareness that will constitute the goodness of my life and all of those whom I come into contact with.

It is my goal to understand and control my own thoughts and emotions, as well as to teach others as an example throughout my day-to-day interactions and experiences in my life.

I know that I am a _____ person aware that my attitudes and emotions in life will affect others and therefore I will do my best every day to create a greater conscious awareness of my thoughts and my understanding and compassion with others.

By signing this paper, I understand that I am committing my life to a positive and uplifting change and promise to do my best to hold this promise to myself.

Date: _____

Signature: _____
(Place this where you may read this every day until committed to memory!)

Exercise: "Seeing *the good in everything*"

Now that you have explored the power of awareness and have learned how your thoughts and emotions are in your control with this new found consciousness, form this simple game and make it a positive habit for the rest of your life.

The worksheet below is a simple game to play with yourself daily!

1.) Track every adversity that comes into your life today and give it a title.

Example:
  • Flat Tire
  • Spouse home late from work today
  • Lost homework
  • Friend died

2.) Positive comment: After titling every adversity write a positive brief statement as to what you've learned from this experience.

3.) Duplicate this worksheet for the next month and use it every day. Keep all of the worksheets filed daily.

4.) At the end of the month review every day's worksheet and see what you've learned.

Keep an extra copy of this worksheet around you so that you may always have it available whenever you need to kick-start your attitude and awareness in a positive direction.

<u>Positive conclusions Worksheet</u>

1. Adversity

1. Positive Conclusion

2. Adversity

2. Positive Conclusion

3. Adversity

3. Positive Conclusion

4. Adversity

4. Positive Conclusion

5. Adversity

5. Positive Conclusion

6. Adversity

6. Positive Conclusion

7. Adversity

7. Positive Conclusion

Chapter 5

The Master of Emotions

Belief is a corresponding communication from all of the thoughts and senses of the mind and body that bring an individual to the realization of perceived truth in our human experience.

Belief is your ability to rationalize all different perceptions and then form a conscious decision based on your feelings. I refer to belief as the master of emotions for many reasons. For example, your perception of anything in life triggers emotions. In return, these emotions control other perceptions. This circling affect is the main circuit for all of the feelings that you manifest in your life. **All of the experiences of each of our lives are developed and form a logical order of what we perceive as truth.**

In many ways I believe that belief is a commitment. A commitment to truth in one's self. If you have adopted a belief then you are committing or creating a promise or pledge to yourself that what you have comprehended is true to you. This becomes an imbedded feeling into your nervous system and gives you either a feeling of positive or negative support for that experience.

Be careful of the true power of belief. For as it may bring you into immense joy and happiness when translated by positive emotions, disbeliefs can tear your world apart, bringing you much anger, depression and self doubt. **The positive and negative thoughts of our minds can free us or limit us completely, based on our perceptions and the emotions that follow.** For this reason, I encourage you to always remember your belief system in life is your toolbox. You choose what to hold in it. What tools work most proficiently for your life's work? If you create beliefs of self-doubt in anything you want or desire in life then you're working with the wrong tools. Get rid of doubt, fear or questions of one's abilities. Replace this with beliefs of complete encouragement and knowingness. This will help you to believe in all that you are, "the master of your own mind, the ruler of your own perceptions of your life, the creator of your realities!"

Mixing Faith with Belief

If belief is a person's self-formulation of truth through the mind, then what is faith? Faith is unquestionable belief! Complete trust or confidence and loyalty! Although this is a great way to define such a powerful word let's redefine it a little more. Belief and faith are very similar mental attitudes but still can be differentiated into two different parts. **Where belief is a mental advancement to the realities of life, faith is a spiritual advancement to the realities of the universe.** View it this way as well, although belief is truth of the mind, you may still lack certainty. It may still deep within you be questionable as complete and real truth. Here's the mystical beauty of faith. Faith is the unquestionable knowingness of truth of the mind and soul. As the world famous author, Napoleon Hill says in his book think and grow rich. *"Faith is the eternal elixir which gives life, power and action to the impulse of thought."* These are such profound words that when pondered, digested, dissected and directed into your life, this will open the doors to complete freedom, success, happiness and so much more. Napoleon Hill goes on to say that *"Faith is the basis of all 'miracles,' and all mysteries which cannot be analyzed by the rules of science! Faith is the only known antidote for failure."* **In all, belief mixed with faith is the painters' vision and brush, the sculptors touch and chisel, the writers thought and pen, the musicians' ear and instrument, which makes the masterpiece that fulfills the soul of one by touching the hearts and spirits of many.**

Triggers and Thought Patterns

Having a higher conscious awareness of our thoughts is an extremely empowering way to change our life in many ways. This freedom will allow us to catch and then observe ourselves when any situation or incident arrives at any given moment in life.

As most all of us know, our thoughts are all connected from one to the next in each moment and scenario that happens like a chain link. From this, many of us have unconsciously created dysfunctional thought patterns that are triggered by previous drama or perceived drama in our lives. These triggers could be seen as a switch that is flipped on whenever an event occurs in our lives that creates a past emotion or a subconscious recollection of a past event or drama that we have experienced before. When this trigger is switched on the roller coaster begins and the ride or thought pattern for most end in a state of uncertainty, sadness, anxiety, anger, resentment, despair, fear, sometimes physical violence or any other negative or dysfunctional process that we have conjured up. As mentioned earlier, this creates our realities and molds our lives and the emotional states of mind that we habitually live in.

One of the most powerful keys to our existence and happiness in life is learning to develop the ability to use our higher state of consciousness or live in this higher state of awareness so that we may become an OBSERVER not an UNCONSCIOUS REACTOR! When allowing ourselves to stay consciously present we then learn to defuse any situation that arises just by looking above it from an observational perspective. By using this tool we can then quickly find many triggers that lead to unproductive or dysfunctional thought patterns in our lives. Triggers can be observed as many different things such as, key words whether in the form of a statement or question, others emotional states along with physical gestures or actions, unconscious touch responses and even visual or sound interpretations that you see or hear while in a particular emotional state of mind. For many people it may be a combination of the above that creates these TRIGGERS of unproductive thought patterns.

So, how do we stop ourselves from being habitually triggered into these negative roller coasters of emotional distresses and negativity? How do we prevent our minds from being taken over and reacting with a wormhole of thought patterns that rob us of our precious daily lives?

BY TRAINING YOUR MIND TO BECOME THE OBSERVER - MOMENT BY MOMENT!

An observer is defined as a person that perceives awareness of things and events through the senses. Thinking above and detaching yourself from triggers that set off any of the senses most importantly kinesthetic or emotional thoughts will allow you to see a whole new world from a "third eye" or nonjudgmental point of view. When practiced often, staying observant in stressful situations will open your eyes and spirit and allows you to release and let go of these dysfunctional thoughts and emotional patterns. When observing yourself in these situations you will automatically give yourself power to defuse sometimes any and all emotional turmoil that may lead to a state of dysfunctional behavior patterns as well. In later chapters we will discuss more of the most powerful connections from mind to spirit that is the master tool for overcoming these triggers and thought patterns; this is the breath, however, for now I will mention that the breath and learning how to slow down during disheartening or stressful situations, to breathe is a wonderful key element to place you in the state of observation. Interestingly enough, the breath has been used in many modern day ad campaigns to allow people to think before they react. One particular ad used for years by the non-profit Child Abuse Agency of America, which sponsored several commercials related to child abuse, taught people how to stop and count to ten by taking 10 calming breaths. In all reality, they were absolutely right. Learning to empty the mind and breathe slowly before reacting is what this is all about. Have you ever heard someone say, relax and take a deep breath! This simple observation is where it starts.

Positive Triggers and Thought Patterns

Not all triggers and thought patterns are necessarily bad or dysfunctional; many conscious and unconscious patterns derive from good habits that draw you closer to your higher self. These thought patterns tend to be connected to triggers that stimulate and promote a spiritual awareness, which we are all naturally drawn to. The most common are the positive stimulus or emotions that come from intrinsic connections of compassion, concern, empathy, sympathy, passion, gratitude, and all other emotional thoughts and or actions of love. Having an observational view of these positive triggers are just as, if not more, important than observing the negative. If we can focus and train our minds and learn to create these thought patterns consistently then the chain linked thought patterns in which we flow through consistently will grow stronger in linking our spiritual self with our physical self.

The True Power of the Mind

The most powerful tool in our human existence is our mind. It's been said buy great men, scientist, scholars, and philosophers that the potential of the mind for all practical purposes could be of infinite intelligence.

I remember as a child listening to Earl Nightingale, one of my favorite authors, who wrote the masterpiece, "Lead the Field."." He discusses a scientific study, saying that if we as human beings would only use half of the capability of our minds, that's probably not even at 50% use, we would be able to speak 40 different languages fluently, memorize the large soviet encyclopedia, and complete dozens of required courses for several degrees at several major universities around the world. Of course, this is only as far as man's understanding of the mind at which we have not even touched the surface. What about the studies of telepathy or those people that have been recorded to use their minds to move inanimate objects. The mind is truly a magical unquestionable phenomenon. It controls everything that we have, receive or give in this human existence. Our mind is the most powerful biological organ at which we have evolved to be the most advanced creatures to inhabit this world and maybe even this universe. With this we develop everything that we see, hear, touch, taste and most importantly feel. **Our minds are our external and internal reality to the world, ourselves and every one and thing around us.**

The mind works on three levels. Most people understand the first level, which is consciousness. This is the first action of the mind. THOUGHT! The second action of the mind is unconsciousness. This second action is thought as well but this thought or mental consciousness is hidden behind the conscious thoughts. This second state of consciousness does not bring immediate response to any of the senses of the physical body. In our first state of consciousness we have developed established patterns or tendencies of response to our rationalized thoughts. These are our emotions. As we discussed in the earlier chapter, our emotions are acted out through the physical realm of our life.

For example, if you see your girlfriend, boyfriend or significant other, kissing someone else our visual sense of sight will input this information into our mind, our thought process will then reason with all of the past thoughts through the subconscious mind. This will evoke a response or feeling; this is the emotion that has taken place. From there, your thought patterns will evolve into the physical. Let's say that your mind registers anger, you may go over and punch that person's lights out. Maybe your mind registers sadness; you may walk away in tears. The brain, like any advanced computer system, in this constant state of multi-tasking or comparison will corrupt or cause glitches in the system of our minds. This will cause our mind to decrease in performance, and sometimes cause our minds to perform illegal actions. To keep using this analogy, I could say that the majority of the mind or our computer is fragmented with unconscious or sometimes even conscious streaming thought that is corrupted. These corrupted thoughts are self-conjured misinterpretations that many times the mind avoids which often leads to unconscious denial. These fragmented stressors and worries in most cases take on dysfunctional thought patterns that create neurotic, irrational or narcissist fixations that are often acted out as a release to our misinterpretations and miscommunications.

Many times these self-conjured misinterpretations of the mind consistently continue to fester and build up until it takes complete consumption of your thought processes, until your mind becomes a scrambled fragmented mess that for some people can cause a lot of discomfort in life and eventually cause a break down. Now, given that most people are not on the edge of a nervous breakdown, I do believe that we all have glitches. We have all, at one time or another, worked ourselves up worrying about something from either a past experience that we continue to dwell on, in which we have no control to change; or maybe a present situation that we have no power to change but insist on obsessing over until we make ourselves physically or mentally sick. Some of us are very good at worrying about things of the future that have not even happened yet. The facts are that the large majority of worries or problems in our lives are not ours to own, not our problems or stresses to deal with but mental delusions that seem to reek havoc and consistently corrupt this magnificent computer of a brain that we have.

A third state of consciousness

Now that we've explained what I believe to be the second state of consciousness, let us talk about the third and most powerful consciousness. Above the conscious mind is a greater level of consciousness. This is what I see as the most infinite level of consciousness that most of us don't realize we have. This is the level or degree of consciousness that directly taps into the spirit. This is the highest level of consciousness that strives for goodness and purity in everything we are made of both in and out of form. This is the master of consciousness that evolves into everything good, positive and uplifting, all of our successes in life, the beauty and wonders that we see, feel, hear, create and share.

With this higher consciousness we can create all the good in the physical world and all the positive energy of the universe. With this highest level of consciousness we can tap into pure enlightenment of the soul and therefore gain the power and knowledge to develop and train our conscious mind to release all of the negative unproductive suppressed emotions, feelings or thoughts of our minds. This is our oneness with self; this is a pure state of being-ness. This is your spirit or eternal being. Although some don't believe that there is such a thing let me give you some discovered scientific fact based on a unique experiment conducted by Psychologist William McDougall (1871–1938). Dr. McDougall developed a highly calculated and precisely measured bed that was designed to weigh every single portion of a human body. This bed was developed as an experiment to weigh people on their last breath of life. In turn the scientist wanted to figure out if the matter or energy of the soul could be calculated into weight. The reasoning was that any particle of matter or energy of any existence or force must have some type of weight. So as people were placed on the deathbed, Dr. McDougall and the participating scientist would measure several different things in order to find any result. In all cases recorded, as each individual took their last recorded breath the body would immediately decrease by an average of ¾ grams. All explanations were carefully scrutinized from the theory of released oxygen to immediate dissipation of liquids and so on. To this day the explanation is an unexplained phenomenon on a scientific level. However the only real conclusion was that as the soul elevated from the body, the weight of the corpse lightened. Dr. McDougall called this phenomenon "soul substance." Although there have been many antagonistic responses to this study, I feel that most people know as I do that we do have a soul and it is pure energy residing within each and every one of us.

In conclusion, in all of these lessons thus far it is the spirit that drives us to better ourselves consistently in life. It is our minds that we are developing as tools to learn a higher awareness as a species individually and as a collective whole. When we train our brains with everyday awareness, whether our choice of attitude, understanding and developing purpose, we will find a better life with every day of this journey that we are on. That is the purpose of all of the exercises in this book. I encourage you to take the time to read on and use this book as a tool for every day life. Develop new thoughts and conclusions as you read and practice and clear the slates to make a better you from within. Remember, you are never stuck in anything at any time. Your mind and the simple faith that you have in yourself and others will always bring you back on track for a better life, no matter what! Take care of you first and others with the same loving intentions and life will become amazing, exciting and powerful in so many ways you cannot even imagine. In later chapters we will discuss how to de-fragment all of these levels of consciousness and live persistently on this third state or higher consciousness moment by moment. However, before we begin those lessons you must first learn how to improve and take care of your life in the physical realm and body. The next section of the book is dedicated to the body and will provide you with what I believe to be many interesting perspectives. All sections will have exercises and outlines to help you along the way; again, please take the time to follow the book in order so that you may enjoy it the way that it is intended to help.

Think to Thank

Just as important as all of the things are that we have covered and studied in this book so far, learning to think correctly in every moment can teach and train you on how to improve your attitudes. These attitudes translate into emotional states of the mind and help you to reach a higher awareness of yourself and your life in the present moment consistently.

Although all of this sounds wonderful and exciting, thinking and acting this way 24/7/365 is simply not always possible. We just can't expect not to have down time or negative emotional states of mind. This is what helps us to see all that we have and allows us to measure improvement. However, one of the strongest tools that I've seen and learned to use in life is the concept of thinking to thank.

When I say think to thank, I really mean remember that when in an emotional state of turmoil or distress; when in times of negative thoughts or despair, one of the best ways to revitalize your natural positive nature is through gratitude. Shift your thought process and find something to be thankful for and dwell on these thoughts instead. Calm yourself and except the truth that although some things in life may really stink and be charged with all types of negative emotions and feelings (they may be complete catastrophes, traumatic disasters with horrible consequences that follow) that when all is said and done they are normally some of the most powerful and positive lessons that you may ever learn from in your life.

I have always said and will always believe that, "Everything happens for a _good_ reason!" Even the worst things in the world we can find positive lessons from. It's just remembering to think about what positive lesson to be thankful for.

Exercises for your mind
Finding time for mental skills development daily is very important. A sedentary mind, as you will learn in the next section of this book, is as bad as a sedentary body. The following are 7 mental skills exercises that I have used for my friends and clients in recent years. I hope you use them all, over and over again and pass them forward to other people you know and love. These exercises are great for not only keeping your mind sharp but opening up your creativity as well. Enjoy!

Mind Exercise 1

Painting a masterpiece:

This mental skills exercise will help you to focus and maintain a steady thought process.

1st Take a piece of paper on one side and at the top write "Masterpiece Exercise." Now close your eyes for a moment and think of the most beautiful scenery or background that you can imagine. Open your eyes and write a title on one side of the page i.e. "Beach" or "Sunset'.

2nd Close your eyes again and begin to paint a vivid image of your masterpiece. Spare no detail and stay there for as long as you like until you have a complete image of your picture in your mind. Using the same example as above: If it is a beach, does it have palm trees? Are there birds flying by? Is the wind pushing the waves in any direction? Are there other people strolling along the beach as well? Where is the sun touching the water? Are you there in the morning for sunrise or in the evening for sunset? The more description, the better, however, don't stress about remembering every thing, just relax and enjoy what you notice.

3rd Gently open your eyes and paint or draw a picture of your masterpiece. This does not need to be a detailed drawing, but rather a simple outline of all of the details you remember. Even if you can only draw stick figures, that's fine, just place the items that were in your picture on that side of the page in the spot that you view them in your masterpiece. When you're finished turn the page over and at the top create a full title for your picture i.e. "My California Sunset" or "My Last Holiday" etc.

4th Close your eyes again and go back to the image in your mind. Focus again on this image and this time really place yourself in the picture: notice, feel, observe and become a part of the image in your mind. Stay here for as long as you like and get as vivid as you can become.

5th When finished open your eyes and begin to write your description of your masterpiece. Now be as detailed and descriptive as you like, write until you have nothing else to write about your masterpiece and you feel that you are finished.

This exercise may be difficult the first few times, but after a little practice you will be amazed at what this will do for you and where this will take you in life. In the future you will be able to take these masterpieces and review them again and again.

Mind Exercise 2

Morning Meditation Journal:

This is one of my favorite exercises and one I think everyone should do; it clears your mind and helps you to plan your day.

1st Find a journal that you feel comfortable writing in, if you prefer to use a computer or laptop remember that when setting up your Account profile with GenerationAwareness.org you will have access to this daily exercise online as well.

2nd Every morning find a regularly structured time frame just to sit and write or type.

Preferably a quiet spot with no distractions.
Make sure to be comfortable and try not to place a time constraint on your journaling.

3rd Sit quietly and close your eyes for a couple of minutes. Focus on just relaxing and breathing. If your mind gets distracted go back to your breath and just observe the rise and fall of the belly.

4th When you are relaxed, gracefully open your eyes and place the pen to the paper and begin writing. Just write whatever comes into your thoughts. Anything that you are thinking is good and just allow yourself to free flow your thoughts. When finished, read what you wrote without judgment. Close your book and begin the day.

This is a very powerful form of meditation that can help you to become organized with your days as well as help you to release stress or anxiety. Again, like all of these exercises, it's good to go back and revisit them once in a while to see your progress or shifts in thinking in your life.

Mind Exercise 3

Brain Strain: Alphabet correlations

This is a great mental skills exercise that I like to do while doing cardio exercise.

1st Begin by reciting the alphabet forwards and backwards a couple of times.

2nd Starting with A and going through Z think of anything that comes to mind and go through the whole alphabet.

Alternate: From A to Z think or things you have or own, you can also use alternate methods such as naming Animals, Cars, Peoples names, foods etc.

3rd As you get better at this exercise you may be able to begin from A to Z with one topic and then go backwards from Z to A in another. This may seem trivial for some people but as you progress this exercise becomes a brain tease for most..

This exercise will really wake up your mind and keep you sharp when it comes to quicker thought responses and better memory skills. Besides, it tends to be really fun when you give it a chance.

Mind Exercise 4

Brain Strain: Number correlations

This mental skills exercise is really the same as the alphabet correlation exercise except for numbers of course.

Examples: You can correlate numbers to dates, birthdays, anniversaries etc. Also simple counting from 1 to 1000 or even 100 and backwards is great for keeping you sharp. Note: Just make sure not to do the same exercise everyday so the mind can keep guessing and it doesn't become stagnant and boring.

Mind Exercise 5

Brain Strain: Revisit your basic math skills

Math is one of the basic tools that we use as kids in school to study memorization and logic.

There are many examples that you can use when it comes to mathematics.

- Counting in Even or Odd numbers
- Simple Addition up through 3 and 4 digit numbers
- Simple Subtraction up through 3 and 4 digit numbers
- Simple Multiplication tables
- Simple Fractions or division

Any math game that you play and test yourself with is great for logic and memorization skills. This will also keep your mind sharp and quick. It's interesting to note that many of us today are so use to the convenience of calculators that we loose these simple mathematical skills.

Mind Exercise 6

Brain Strain: Color your thoughts

This exercise is one of creative descriptive thought and will require color pencils, paint or even crayons if you like. The objective is to think of one object and visualize the colors in detail.

1st Get a piece of paper and write down one item that comes to mind that is colorful. This could be anything that you think of but try to think of something with several colors.

2nd Close your eyes and visualize in great detail all of the colors that you see in the item that you wrote down. Again, this requires practice in order to create a vivid imagination that will see all that you want to see. View all of the colors and the shades and placement.

3rd When finished, open your eyes and color, paint or draw in detail the item that you had created in your mind. Do your best to make it look just like your mental image. So what if you're not Vincent van Gogh just do your best and don't stop until you're finished.

This exercise will help you to release your more creative hemisphere of the brain that can open the mind up to more creative thinking processes. I encourage you to do this at least once weekly.

Note: If this is too difficult for you to do at first find a picture that you like and use it to assist you in the exercise. Start out by just viewing the image next to your blank sheet of paper and copying as close as you can. Next time try turning the picture over at intervals until you need to view it again. This is a great way to train yourself to do this exercise.

Mind Exercise 7

Think how they think:

Here's an exercise that is really powerful as well as fun and some-times quite comical. **I learned this from the great Napoleon Hill.**

1st Find a person that you like, admire or look up too in any way. Visualize the person and their mannerisms. How do they speak, think, talk or act? What makes them unique in character? How do you think they would respond to you and what type of conversation would you like to have with them?

If needed write down your questions or the topic of interest that you have for them.

2nd Reenact your imaginary conversation with them playing both roles out loud and using their voice tone, vocabulary and more to complete the character.

3rd Complete your conversation and walk away on good terms stating to meet again. Develop your character and role-play with this person. When you have a tough issue that's going on in your head, take a walk with your character in your mind and ask for advice. You would be amazed at some of the answers and results that you may get with this exercise.

Remember this person can be an individual that is alive now or someone that you never even knew. I've had conversations with some of the greats like Thomas Edison, Martin Luther King Jr., Napoleon Hill, Bill Moyer, Joseph Campbell, John F. Kennedy, Zig Ziglar, Ronald Regan, Earl Nightingale, Nostradamus, Eckert Tolley, James Redfield and even my girl, Oprah Winfrey. For the record, this doesn't mean you're crazy because you're talking to dead people or people that you've never met but rather you're using your imagination to create an idea of their intellect and responses. It's a way of sparking your own subconscious intellect and using it for what it's worth.

Please remember that these are just a few exercises that you can use to keep your mind sharp. Find whatever interest you have whether cross word puzzles, Sudoku or my personal favorite "Reading Books"! The idea is to incorporate these daily exercises into your lifestyle and keep your mind focused on something that you can accomplish daily. The following link will guide you to several mind exercises and games that you can use daily if you like.

Go to: www.generationawareness.org/mentalskills/exercises

BODY

CHAPTER 6

WE ARE CREATORS

From conception to our first breath of air to our first thought, we are perpetual beings in motion, as mentioned in the last section. Mentally, we are creating thought constantly. Moving our bodies on a conscious level and reasoning on a subconscious level as well. However, in this mental dimension of our existence it is obvious to realize that in order to use our minds we must also physically pump blood, create cells, rejuvenate organs and a million other things all at once in the physical body. We are a moving being in constant action. The question to most is where does this action arrive from?

ENERGY

That's right! We are nothing but raw harnessed energy working in conjunction with each realm of dimension within our existence. In modern science today we have discovered many things about the body's energy. If you were to look at an ultrasound or brain scan you are looking at different degrees of warmth or energy throughout the body. If you were to see a cat scan you would see many different aspects of energy being seen in the physical. But did you know that the energy of the body is not only seen in new science but heard as well. Science has found that the energy of the body creates a vibration or hum through different parts creating an orchestration of many different sounds. In many ancient cultures, there is history of the study of energy. From meridian lines which are believed to be energy lines throughout the body to charkas which are said to be spinning energy forces representing different parts of a being's existence and having several different sounds or vibrations as well. Whatever belief you have adopted, it is true that we are nothing but a self-perpetuated flow of energy, never ceasing to exist. Think of it, even if we disintegrated into fertilizer, we are still moving through the world creating more and more and more.

As I mentioned in previous chapters, in one of my favorite books by Earl Nightingale "Lead the Field", he mentions that nuclear scientists have come to the conclusion that the human body creates such massive productions of hydrogen energy in the average humans life that if transformed or harnessed could provide enough energy to run a small country for a week. In dollar amounts they mentioned this would make the energy level for a human body worth about 85 billion dollars. I'm sure that has risen since the average life expectancy has skyrocketed in the last 30 years as well as the tremendous rise of inflation.

The energy of the human body is a fascinating subject that we could write an encyclopedia of information about. However, the purpose of this section of the book is to provide you with basic knowledge and understanding of the physical elements of you as a human being. In this chapter you will learn the fundamentals of how the body works and how to improve it into optimal condition. Each source of energy will have an exercise that you should complete before going on to the next. Many of these exercises can and should be done on a regular basis whether once a month, or 2 to 3 times weekly or even daily. I encourage you to make them all an important priority in your life for healthy living. Let's begin!

The Ten Sources of Energy in Life!

The energy needed to perpetuate human existence, I believe, is divided into ten parts that must all be used in order to create a sufficient quality of life. Sunshine, air, water, nutrition, exercise, flexibility, recovery, touch, belonging and balance. These are the basic fundamental physical nutrients for growth of a human life. With the combination and balanced moderation of these required sources of energy the body can reach optimal health and physical and mental excellence.

1. SUNSHINE

In the beginning there was light! Light is the essential celestial force of positive energy that gives warmth and promotes the earth and every thing that lives and grows. It is amazing to learn that hydrogen gas is what gives the sun energy and, as mentioned previously, we as human beings internally produce the same hydrogen to perpetuate life ourselves. **Fascinating!** Sunshine is the first ingredient for human existence and survival, our energy sources are one in the same. For the earth to flourish with life it survives first with sunshine, without this basic element of universal nature this planet would be a cold dead rock hurling through the universe and human beings would have never existed.

Why is the sun so important to human health? The sun is not only the main candle for vision as well as the heater for our global atmosphere, but just as importantly, the sun provides a valuable nutrient to the human body. As we derive many nutrients from our food such as vitamins A, B, C and E, most people are confused as to where our true source of vitamin D comes from. Well it is certainly not from cows' milk, but if you've guessed the sun, you're absolutely right! The only natural source of vitamin D comes directly from sunshine. You see, as ultra violet rays penetrate the skin they come into contact with fluid known as ergo sterol. This combining effect of the sun and ergo sterol forms vitamin D which is absorbed right into the bloodstream and circulatory system. As remarkable as this phenomenon is, we as a human species are being bombarded with false information as to the damaging effects of sunlight. We are told to stay away from the light of day and scared by research studies that show overwhelming statistics of outrageous sorts including several newly named skin cancers that can eat you alive. As a quick note to the average Barney and Wilma out there, when you see these statistics in the magazines and newspapers, do you ever question their validity? I hope you do because it is only common sense to realize that studies for research projects in any field are well-funded for a reason. In many cases these reasons are to sell a product or service and in most statistics there is a fear-based ethic that comes from the scientific studies that are manipulated by so-called professionals. Think of it this way, most scientists or university science labs must be funded for survival. It's a company that pays them or funds their projects, right? To sum it up in two words, when it comes to skin cancer its "Big Business!" Ah, I'm sure now you're getting the picture. It's all about showing them the money and trust me they've scared enough people with their research since the 1960's to become an annual billion dollar industry. Even more disturbing is the number of carcinogens that are in most of these sunscreen lotions, which this big industry forgets to tell you or warn you about. So in all, make your own research judgment with common knowledge and reasoning. However, please do not take this information wrong, skin cancer is real and can be devastating to anyone's life. I feel the need to say again, that **anything in life abused and not consciously moderated has the ability to harm and or affect your health.**

Although skin cancer is a real thing, so is osteoporosis, which is one of the biggest bone malnutrition deficiencies related to the human species and our lack of sunshine. To understand this better you must first realize that vitamin D, when absorbed, into the bloodstream is the main transporter for calcium to the bones. When vitamin D is lacking from its natural source then a calcium deficiency can occur.

Another problem from a lack of sufficient sunshine is what is called winter depression; this is a mental deprivation of day light sunshine. In many areas of the world including the U.S., when people are confined to stay inside because of the cold weather, this mental state is many times a reality. Some people become extremely irritated, depressed, frustrated and in many cases this leads to a lethargic state of mind and body. I remember as a child living in the cold winters and being stuck inside - I sometimes felt defeated and sad.

With this information in mind it is only common logic to get your share of sunshine daily. 10 to 20 minutes of sunshine should be more than enough to provide adamant energy and optimal health to your life. However, remember that it's important to be conscious of the best times of day to sunbathe, morning hours until 11am and afternoon hours from 5pm until sunset. Avoid the times of the day when the rays of the sun are most potent (11am to 5pm) and make sure not to overdo it. There is nothing worse than a stinging sunburn! Let the rays of the sun touch as much of your skin as possible and don't cover up with any sun block, sunscreens or other chemical junk. Give your body a chance to soak up a little sunshine but remember in moderation as well. If you are in a place that the winter months don't provide much sun light then improvise. Go to a tanning salon and relax in some modified sunlight for 5 to 15 minutes. This is certainly better than nothing. (Please don't burn yourself!) Better yet, find a window and bask in the sunlight from the inside.   I must also mention that as the rays of the sun are potent if over indulged remember to protect your eyes as well. Although the eyes are a significant source that the sun actually goes into, it is important to protect your eyes. (They're the only ones you have.)

If you are not comfortable with direct sunlight then it is just as effective to open the curtains or blinds when indoors or go outside and sit in the shade with your sunglasses off. This will allow you to absorb light through your eyes without being directly in the sun's rays.

Remember, the sun is the first source of life. Without it we wouldn't exist. So get in your daily dose of sunshine. With the sun in moderation you will improve your quality of life both physically and mentally. You will see that providing sunshine to your body is as important as breathing air into your lungs, it's only a natural part of life.

SUNSHINE EXERCISE

This is an awareness exercise that can be extremely powerful and relaxing. Although sunshine may not be available to you every day on the days that you need it most, this is an exercise that will make you feel great. Whether inside or outside take just a few moments to stand or sit in the sunshine.

1st Sit or stand in a quite comfortable spot.

2nd allow the rays to touch your face, palms of the hand and feet, if possible.

3rd Quiet and relax the mind, breathe in your nose and out of your mouth. When you're ready, gently shift your awareness to the sensation of warmth on your skin.

4th Visualize the sun penetrating through the skin as you breathe in the purest source of energy. Imagine the sunshine as it hits your skin filling up the body, from the bottom of your feet, through the legs, up through the torso, into the spine, up through the shoulders, into the arms, until it fills up completely to the neck and tops off at the top of the skull. Allow the rays of the sun to completely emanate from every pore in your body until you visualize your body glowing as bright as the sun or as a white-hot light.

5th Finish this exercise by journaling your thoughts immediately after you have filled up with sunshine. Keep these journals for a rainy day so that you may bask in the sun and review them like a refreshing ray of light.

Sunshine Journal

Journal your thoughts after this exercise, write whatever comes to mind.

Chapter 7

2. AIR

As the sun spins the earth into a gravitational pull, the warmth develops the atmosphere of gases that are exchanged and stimulate growth and life for everything. The earth's atmosphere is made up of about 21 percent oxygen; the main tool used to support most all living animals on the planet. Oxygen is the starting point of life. From beginning to end, oxygen is inhaled into the lungs with one main purpose; to oxygenate and give life to the blood cells and cleanse them while creating stimulation throughout the body, also known as the circulatory system. Oxygen is the bodies' first measure of detoxification. When air is exhaled, the body releases an extremely poisonous gas called carbon dioxide. This exchange of the respiratory system acts as a purification system and a natural law or trade off of life.

If you were to step back and ponder on the total importance of this autonomic impulse that is the core of our existence as a species, it is of value to remember the importance of the quality of every breath we take and what we can do to protect and improve the air and environment that we live in.

Cardiovascular exercise or aerobic conditioning exercise is one of the greatest assistants when it comes to purification and efficiency in oxygenating the blood and promoting better health in life. In order to improve the quality of air that you breathe, it is first important to avoid the every day toxic pollutions that we live, work and sleep in. The first pollution that most of us consciously avoid is industrial pollutions that are inhaled while living in heavily industrialized areas. Although most may think that this type of toxic pollution is more so related to big cities, this is not always the case. Many rural towns financial lifeblood is through industry related plants and factories of all kinds. The smaller the towns are the more people not only live down the block from these big company pollutants; but, also work and breathe in the same factory, day in and day out. If you are one of these people that are living and or working in close vicinity of an industrial plant, take charge of every breath that you, your neighbors or your kids take. Do your research and find out what the quality of your air is like. The internet is a wonderful tool that can help you not only research the industry you're going up against but can also provide you with environmental protection information as well. This will give you the power to take action and protect yourself and the children. There are many organizations that are available to help you with controlling pollution and its deadly effects. Get involved in your community, city and/or state and take action to protect our fresh air. Here is a link to connect you with some organizations that are doing fantastic work in this area.

www.generationawareness.org/air

Although many people say that there is no such thing as clean air anymore, we should do our best to keep our neighborhoods as toxic-free as possible.

Another every day pollution that many of us are guilty of contributing is carbon monoxide gas. While we are driving to and from the mall, work or the corner grocery store or wherever else, we are filling toxic poisons throughout our towns and cities and in many of our lungs as well. Carbon Monoxide is an extremely dangerous substance that when ingested even in small portions can asphyxiate and kill a human being in a matter of minutes. Car pollution is probably just as bad as big factory pollution because it is so close to our everyday lives. Some of the best ways to avoid this pollution in a heavily congested area of traffic is to make sure to role your windows up and block the circulation duct preventing air to come in through the outside. There are many car companies that are now providing air filters and purification systems for air conditioning systems within their lines of motor vehicles. There are also other alternatives as well, such as **air filtration and purification systems that plug right into your cigarette lighters** and allow you to breathe pure air while driving down the road. Isn't that great to see: something like a cigarette lighter which is normally used to poison your lungs used now to promote clean air and good health, I love it! I often get clients that ask me for recommendations when it comes to this type of technology in what works best. I consider you a part of the family now that you are reading this book; so, I have provided all of these answers on the following link below. At some point, if you would like to visit my website and sign up for the newsletter, I will provide you with the most updated list of all this information, not to mention all of the links that you will find referenced on each subject that we speak about. Please keep this in mind, now let's continue.

Although modern civilization has advanced so far, it still stuns me to see the alternate defeating routes that we take as an intelligent species. The automobile industry is a perfect example of a good thing gone bad. Henry Ford, one of the great pioneers of human convenience, had his claim to fame by helping to invent a combustible engine and mass marketing the automobile as we know it today. I'm sure that his interest did not lie in polluting the streets with toxic gases and raping the earth of her natural resources. I'm sure that Henry Ford's dream was not to reap the American society of their good health and economic dependency. But unfortunately the automobile industry is killing the earth by being a major contributor to problems in our ozone layers.

If Henry Ford had taken some advice from his good neighbor and mentor, Thomas Edison, who invented the first steel alkaline battery, we wouldn't be in as bad a polluted mess today. Although many people believe that Mr. Ford was the inventor of the first automobile, this is incorrect. The first recorded automobile invention dates back to 1769 by a Frenchman named, Nicolas Joseph Cognut. This vehicle was a steam driven vehicle. The next two automobile inventions were both battery operated. The first was invented by Robert Anderson of Scotland from 1832 and the second in 1891 by a gentleman named William Morrison from Des Moines, Iowa. The truth is that before Mr. Ford's invention of the Model T, there were many attempts at gasoline driven combustible engines. What Henry Ford truly invented was the ability to mass-produce gasoline driven vehicles. It is interesting to note that in the very early 1900's, one third of all vehicles driven in all major metropolitan areas of the US were electric cars. In that day and age the majority of taxi's in New York City were electric cars as well.

Today, many car companies are stepping up and creating several different hybrid/electric cars as well as vehicles that run on natural gas and even air compression systems. Let's hope that these vehicles become the norm sooner rather than later for the sake of our atmosphere and our children. Go to www.generationawareness.org/cars to find out more about the technological advancements in automobiles.

Household pollutants are also a major contributing factor to unhealthy and unpleasant air quality that we literally breathe in every day. Many of the household supplies that we cook, clean and maintain personal hygiene with have toxic fumes that are masked to appeal to our senses. Heck, even ammonia for bleaching your white clothes has a flower or fresh lemony smell to it. That's certainly one flower I wouldn't want to smell too long! I'm sure some of you are saying, "Well I only use it once in a while" and other than that it's safely tucked away in the utility closet or such. Well unfortunately that doesn't really mean much! Let me put it this way. If you only clean your house during spring cleaning that is still one time too many. Let's break it down a little better.

1st) Clean the bathtub, toilet or shower!

2nd) Clean the stove or range.

3rd) Vacuum the carpet or mop the floor.

4th) Dust and wax the furniture.

5th) Do the laundry.

These are normal cleaning rituals that include, for the majority, toxic chemicals and can be hazardous to your health. Be aware of the household cleaning supplies that you have and make a conscious effort to find natural products that you can substitute them with to do your cleaning. And if you continue to use these products protect yourself by wearing a breathing mask of some sort. If cleaning on the weekends with children in the house, send them outside for a little fresh air and sunshine. Making a conscious effort to do small things can stimulate more of a conscious effect for bigger things as well.

Recently I have found a company on the forefront of household clean-ing supplies, providing the best enzyme based non-toxic products that I have personally tested. At this point they provide a dozen products ranging from dishwashing liquid, laundry detergent, toilet bowl cleaner, carpet upholstery and even a stain pen. And the most amaz-ing thing is that all of these organic cleaning supplies work just as good if not better than what you would buy in your local grocery store and cost the same if not less. I love to see this technology, it truly amazes me. It is quite obvious that this organization did their home-work and will thrive because of the good intentions behind there research. For more information follow the link below to find out more about these and other personal hygiene products that we endorse through generation awareness.

www.generationawareness.org/wowgreen

FINDING FRESH AIR

Although some of us are fortunate enough to live in healthy and breathable areas with little pollution, many of us have no choice but to live in the city with the smog and poison under our noses. However, if you are subjected to higher amounts of air pollution, then make the effort to take frequent trips to areas of cleaner air. You may be asking yourself where clean air can possibly be in your area and see it virtu-ally impossible to find fresh air, but don't give up. Mother Nature is a very powerful source and is always cleaning the air that we breathe. The three ways that Mother Nature cleans the air will guide you to the cleanest breathing. The first way is by what I call the great trade off of life. As human beings inhale oxygen and exhale carbon dioxide, plant life does the opposite. That's right, plants actually use our carbon dioxide as energy for their breath and exhale or emanate oxygen. This wonderful trade off allows us as a species to provide life to our surroundings while our surrounding plant life supports and sustains us as well. This is why I suggest that you find a vegetated area whether the woods, forest, mountains, etc. Taking a relaxing walk through a deeply vegetated area will help not only to clean your oxygen intake up, but can be very magical in helping you connect to nature. If you live in a big city and there is no way to get out then take action by either going to a local park or botanical garden or even getting some plants in your home makes a difference. Spider plants are great because they expel a fair amount of oxygen and can help keep the air clean in your home as well. Another great cleanser of our air is large bodies of water like the ocean or even lakes or rivers. If you can get away take a walk along the beach or near a local lake or body of water. These areas tend to be great sources of fresh air and support healthy, quality air. If you don't have any of these areas available to you then you can always take a brisk walk after a rain shower. This is also another way of Mother Nature's ability to purify our air.

Breathing is an absolute necessity in life! If you don't believe me try going without it for a few minutes. With this knowledge in mind, take the time to find ways to improve the quality of your air. Go for frequent walks in the fresh air, get adequate cardio exercise and purify your blood. Buy some plants and keep them in your home, get an air purification system, and once in a while just open your windows when it's nice outside. Make sure that you become conscious of and avoid obvious pollutants both outside and inside your home. Teach others of your experiences and help them to breathe free of toxins and pollutants and remember that breathing is the essence of healthy living. Also get involved with organizations that protect our natural forest and bodies of water and make a difference, whether you go out and help clean a shoreline or pick trash up that you see as you walk down the street. Take responsibility for our earth and make a difference!

HEALTHY AIR EXERCISE

This is an exercise in planning and following through.

1st Pick the most appealing location to find fresh air.

Place: _____

2nd Choose the day that you plan to go to this location.

Day: _____

3rd Give a specific time that you plan to participate in this exercise.

Time: ___:____AM or PM

4th Allow yourself a minimum of 30 minutes at this location to observe and enjoy the quality of air.

5th While there journal your thoughts on this wonderful experience! *(Don't forget your pen or pencil and paper.)*

Healthy Breathing Exercise

Journal:

Chapter 8

3. WATER

Water the essential liquid of life. It provides life to everything on the planet whether directly or indirectly. Water is our main source of life, without it we would be a simple pile of dust. In my study of water I have found a very fascinating correlation. In many scientific studies of the body and water, most agree that the body is roughly made up of about 70 percent water. From our brains, kidneys, livers, muscles and so on, our bodies maintain an average of 70 percent water. I recently found that the earth is also covered with approximately 70 percent water. In total it is estimated that the earth's surface holds on it 326 million cubic miles of water. If you still can't picture that, imagine walking around a country block that is 1-mile distance to every corner, then take each of those corners and lift a wall 1 mile high and fill the center with water. This is something you certainly couldn't do with your back yard hose. Why you might ask? Well it takes a little over a trillion gallons to fill that one cubic mile of water, so you might be there for a while. To imagine 326 million individual cubic miles of water on the face of the earth is amazing. Now isn't it interesting to notice as well that the fruits and vegetables that we consume are also made up of about 70 percent water as well. This fascinating correlation leads me to believe that water is truly the lifeblood of everything that lives on this planet. It is the balancing act that creates energy and keeps our life and our world in fluid and physical motion. Without it we are non-existent. Water also helps to create our atmosphere as well. Each day 280 miles of water evaporate into the atmosphere moving and eventually dropping somewhere.

Water is also harnessed and provides energy to the world in many places, but most importantly, water provides energy to human beings and the foods that we eat to survive. With all of this in mind it is pretty easy to assume that our water is one of the most important tools for survival in our lives. The big question that is posed is that of pollution or sewage; if our water is that important to us then why is it that we continue to allow big businesses and industries to contaminate and pollute it with toxic substances?

THE AGE OF INDUSTRY

In the mid to late 1800's, with the evolution of our modern day living came the industrial age of technology. From Andrew Carnage's development of steel to John D. Rockefeller's mass production of petroleum and lets not forget dear old Henry Ford. These gentlemen are just a few of a multitude of the massive factories of production spawned over decades of our history. In most of all these factories toxic byproducts were produced by their end products. In the beginning of this age of industry, there were few rules and regulations regarding pollution. Most big business, up until the early to mid 1900's, just disposed of toxic residues either in holding ponds in the back of their factories or some even dropped it right into flowing creeks or streams of water nearby. It wasn't until 1969 when the Cuyahoga River off the coast of California literally caught on fire from a large oil spill that our government really started to look at the seriousness of pollutants in our waterways! In 1972, Congress passed the Clean Water Act that vowed to clean all waterways throughout the United States that people fished and swam in, and to completely eliminate the discharge of pollution by the year 1985. Although we have set laws and made some extremely great calls-to-action we are still far away from our 1985 goals. Year to date it is estimated that nearly 40% of our waterways are still unsafe to swim or fish in. In the last ten years there have been nearly 30,000 beaches closed due to contaminated water and many fish consumption advisory warnings because of such high toxic levels of chemicals in our waterways. Although our government has placed strict fines for these giant industries polluting our waterways, the EPA (Environmental Protection Agency) has had a tough time keeping up with them. It is estimated that in 1997 big business dumped 270 million pounds of toxic chemicals into our nations rivers, lakes, and streams. Almost 30 percent of large industry plants are just downright non-compliant to the clean water act of 1972 and the goals that the act implies. It's as if these big industries greed for profit allows them to weigh the risk of getting caught and the fines they could incur, versus the minimal fines that in many cases are not enforced. The government's lack of persistence with the Clean Water Act creates a serious problem for our society and future generations to come. The Natural Resources Defense Council (NRDC) recently gave a press release stating that the previous federal administration had launched one of the worst attacks on environmental safeguards in modern history. The NRDC reported significant cutbacks on some of the nation's most important environmental programs including public lands, wildlife, forests, our nation's air pollution, and as importantly, our nation's water treatment systems. In many ways, I feel that our government has helped us to become the wonderful nation that we have become and in others I feel tricked and deceived. Believing that the government is "by the people, for the people" is like believing that a used car salesman is just really giving you the car at his cost. Yeah right! When it comes to government and big business, the government is the manufacturer, big industry is the car dealer and the people are the suckers that just bought the lemon that broke down the next day after the warranty.

In the industry of water pollution, why is it that our government can prevent big business from dumping toxic chemicals in our waterways, when our government, in part, uses toxic chemicals to treat our drinking water? In addition, taxpayers' money buys toxic chemicals from big businesses, which are in turn used in our water treatment systems. Chlorine is the main chemical used, which I would like to discuss.

Chlorine is a legitimate "move gone wrong" by the United States Government. As water became increasingly polluted due to the large industrial movement of the earlier 19th century, the battle with microbes (viruses, bacteria and parasites) became more prevalent. Hence, the U.S. Government began experimenting with chemicals to kill these illnesses, which in some cases caused death. The solution was "Chlorine!" They found this chemical actually cleaned up the water by killing all living or potentially threatening chemicals or microorganisms. However, there were not many studies done on the adverse effects of chlorine. By 1974, our government passed the Safe Drinking Water Act regulating and setting limits as to the amounts of harmful chemical, bacteria and metal levels that were allowed in our drinking water. Today, we are finding out more and more information about chemicals we have been drinking in our water systems for years. Most importantly, we now know that chlorine, when combined with other natural elements in tap water create toxins called "Trihalomethanes" such as Chloroform, Bromoform and flouroform. These toxins are considered carcinogens and have been known to cause liver, kidney and bladder cancer. Other illnesses related include, asthma, eczema and heart disease. The kicker is: now with the knowledge we have about chemicals in our water systems, most all of us turn a blind eye right along with all of the federal and local agencies. What do we do? We feed right into the fear-based consumerism and buy purified water instead. Did you know purified water is quickly becoming a real competitor to diet sodas, with hundreds of millions of dollars in sales yearly in the United States? So this question always comes to mind for me when I think of the water treatment plants in our local communities: Why is it that large corporations like Pepsi and Coca Cola can build huge factories to purify water in massive quantities, but our government can't find a solution for treating our local city water systems?

Hopefully in the near future a more conscious government can look into that with a little more urgency. Until then it is important to always make sure to do the following for good health. If at home drinking from the tap, make sure to have a purification system connected to your water. Even in the shower or bathtub, it's important to use purified water. Remember that your bodies' largest organ is the skin, which is like a large sponge that absorbs anything topical that you put on it, most easily water. If going out on the run or to public places make sure to take purified water or ask for it when dining out. For those of you with well water systems, take extra care of all of your water and treatment systems. Most purification systems are good nowadays; however I still think that the best purification system is reverse osmosis. You can go to the link below to find the brands that we endorse at www.generationawareness.org/purewater.

The big question that most people are not quite sure about: How much water should I drink daily? Science says you need to drink at least eight 8-ounce glasses of water a day (2 quarts), more so when you exercise. Now this 8-ounce stuff is based off of an average. I mean how can you tell someone that is a healthy 90lbs and someone who is underweight at 190lbs that 8 ounces is what they need. The equation is the following for determining how much water you should consume daily.

Your Body Weight divided by 2 = Ounces of water a day you should drink. Pretty simple right! For Example I weigh 175lbs / 2 = 87.5 ounces daily. Make the equations in the space below for yourself.

I weigh _____ lbs. /2 = _____Ounces daily

Water Tips:

It's always a great idea to have a glass of water first thing when you wake-up. After all, most of us sleep between 5-9 hours daily and during those sleeping hours we are using up a good portion of water to detoxify our system.

Coffee drinkers make sure to have an equal amount of water for each cup of coffee every morning. Since we know that coffee is a diuretic and makes us deplete our water supply and not feel thirsty. (Natural Sources of Herbal Teas are better)

Test your hydration through your urine! This sounds a little strange but a great way to make sure your body is hydrated throughout the day is to view your urine to make sure that it is mostly clear like water. When dehydrated your urine will become a much darker yellow and may have a stronger odor.

If having trouble drinking regular water, find flavored water or anything that doesn't have a lot of sugar or carbohydrates in it. Revisit the previous link to explore options if you like.

Which water is best to drink is a big issue in our society today. I really do recommend that you never drink out of a tap if you can help it. The purer the water, the better. Don't be fooled though, a lot of bottle companies hoax people into believing that some waters on the grocery store shelves are purified when they're not. For example, in most supermarkets you'll find 4 types of water choices:

1) Purified

2) Spring Water

3) Drinking Water

4) Distilled.

I suggest that you always focus on purified or distilled water since you know that the words themselves equal a purification process. Drinking water and Spring Water are very questionable.

Chapter 9

4. NUTRITION

In this chapter we are going to talk about one of the most troublesome subjects of the western civilization and its influencing culture in this day and age. However, before we do, I would like to introduce some facts that you may not be aware of:

Fact: 1 in 3 people in the US are considered obese. With the population at 328 million, that is an estimated 109 million Americans.

Fact: 1 in 5 children between the ages of 6 to 17 in America are overweight.

Fact: Overweight/obesity is one of the most prominent known risk factors for all of the following conditions and diseases.

- *Diabetes*

- *heart disease*

- *high blood pressure*

- *gallbladder disease*

- *arthritis*

- *breathing problems*

- *several cancers*

It is an absolute shame how people of this century have forgotten or have not been educated on just how basic eating right really is. It is no wonder with all of the marketing and advertising for healthy eating on one side and the other side snapping the whip of consumerism to work longer, harder, faster and eat processed or junk food in between. Not to mention there is a take out, drive thru or to-go-around pretty much every corner; all processed so cheaply for preservation and profit that most of this food has very minimal nutrition at all.

You've got a fast food joint promoting fast, cheap processed food; a gas station selling quick pick-me-up sugary drinks or candy bars; and a drug store selling fat loss pills right next to the pharmacy all at several intersection in most every town in the country. If you ask me it seems to be a big racket. Let's go back to the basics and start from the beginning of common sense eating and nutrition.

Five Basics of Simple Nutrition

1st You are what you eat!

The importance of nutritional value in each meal is the absolute cornerstone to conscious healthy eating and longevity in life. For all of you that remember, this old adage of you are what you eat, it really rings true. If you consistently consume fattening greasy foods with additives that are processed for quick sell or easy and fast consumption, more than likely you will end up becoming a statistic sooner rather than later and I mean that in a dead kind of negative way.

It really is that simple; be aware of everything you stick in your mouth and avoid processed foods to a minimum. Eat healthy organic fruits and vegetables, as well as organic meats if you choose in moderation. You will become much healthier; your body will begin and continue to naturally regulate and re-proportion itself. Remember these questions before sticking that piece of food in your mouth.

☐ What true nutritional value does this food have for me?

☐ How is this food prepared and has its preparation effected its nutritional value?

☐ Is there additives or by products that I can avoid if possible?

☐ Is there a smarter way to prepare this food?

The 4 Basic Questions to Good Eating

1. What true nutritional value does this food have for me?

2. How is this food prepared and has its preparation affected its nutritional value?

3. If possible, are there additives or byproducts that I can avoid?

4. Is there a smarter way to prepare this food?

Place this on your refrigerator door and read each time you open.

These common sense questions should start the ball rolling and allow you to consistently become aware of all nutritional value to foods and their preparations as well as alternatives and foods to avoid altogether. Here's a list of foods that you should avoid if at all possible.

☐ Deep-fried foods of all kinds

☐ Foods high in refined sugars (Ex: Cakes, Cookies, and Donuts etc.)

☐   Foods high in sodium or sodium glutamate (Ex: some Chinese foods)

☐   Daily Animal Protein ingestion (Ex: Milk, Cheese, Chicken, Red Meat & even Fish)

Remember that the largest most processed food products used are refined or bleached sugars, flours and dairy ingredients. It's also important not to fall into the trap of 'enriched foods,' this basically means these foods have been stripped of much of their nutritional value during the refining process and then supplemental synthetic vitamins and or minerals are added back to the food. Many large food companies are now also "Fortifying" food, which means that they are basically adding additional synthetic vitamins and or minerals to their products to create the appeal of better health. Unfortunately, neither Enriched or Fortified food products work well with the absorption of our bodies and we normally internally reject most of this.

In saying this, make sure to find whole foods that are as unprocessed as possible. If you need to find a store that has these products you can go to www.generationawareness.org/healthyfoods/localstores to research a healthy place to eat or purchase food in your neighborhood. If I don't have the info then I'll find out and help you. It is my goal to help as many people as possible to develop and clean their bodies from the inside out.

2nd Portion control and frequency of meals

How much and how often you should be eating throughout the day - This is an old concept that is cycling back through nutrition programs with new science sustaining it for good. First, regulating portions is as simple as forming a new habit, right? Not so easy though! The facts are that eating small nutritionally valued meals every 2 to 3 hours daily trains the body's metabolism to run extremely efficient. Think of it this way, if you eat the 3 square meals that have been beat into many societal cultures heads for centuries, then this allows your body to slow way down. With each heavy meal consumed, the body secretes hormones and pulls blood towards the stomach and digestive track. When this happens the body becomes overwhelmed with work and excess calories that it cannot use. Eventually all of this food is broken down into its proper value whether carbs, being broken down into glucose or what you would call sugar, our fastest source of energy; or proteins broken down into amino acids, which repairs muscles, organs and bones in the body. Of course, fats are being broken down into our back up energy source, also feeding the brain and organs with vital cushioning and energy as well. What happens next is really interesting, as all of these three macronutrients are broken down, the body will pull or absorb the micronutrients, which are vitamins, minerals, fiber and water through the intestines and into the blood stream. Once this happens, all of these calories will be processed through the liver in which it will determine whether to store it or use it. This is where the problem comes into play with a big meal, too much of all of this food at once, the body will have no option but to convert and store excess carbohydrates, fats and protein into its fat reserve for future use.

Now let's look at training your body with small portions consistently 4 to 6 times daily. If the body is only allowed to process and absorb a regimented amount of food every few hours then this is what the brain is being told and relates to the rest of the body and organs being used. The brain says, *"OK! I see how it's going to work, My Body is giving us these small amounts so let's use what we get and start lowering some of these reserves that we've got around our legs, hips, belly, back, arms and around the organs inside. Did you hear that body, we're all going to have to expend a bit more energy to sustain our normal ways so let's get busy! "*What you're really doing is giving the body a swift kick in the butt, It processes less and runs more efficiently. And with an added exercise regimen that promotes and expends more energy, the body will look harder for energy reserves to help it run consistently and efficiently. We'll get more into this later!

3rd Food Combination and what to avoid!

Downfall of mixing meats with complex carbohydrates - The third part of simple nutrition goes against everything that most generations

have been taught especially in modern days. All of the good old traditions that we relate to being a part of food and culture, from baseball
and hot dogs, to Philadelphia and cheese steaks, cook outs and ham-
burgers, Chicago and pizza, meat and potatoes etc. The one thing
that all of these foods have in common are the wrong combination
between dense protein and heavy complex carbohydrates. Mixing
any meat such as chicken, turkey, cow, pig, eggs, cheese, milk and
nuts, with heavily starch foods such as pasta, bread, potatoes, cere-
als, sweet fruits or sugary processed cakes and candies releases special individual enzymes and acids that help breakdown foods for
digestion and processing for the body.   When animal protein is
ingested into the stomach it triggers a release of heavier portions of
hydrochloric acid to be released to break down the substance while
passing through the digestive system. When starchy foods are
ingested, an immediate release of the enzyme called ptyalin begins to
break down the starch in the mouth and throughout the digestive
track. This enzyme creates an alkaline base that coats the stomach
to help breakdown into the small intestines. Because of the mixture of
acid and alkaline secretions, this creates a canceling effect for the
food being processed throughout the digestive system. Many times
this dormant food can spoil and rot while processing through the
body. Some research has found the lack of proper breakdown of proteins, when the body only breaks down the molecules on a macro
level and not all the way down to the true amino acids (micro level)
that rebuild tissue, can cause major toxic conditions in the body.
These conditions may cause a number of immunologic reactions that
could lead to allergies and diseases of all kind. To add to this mess,
when the body is using this enormous amount of energy to process
these neutralized foods through the digestive track our metabolism
becomes lethargic and sluggish. This adds more stress to the liver,
which trains the body to store more fat reserves. This downward spi-
ral sets the stage for obesity and eating with these combinations also
prevents people from losing weight when they really want too.

Remember to eat fresh vegetables or simple carbohydrates with
your proteins. Don't combine animal proteins with fruit either, this will
honor the body's natural digestive processes which leads me into the
next nutritional concept.

4ᵗʰ Honoring your Circadian Rhythms – The fourth basic nutritional idea that I would like to teach you is the idea and study of *Circadian Rhythms*. This is one of the most fascinating subjects that I have studied and learned in recent years. However, in keeping with the simplicity of this lesson I will not go into great details, rather, I will stick to the basics. If after reading this information you are interested in studying more on these and other nutritional concepts, I have listed some books that you can check out at www. generationawareness.com/books/ nutrition.

About 3000 years ago when scientists were philosophers and doctors as well and they began recording and studying the human body in many ways; when hospitals were facilities that were peaceful and serene community bay sides with fresh sea breezes blowing through uncontaminated winds is when holistic wasn't holistic but rather just a clean way of life. Scientists and doctors began to notice certain qualities in human beings and other mammals on the earth. They saw that human's were not just creatures of habit but also creatures of light and darkness. They noticed the energy levels of human beings were mostly at their highest when the sun was at the highest as well. They also noticed most human beings craved food or ingestion at these times.

INGESTION - We will call the first rhythm - ingestion. This is from 12 noon until the sun begins to set and this is the best and most appropriate time for us to eat. Now, bear in mind that eating small portions as discussed previously in frequent meals every 2 to 3 hours is optimal for a higher and more effective running metabolism. This first natural rhythm of the body, when you think about it, is pretty much common sense. Unless you have trained yourself to be a night owl, it's obvious for most of us that we are up and running during the day and therefore require food as energy to sustain ourselves and keep going.

ASSIMILATION - It's also quite obvious, that when the sun goes down our metabolism begins to decline and then we begin to go through the next phase or circadian rhythm. In the evening the sun sets and eventually we shut down completely and fall asleep. In this time, normally from 8pm until we get up or the sun rises, this is called the assimilation process. Imagine for a moment that your body is a factory that runs 24 hours a day. During the day we open the doors and place all of the materials inside, as the sun sets and we fall asleep the doors shut and our internal factory begins going to work on itself. This means that the body shuts down completely. Your respirations go down, your heart rate and blood pressure slows the body and goes through the REM stage, which is the rapid eye movement that our brain uses to prepare the brain and nervous system to relax. All of this takes place and the body or factory begins to go to work inside on a microscopic level. This is the time when the body replenishes and restores and regenerates itself completely. This second phase is affected though when the body is not given proper nutrients such as natural sources of vitamins, minerals, proteins, fats, and carbohydrates. If we give the body minimal materials and or ingredients to rebuild then things will begin to breakdown and never truly repair. As mentioned above, this is why nutritional value to the food you ingest is so important. If you eat processed foods high in a lot of things that you can't even pronounce and synthetic vitamins; then as you age and your hormone secretion naturally begins to decrease you will be more prone to sickness, disease and injury in your life. The third circadian rhythm is but yet another common sense item if looked at as well.

DETOXIFICATION - When the sun rises and you begin to wake after being rested and re-energized you will notice a few very common things that happen. First, the pit stops to the bathroom as one of the primary, if not first, thing done. Next you'll notice the bad breath, the crust in the eyes or ears. These are all common parts of detoxification and this is our last phase of natural processes of the body. If we go back to the analogy of the factory, when all is done by the end of the night and the body or product that we have so steadily worked on internally over night is accomplished, then it's time to take all of the scraps or byproducts, open up the back door and push them out of the factory. It's actually easier and better to sweat in the morning because the body wants to naturally detoxify. This leads to a very important question that most all of my clients always ask when discussing circadian rhythms. "What do I eat in the morning?" Well in order for your body to push excess junk out of your system it's using your circulatory system or blood to do this effectively. So the last thing you want to do is bog that process down. Although having a healthy breakfast may be important, eating lunch is just as important too. If your body is naturally trying to detoxify in the morning then why are we going to slow it down with a big hardy breakfast full of stuff that we're trying to get rid of. If we know that eating a large breakfast will likely combine the wrong kinds of foods and slow our metabolism down, as well as pool a large amount of blood to the digestive system, which will put a halt on our natural detoxification state; why not honor that natural rhythm by allowing the blood to flow and keep doing its job while waking up with sunshine and eating a piece of it as well? I'm talking about fruits. Most any kind of fruit is full of so many different vitamins and minerals and is light on the digestive system. Berries, melons, apples, bananas, oranges and many other fruits are really the nectar of the Gods, not only are they extremely natural when eaten raw but they also process through the body really easy. Most fruits will process completely through your body within 30 to 50 minutes and transport nutrients that fast because they are simple carbohydrates that don't take a lot of energy to process. This means that by eating moderate amounts of fruit first thing in the morning, you will honor that detoxification rhythm and stay healthier in general at the start of each day. However, remember if you are eating properly by eating every 2 to 3 hours, this should give you time to also have a small bowl of healthy carbohydrates as long as it's later in the morning and not a large amount.

Remember the three Circadian Rhythms and honor them for optimal nutrition.

I.   Ingestion Phase – Eat during the day in small healthy portions. Try to avoid mixing proteins and starches. Eat small portions often, every 2 to 3 hours.

II.   Assimilation Phase – Don't eat after dark and get adequate rest for your body. Remember that healthy foods during the day equate to healthier internal recovery of all the important working parts of the body.

III. Detoxification Phase – Eating healthy will give you less byproduct to release in the morning, never eating a large breakfast will help honor your detox stage. Exercise in the morning if you can, do something that will make you sweat. Be aware of your body's actions and help it to detox by drinking plenty of water in the morning as well. Start your day off with a healthy piece of fruit.

When you begin to become aware of all of these natural processes that the body should go through daily, you will begin to understand the importance of nutrition in so many ways. This will allow you to see that nutrition isn't really difficult at all, it's just a game of new habits over old ones. With a little knowledge and discipline you'll get there fairly fast.

5th Plan your work and work your plan!

Nutrition really is all about changing bad or old habits and creating new ones. One of the easiest ways to do this is by planning what you are going to do in advance and then following through with your plan. This is probably one of the best things that was ever taught to me and stuck. **When it comes to nutrition, most people are lazy because of the order of importance that they have given food in their lives;** all the while not using common sense that it's the food that affects our overall health and therefore everything else we see as important anyway. Isn't it interesting we can plan a week or two vacation with great detail and months in advanced; plan a business meeting with all the bells and whistles and take hours to do this; plan a career even with a ten-year degree and so forth, but we just can't seem to plan on what to eat for dinner or for the week in most cases. Planning really is a way of life in many things. Why shouldn't your nutrition be an important part of these planning regimens. In the following information you are about to learn, I hope to educate you to some interesting concepts and most importantly teach you some skills that I use to help others improve their awareness and recreate their eating habits. But first, let's talk about the three parts of food that create energy, both the good and the bad, Protein, Carbohydrates and Fats.

Proteins – are the building blocks for tissues and are responsible for all the muscles and growth and also repair the body. Proteins, when processed, are made up of twenty-two different amino acids. Thirteen of these amino acids your body can produce; the other nine your body cannot produce. These are called essential amino acids, which must be included in your daily intake and are divided into a few basic sources of protein.

Plant Proteins – vegetables, whole grains, beans and nuts – these proteins are the most natural sources for the body, although most all of these have great sources of protein, it is minimal in comparison to other sources. However, striving to obtain all nine amino acids needed when eating plant proteins is possible. By combining different sources of these proteins you can complete all nine amino acids in the chain. Here are some popular examples: whole wheat bread and almond butter, corn bread with beans, rice and beans even green vegetables with these sources work well.

Animal Proteins – meat, poultry and dairy – although all nine essential amino acids in a single source will supply more than enough per meal, lets discuss the disadvantage that we are at with saturated fats within these high protein sources. Americans ingest two to three times or more the suggested daily amount of necessary proteins based on their energy expenditure. Guess where most of it comes from? You guessed it, ANIMAL PROTEINS! The wealthiest country in the world (Super Power), more advanced in so many fashions than others. Yet, with all our technology and science we are just now getting a small view of the big picture when it comes to the epidemic of diseases and sicknesses that are being perpetuated by some pretty big hitters in the world's economy. *(If you're following me you know whom I'm talking about, The D and M Industries! You can guess for yourself what D and M stand for!)*

TO BE CARNIVOROUS OR NOT TO BE CARNIVOROUS
THAT IS THE QUESTION!

Although some scientists argue that man is, for the most part, omnivorous, (meaning a meat and veggie eater) it's obvious that our anatomical structure as a species proves different. For discussions sake, let's paint a scenario for a moment and imagine that you are sitting in your backyard feeling your stomach rumble and realizing that you're hungry. As the hunger cramps increase, you suddenly notice a small wild bunny rabbit hopping along and minding its own business. Let's say that for some crazy reason your natural animal instinct jumps out of you and you are then able to swiftly chase this rabbit down and catch it. Not likely right! OK! Let's say that your animal intellect allowed you to carefully devise a plan to trap the rabbit. When trapped, you carnivorously grab the rabbit and immediately try ripping and biting into the rabbit's skin and flesh. First of all, do you think that you could actually tear or rip through a rabbit's skin with your hands and teeth? Probably not! Again, intellect would say to use a sharp object or perhaps a knife. Let's say for argument sake you were able to do this and then you began to eat the meat of this rabbit. The muscle, intestines, heart, organs etc, what do you think would happen? We'd probably be absolutely grossed out not to mention at a very high risk of getting sick from some type of bacteria or possibly a disease that the rabbit was carrying. Intellect or experience would tell us to cook this rabbit in order to protect ourselves from any sickness or disease while increasing the tenderness of the meat. Now what if you were a lion or a tiger or a bear. OH MY! Then what are the processes of this natural hunt and the digestion of this soft little furry bunny rabbit. First, the lion is designed and has the ability to catch animals of prey; he's designed to do this. Second, when the tiger catches his prey he has special teeth called canines (you knew that!), which allow him to rip through the skin and flesh of this animal. Third, why is it that the bear can eat raw meat and not worry about the illnesses that we would? Because he has an acid based saliva that automatically kills any of these bacteria's when ingested. Finally and most importantly, why is it that lions, tigers and bears are not suffering from the enormous amounts of cancers and illnesses that human beings are on this earth?

SO LET'S MAKE SENSE OF THIS AS A SPECIES:

- **We have no claws or canines to successfully kill and eat another animal**
  (Hint, try chewing a piece of raw meat sometime)

- **We have alkaline-based saliva, not acid-based, preventing us from killing bacterias.**
  (Our stomach acid is over 20 times weaker than carnivores stomach acids)

- **We have very large intestinal tracts that are up to 27 feet long.**
  (Carnivores have very small intestines designed to quickly digest meat)

- **We perspire through our skin and control our temperature in this fashion.**
  (Carnivores perspire and regulate temperature mostly through their tongue)

In all reality, we have more similarity of a herbivore rather than either an omnivore or a carnivore. Our anatomical makeup just shouts it. Why is it that most human beings eat meat and how did this habit start?

THE EVOLUTION OF HUMANS AS CARNIVORES

In recent years we humans have found some extremely fascinating things that make a lot of sense when it comes to this subject of man eating meat.

It started with an archeological dig in the province of Georgia, bordering south of Russia and north of Turkey. As most know, the earliest findings of mans existence was with the cavemen, or pro magna, which were recorded millions of years ago. However, the recent find in Georgia was of a tribe that was named Magnus Erectus that dates back to be the oldest existence of man that ever lived. The information that was gathered was astonishing and made me a believer in moderate animal protein ingestion.

Some scientist are more convinced that through these digs and the history and placement of bones, our advancement and intellect by eating animal protein has finally come full circle to find its beginnings. Keep reading and you'll understand what I mean soon enough!

You see, the early human beings were indeed designed as herbivores but as the earth began to shift and mold itself by developing seasons, both warm and cold, these earlier humans began to migrate. As I began to understand this history lesson it was quite obvious that most could not migrate fast enough. Not only because we don't have enough hair or thick enough skin on our bodies like most mammals to stay warm but also because naturally as a herbivore we didn't have enough body fat. In order to survive, these early humans became scavengers and would pick off of leftover meat when carnivores would leave eaten up carcasses. This is where it begins to make sense. As the creatures began to eat meat (I'm sure that a lot may have gotten sick or it may have taken time to adapt but remember there probably wasn't near the amount of disease back then either and the will of man as a species is incredible) they began to become more and more intelligent. Remember that meat is protein and protein breaks down into amino acids, which build and develop muscle. Organs are muscles; the brain is a living muscle as well and requires fat and amino acids to grow and function. Now think about this, back in those days it was all about survival of the fittest in the wild and who do you think were the strongest? Carnivores! Why? Not just because they had large teeth and acidic saliva but rather because they were hunters. They had the intellect to track and kill other animals, which made them stronger and more intelligent.

As the early humans began to develop more brain capacity, they probably began to follow and or mimic the carnivorous animals becoming territorial and aggressive on a smaller scale while learning to defend themselves in the mean time from larger predators. We have even retrieved tools that they would use for butchering and hunting to prove this as well. I know this may be farfetched for some of you, but think of this for a second. Think of an animal in the wild that is a herbivore and now think of a predator that may see this herbivore as its prey. Which is more intelligent and which, more than likely, will survive? If you're thinking along these lines then its plain to see the predator will stay on top of the food chain and come out alive in most cases. Remember the dinosaur movies as a kid and you will quickly remember a carnivore chasing a herbivore.

Human beings today are by far the most intelligent creatures on the face of the earth. We have a body that is physiologically evolved from a herbivore into an omnivore. Both Plant food and Meat sustain us pretty well. Although it is possible that eating meat has helped us to evolve faster and become the intelligent creatures that we are today in this world; why is it that our lives are so full of disease and sickness in this day and age?

To finish the archeology dig and the results, as researchers began to discover many of the bones they found the remains of an old man. Through technology, the scientist found that the bones of this particular fellow indicated, possibly, the first case of arthritis. Although the earlier human being had lived much longer through this stage of evolution by becoming a meat eater, he had also suffered the effects of it as well. Today it is common knowledge that saturated animal fats leach to bone, which create less density and circulation to the body. Some scientists even say that animal fat including dairy create osteo-porosis and can also be leading factors to arthritis and, of course, we all know about heart disease. The lesson all comes back to modera-tion and balance in life.

Just for the record, there have been several studies by some of the top scientists in the world relating all different types of cancers and illnesses with the consumption of meat. From most every organ that we possess there's a correlation of cancer, and as mentioned above, probably the most prominent is the correlation related to heart dis-ease. But let's not just blame this on meat eating alone. What I like to call _DIRTY SCIENCE_ has a lot to do with this too. This is the part of our intelligence that really stinks. As we began to become smarter and to develop ideas of societies and cultures in our humanity, survival of the fittest turned into something more than just trying to make the kill and have our bellies full. We became a world of wealth, which led to greed. If you go back to meat for a moment, when you really look at the trends of our society, meat was a rare and somewhat expensive item to have on our plates until we had refrigerators and freezers. Until the age of industry we were for the most part lacto vegetarians. Even back in biblical time's, meat was eaten most often by royalty because they were the only ones who could afford or store it. Salt was an expensive commodity and was one of the most common ways to cure and keep meat at that time. If they could only see us now!

When we began to develop our intellect over the years, we have found several ways to improve and increase production of everything including animals. Such as synthetic hormones for faster growth, which increase production of these animals and in turn creates more products of which prices are lowered so more people can afford to purchase greater amounts. This is big business and has made the meat industry one of the largest businesses on the face of the earth. Unfortunately, the drugs and hormones that are given to these animals are creating illnesses in us as consumers. A great example of this is also in the dairy industry. For many years most Dairy Farmers would inject their cows with a special hormone called rBGH (recombinant bovine growth hormone) in order to increase their milk production for market. Although the government will not post the 30 day test results of the rats tested in the short study, it was quite obvious that it was not only bad for the cows themselves, but for humans drinking cows milk as well. These hormones trigger many problems in these cows such as a shorter life expectancy, developing mastitis, and infection of their utters which grow puss pockets internally and leak into the milk. When a human has an infection what does the doctor give them? Antibiotics! Guess what the cows get to mix to their chemical soup milk, a more potent source of antibiotics suitable for a 1000 pound cow, which is being pumped into our breakfast cereal, given to our babies in their bottles and used to dip our chocolate chip cookies with. Don't forget all of the processed foods that use large amounts of milk, which are shipped by the truckloads. This is just one example of dirty science. Now think about over-crowded stalls of all types of beef, chicken, pork etc. that become unsanitary and infested with disease. How many more millions and millions of pounds of animals do you think are injected or fed each day with hormones for fast growth and excessive antibiotics. Here are some scary facts that you may want to know. The following information comes from www.mindfully.org and for more information you can visit www.gracelinks.org too.

- *National Institute of Allergy and Infectious Diseases, "Antimicrobial Fact Sheet", May 4, 1999* - Overuse of

antibiotics in animals is causing more strains of drug-resistant bacteria, which is affecting the treatment of various life-
threatening diseases in humans. The Institute of Medicine at
the National Academy of Sciences has estimated the annual
cost of treating antibiotic-resistant infections in the U.S. at
$30 billion.

- ***American Medical News, "FDA Pledges to Fight Overuse
  of Antibiotics in Animals", February 15, 1999*** - Fifty million
  pounds of antibiotics are produced in the U.S. each year.
  Twenty million pounds are given to animals, of which 80%
  (16 million pounds) is used on livestock merely to promote
  more rapid growth. The remaining 20% is used to help control the multitude of diseases that occur under such tightly
  confined conditions, including anemia, influenza, intestinal
  diseases, mastitis, metritis, orthostasis, and pneumonia.

- ***Risk Assessment of Fluoroquinolone Use in Poultry,
  Food and Drug Administration, February 2000*** - Chickens
  are reservoirs for many food borne pathogens including
  Campylobacter and Salmonella. 20% of broiler chickens in
  the US are contaminated with Salmonella and 80% are contaminated with Campylobacter in the processing plant.
  Campylobacter is the most common known cause of bacter-
  ial food borne illness in the US.

- ***Newsweek, March 7, 1994*** - Antibiotics in farm animals
  leave behind drug-resistant microbes in meat and milk. With
  every burger and shake consumed, super-microbes settle in
  the stomach where they transfer drug resistance to bacteria
  in the body, making one more vulnerable to previously treat-
  able conditions.

Now, I am not trying to scare you into changing your way of life and
become a diehard vegetarian. NO! I honestly believe that this is not
my place. However, with the information that I have given you, I hope
that you can realize that eating meat for every meal or every day is not
a very smart thing to do. Therefore, I suggest that you limit your
portions of meat, poultry and dairy. Take several days off during the

week and be aware of how you feel afterwards. This could honestly add years to your life. Remember that most every plant source has protein in it and when eating a healthy selection of fruits and vegetables your body will get its needed amount of not just protein, but vitamins and minerals as well. Also it's good to point out that there are a growing amount of farmers that are becoming aware of this problem and dedicating their businesses to raise organic raised animals, using healthier grains and feed and pledging not to give steroids or antibiotics but to take a more holistic approach at all cost. Given the price of the meat or dairy may be a bit more expensive but it does cost a lot more to raise these animals with sufficient space and in a clean healthy environment. If you'd like more information on local stores in your area that provide organic meats and dairy products go to: www.generationawareness.org/healthyfoods/localstores/organicmeats.

Soy Proteins – Soy! unlike many of the other plant-sourced proteins, provide all 9 of the essential amino acids and have no excess saturated fats. Soy protein although controversial for some has gained much popularity by many. Soy protein can be used as a complete protein source in moderation, or used with other plant sources as well as supplementing animal proteins and human's dependency on meat consumption.

Soy has been a common source of protein in most Asian countries for centuries. Although many people believe that in Japan and China soy is the main source of protein in most people's diets. The truth is that in these countries soy is used as a condiment and doesn't normally replace animal proteins at all. Soy protein's popularity in recent years is due to the growing epidemic of, as mentioned earlier, animal diseases and a better understanding of the effects of antibiotics and hormone residues in expedient genetically mutated commercially-raised animals. In moderation it can be a great alternative!

Myth: Soy is hard on the kidneys?
Animal proteins are much more difficult to digest then any vegetable protein. However, it is uncertain that excessive protein is very tough on the kidneys, which we'll talk about shortly.

Myth: *Soy depletes bones of calcium?* Some people have heard that soy is extremely acidic and can deplete the bone of its nutrients. This is false, and for good reason. Soy is considered a neutral food and is neither acid nor alkaline based. The problem here is when the oil is depleted out of the bean. This is done by some manufacturers that make soy powders to prevent the soy from going rancid or spoiling fast. When this is done it does make the soy acidic. However, most manufacturers are now adding calcium to balance this problem and make the soy neutral once more. So make note of soy powders and check to see if there is an adequate amount of calcium added to protect you from this problem.

PROTEIN TIPS:

CAUTION: Like anything, some people are allergic to soy and have adverse reactions. (These are few and far between.)

It is also cautioned for women with estrogen-sensitive cancers to speak with their doctors before adding soy to their food list. The isoflavones in soy may interfere with the action of tamoxifen. **(tamoxifen – this is a chemical compound that although non-steroidal is still a physiologically active estrogen antagonist. In most cases tamoxifen is used to treat postmenopausal breast cancer.)**

On the other hand soy can actually help men suffering from prostate cancer from developing severe hot flashes.

Caution: Soy should be eaten in moderation because of the high isoflavines that mimic estrogen which also act as phyto endocrine disrupters. It's estimated that just 30 grams of soy per day in your diet can cause lethargy, hypothyroidism, weight gain, constipation, fatigue and may be related to increasing cancer cell growth. In all, soy protein should be used in small amounts for good health.

NEW SCIENCE ON PROTEIN

There are many arguments in nutritional science today that view protein ingestion from one side of the spectrum to the other. However, what we know is that the body will absorb a significant amount of protein based off of its needs. If you are an extremely active person involved in sports or weight training it is obvious that your body will need a significant amount.

In order to make protein work for you at its most efficient level, you need to be aware of two things. First, calorie consumption is mandatory. If you consume too few calories and you start to optimize your metabolic rate and get your furnace started in the body without enough nutrients, the body will go for the closest and most abundant source of energy that it has. Your Muscle! Yep! Without proper amounts of (Fruits, Veggies & whole grains) nutrients in calories the body will turn on its self to survive. This happens more than you would imagine with most very active people whether young or old. An example of this would be those people with normally high metabolisms to begin with. The second thing to be aware of is that increasing protein intake also means that you should increase water consumption. This helps with protein synthesis and digestion.

In my research, I have found what I believe to be one of the most important scientific studies in the history of man and nutrition, the Holy Grail of Science and Nutrition if you will.

"THE CHINA STUDY", is a wonderful book written by Dr. T. Colin Campbell Ph.D. and his son Dr. Thomas M. Campbell II. This study is so profound to the correlation between animal protein and many of the largest problems that plague Western Cultured societies today, including the two top killers in America, Cancer and Heart Disease as well as the major epidemic of Diabetes that exist in our world today. The little that I could say about this book would never give it the justice that it deserves. However, for those of you that need UNDENIABLE SCIENTIFIC STUDIES FOR PROOF before changing your nutritional habits this is the information that you have been looking for all of your life.

In "The China Study" book, Dr. Colin Campbell brings together 40 years in nutrition research that leads to the largest single study ever completed on nutrition and disease. This scientific study is so massive that it involved a population of 880 million people in 116 counties throughout China which produced a whopping 8000 statistical comparisons extremely significant to everyone on this planets good health. The results of a "Plant Based Whole Food Diet" has proven to be astonishing in preventing and reversing disease by decreasing all animal proteins from 10% to 0% in our daily diets. This easy to read and comprehend master piece and the valuable information and research that Dr. Colin Campbell shares in reference to the disorder and disarrangement of nutrition in government, corporate America and as he titles it, "The Dark Side of Science", which provides many insights from his colleagues, mentors and his own personal experience in government committees unethically infused with major food industry supporters in many industries. Most importantly Dr. Colin Campbell's raw sincerity and passion for his life studies revealed from page to page offer true hope for humanity in finding a healthier way to eat and live in our world today. I certainly encourage everyone to read this book and set with the information presented and go with your heart on this one. POWERFUL INFORMATION for the quality and quantity of your life.

In all, I believe that animal protein has come full circle in the evolution of man on this ever changing planet. The one thing that may have possibly sparked our intellect as it did the predators we feared millions of years ago has now made our species the most powerful and intelligent creatures that walk this earth today. But with this intellect we are paying a huge cost that involves bad health, earlier death rates and poor quality of life. For more information on The China Study Book go to www.GenerationAwareness.org/ChinaStudy.com

Carbohydrates – are the body's fastest and most efficient source of energy. There are two types of Carbohydrates: simple and complex.

Simple sugars actually save the body the extra step of breaking them down unlike compound sugars. Simple sugars are usually processed foods that have been refined. But don't think that only candies, cookies, sodas and cakes are to blame for weight gain; processed foods can be white rice, white bread and many pastas that you would see on our grocery shelves. These simple sugars are broken down super fast, which cause a rapid blood sugar increase and spike insulin production in the body.

Complex carbohydrates are whole grains, good fruits and vegetables that contain healthy fibers, which slow down the process of sugar. In all, carbohydrates break down to the simplest form of energy in the body that is stored in the blood stream and the muscle tissue called glycogen. When the body is overfed, either simple or complex carbohydrates, it automatically stores excess glycogen through insulin production and converts this sugar into fat as mentioned previously.

These discrepancies, combined with the fact that many people find the glycemic index a difficult concept to understand and use, mean that many nutrition organizations are reluctant to recommend it.

What about the Glycemic Index

The glycemic index is a fairly new diet craze word that is leaving many people very confused as to what type of carbohydrates are good and bad. When the glycemic index was originally developed it was a food chart for people suffering from diabetes. The index provided diabetics with an established chart showing carbohydrates that were high or low in sugar. It wasn't until just recently that some diet books have shown this as a way to help the average person lose weight.

However, this science is fairly new and has many varying factors. It's safe to say that although the glycemic index is a great concept and certainly doesn't hurt to follow, the index is based off of averages and therefore cannot be extremely accurate. Here are some variances that make a big difference:

☐ Type of processing for food

☐ How the food has been stored or ripened

☐ How the food has been cut or diced

☐ How the food is cooked and prepared

☐ Added chemicals or enrichment process

These varying factors can make a big difference in a single food item and can affect its glycemic level tremendously. Think about it, if you have to find out how thick your pasta is if you're going to eat it or just how to cut or dice your food just to be somewhat accurate, that's tough!

The truth is that it's totally irrational to think that we can tell how high or low the glycemic level is and how our body will react at any point of the day to foods, unless we continue to prick ourselves with a glycometer before and after each meal all day long in order to test our blood sugar and track the steady results over time. I don't think most people are interested in doing that either!

Although it is true that low glycemic foods have a low energy density, the importance is mostly in the high fiber. Foods high in fiber allow the body to break down at a slower pace and prevent the pancreas from secreting too much insulin at once. This is the goal in order to allow the body to process and collect the important nutrients of carbohydrates at a decent rate and allow less glycogen reserve to be stored as fat.

Keeping Processed Carbohydrates to a minimum

Processed carbohydrates normally have minimal vitamins and minerals as well and trigger a part of the brain called the appestat to send a message to the body that it still needs nutrients. The appestat is like a dipstick into the bloodstream constantly testing for sufficient vitamins and minerals this is also what tells you if you are hungry or full. A great example that always reminds me of this is when you eat Chinese food and your hungry again shortly after. Since this type of food is normally a large portion of white rice with minimal vegetables and or meat topped over it, the body reacts to the empty, refined, bleached white rice and although a proportional amount of calories were ingested, it can still find minimal traces of nutrients. When this happens it creates a cycle of mixed messages to the brain, creating carbohydrate cravings or sugar rushes, which in return keeps the body in frequent insulin spikes. This may eventually lead to lowered insulin production and increase the production of stored fats. Scientific research is studying the effects of high sugar eating and it's believed to be one of the leading causes of Diabetes II. This type of diabetes is when your body makes the insulin but the body's cells stop reacting. Bad News! This should encourage you to stay away from processed foods, especially junk foods. Remember, you are what you eat and you certainly don't want your body to turn into junk!

Fat – is the body's reserve of energy production and protection. Fat is a mandatory part of good health and helps us to protect and maintain our organs. Fat provides a healthy nervous system, good skin and hair and is absolutely essential for Hormone production.

Myth: All fat is bad for you!

The good the bad and the ugly Fats:

- **Saturated fats** – UGLY – These fats come mostly from animal foods and contain cholesterol. I suggest that everyone minimize consumption of these fats because they contain a lot of the "bad" cholesterol, LDL (low density lipoprotein). Examples of these fats are, bacon, fried foods, chuck ground, T- Bone Steaks, whole dairy products etc.
- **Unsaturated fats** – There are actually two types of unsaturated fats.

1st) Monounsaturated Fats – GOOD - This type of unsaturated fat is mainly derived from vegetables. The two most popular sources are from cooking oils such as canola and olive oil. (Olive Oil being the best) These oils contain no LDL (Low Density Lipoprotein). This source of fat actually contains antioxidants (Vitamins and Minerals) that prevent and protect against heart disease.

2nd) Polyunsaturated Fats – GOOD and BAD - These fats when eaten from the right sources are excellent sources of fats and actually help to improve the body's functions, in particular, the brain. Broken down into their natural source, they are called Omega 3 fatty acids. They are found in many things such as; fatty fish i.e. tuna, salmon, sardines; you'll also find them in some grains and seeds like sunflowers, safflower, and flaxseed, even corn. These fats transform into bad and dangerous stuff once they have been processed or hydrogenated. After that they turn into what are called trans-fatty acids, these are shortcuts to processing and preserving foods. This transformation of fats raises blood cholesterol levels and has been attributed to helping increase heart disease along with other types of cancers.

Fats are the body's natural source of stored (not immediate) energy. Your body will use Fats as a second energy source. Although good in many ways, as we have just explained, why is it that people gain excess fat? Excess fat that leads to obesity is normally caused by one or three reasons.

1) Bad food choices – Eating processed or high fat foods will send the body a signal to store.
2) Whether eating healthy or unhealthy foods over consumption of any foods can cause you to gain weight.
3) Under eating – (Caveman syndrome) can throw the body into a state of starvation sending mixed signals that it needs to conserve as much as it can once ingested after long breaks between eating.

So like everything else when it comes to nutrition and fat consumption, it's important to stay aware of what you eat, how often and how much. Here are a few more tips when it comes to understanding fat in your nutritional habits.

- Fats have twice the calories per gram than proteins and carbs. 9 calories per gram of fat to be exact vs. 4 calories for carbs and protein.

- Did you know that the only way to raise your level of HDL is by exercising, there are no known foods that contain HDL's.

- Fat-soluble vitamins include A, D, E and K, be careful not to consume too many fat-soluble vitamins because, since your body can store them, they can reach toxic levels.

A FEW OTHER THINGS THAT CAN MAKE A BIG DIFFERENCE WHEN IT COMES TO

GOOD NUTRITION

Avoid Alcoholic beverages with food – Although it is a common social habit to drink alcohol and eat at the same time, it's really not a good idea to do so. Most people ask why not, it helps to absorb the alcohol and taper my buzz. I do understand that a piece of bread may soak up some of the liquor in your stomach, but isn't the whole reason that you are drinking is to get a social high? Most people hate it when I mention the words social and high. The facts are that alcohol used to be an illegal drug back during the prohibition area and it does make you high, tipsy, drunk or stoned, call it what you will but it lowers your inhibitions. From a nutritional standpoint drinking alcohol tends to slow your bodily functions down as well as your digestive abilities. So while you eat, not only is it easier to say oh just give me a little extra of this or that, but also one more drink. This is the pattern that a lot of people fall into when drinking and eating in a social environment. When drinking and eating together, our bodies slow down and process less. Like the food combinations, alcohol when mixed with food, strips a lot of the nutrients from the food that you are eating so it tends to be a wasted meal anyway.

Follow the rule of drinking alcohol at least one hour before your meal and consume plenty of water during that hour as well. This will do two things for you. First, help dilute your alcohol so that your metabolism will not slow all the way down. Second, the water will prevent you from dehydrating your body as well to curve your appetite.

Keep Drinking Alcohol after dark to a minimum – As mentioned earlier, the second circadian rhythm begins in the evening when the sun goes down. When drinking alcohol during this slowing phase the body becomes lethargic and toxic. It takes away from the internal process of recovery that you allow your body to go through when healing. With this note I would like to add a comment about wine and its nutritional value. Although it's a scientific fact that wine has many good antioxidants and some say that it's really good to have a glass of red or white wine each day, please remember that it's refined sugar that adds to your daily caloric intake and can lead to excess fat and, for some people, bloating and discomfort. Drinking a shot of vodka may be better!

Out-to-Eat Rules – Here's a simple rule that I've attempted to teach all of my clients over the years that works well for those of you that like to go out to eat often. First of all, make sure that like everything else, you plan your dining out and prepare yourself for the restaurant and the types of foods that you plan to indulge in. Remember, no excuses! Just because you are going out to eat doesn't mean that you can't eat healthy. Most restaurants tend to have healthy items on their menus now-a-days, so take advantage of the healthy items available and if not, don't be afraid to ask for a more health conscious meal. After all, they're there to service you and believe me they want you to come back. OK! On with the out-to-eat rule...when eating out even if healthy or not, only eat half of your meal, save the other half for another meal later. Personally, my wife and I tend to split our meals because I'm not real picky and tend to like most foods... As long as they're healthy!

Earn your dessert – In recent years there has been an influx of nutrition books that teach you about a cheat day or meal that you can earn when training and eating well during the week. I've taught this and used it often myself and honestly it tends to work well for most. However, instead of planning a whole day of cheating, I would recommend a couple of meals weekly. Remember a small portion with anything is still important. To have a slice of cake is one thing, but sitting down and devouring a complete cake is another.

Move around after you eat – One of the best things to do after eating is to walk. Whether it be a brisk walk on your lunch break, a cardio class or an evening stroll after dinner, walking is a great way to stimulate the digestive system. It also prevents you from getting the couch potato syndrome.

Eat dinner early – This is an old concept that still holds true; as you read earlier the second circadian rhythm, which is assimilation, Remember that eating late takes a lot of energy away from this process and prevents the body from honoring this rhythm. On top of that the body is more apt to store much of the foods you eat late as fat reserve since the body is in a lower gear. Make sure that you eat a small healthy meal about 1 to 2 hours before sunset. To be safe, make this a habit and this will take you a long way in the weight loss and maintenance department.

Stay disciplined, but don't be so hard on yourself – Remember not to be so tough on yourself. If you mess up just dust yourself off and try a little harder. Just don't give up and do your best to follow these five basic rules of nutrition. Before you know it, this will become second nature and your body will begin to change. After seeing how easy it was to get the results you'll be on your way to living a better healthier life.

Water, Water, Water – Drinking a sufficient amount of water throughout the day is probably one of the easiest ways to curve your appetite. So planning to drink one or two full glasses of water 20 minutes before each meal will keep you right on track, not only with your hydration, but also with any sweet tooth or salty carbohydrate craving you may have. Also, if you didn't know, staying hydrated makes it easier to lose weight for most people.

Conclusion: Although nutrition is a science in many ways, unless you're a scientist don't treat it like one. For the most part, food and nutritional concepts are not meant to be difficult. Eating should be enjoyable and fulfilling; it is the natural process of our lives and completes us as a species. Being responsible with the food that you eat is really the most important part of nutrition. Make sure to keep it simple and follow the simple ideas that I have listed in this section. Just stay persistent with these habits and make eating healthy a lifestyle habit of importance.   Below is a meal tracking worksheet that I have designed for my clients that will help you become aware of your eating habits and trends. This is a magic worksheet that will help you in many ways to form the habits that you need for healthy eating.

Follow these simple steps and watch your nutrition improve dramatically. Please don't pass up reading about nutritional supplementation that follows these worksheets. I've recently found some fascinating information that everyone must read.

Food Planning Worksheet
Part I

7 Simple Food Ideas

1st Breakfast – Write down 7 easy foods that you would like to eat over the morning hours, fruits and whole grains are good to consider.

1.
2.
3.
4.
5.
6.
7.

2nd Lunch – Write down 7 simple meals with portion control and proper food combinations

1.
2.
3.
4.
5.
6.
7.

3rd Snacks – These 7 items need to be convenient and healthy snacks moderate in protein and carbohydrates. Preferably, something that can be kept in a purse, car glove box or your pocket.

1.
2.
3.
4.
5.
6.
7.

4th Dinner – List 7 meals that again are moderate to small in portion control as well as proper food combos.

1.
2.
3.
4.
5.
6.
7.

Go to: www.generationawareness.org/forms/printable

Food Planning Worksheet
Part II

Good & Bad List	
Healthy	*Unhealthy*

Directions: Make a list of all of the foods you listed in part one and separate them into healthy and unhealthy.

Go to: www.generationawareness.org/forms/printable

Food Planning Worksheet
Part III

Healthy Grocery List

Fruits

Veggies

Complex Carbs

Proteins

Snacks

Liquids

Directions: Take all of the foods from part two of your food-planning list and make a grocery list divided into sections of the grocery store:

Note: It may be good to also list amounts and pounds of certain items so you don't over shop. Stick strictly to this list and do not buy anything else.

Food Planning Worksheet
Part IV

Daily Meal Tracker

Date _____	Proteins	Carbs	Fats	Calories
Breakfast/Time:				
Snack/Time:				
Lunch/Time:				
Snack/Time:				
Dinner/Time:				

Daily Nutrition Check list

Oz of Water _____ Complete / Ate Dinner before Dark **Yes** or **No** / Alcohol with food **No** or **Yes**

Grams of Protein _____ Complete / Out to Dinner Rule ½ or **Full** / Alcohol before dark **No** or **Yes**

Grams of Carbs _____ / No Mixing of Complex Carbs and Meats **Yes** or **No**

Rate your Nutrition in total today: **(circle one)**   *1   2   3   4   5   6   7   8   9   10*

Bad   *Average*   *Excellent*

Go to: www.generationawareness.org/forms/printable

The Truth about Nutritional Supplements

I have to be honest with everyone reading this book; this is the one section of the book that I have waited to finish last. Why you might ask? Well, the truth is that the research involved in nutritional supplements is as vast and misleading as any other subject on the planet. Nutritional supplements are entangled with modern medicine and healthcare in such a way that they are misleading the public to believe that a synthetic pill can replace healthy eating habits. Also by allowing such obvious pharmaceutical drugs to be accepted with minimal testing while blatantly kicking natural cures and preventative resources to the curb, some which have existed for thousands of years, it saddens me to see such greed surrounding human life. When you think about it, the pharmaceutical industries have formed a monopoly and have pushed western medicine out to many parts of the world. Given, there are medical drugs and advancements that truly do save lives in emergency situations as well as help to sustain life. However, if you view the big picture of western medicine, you will find some troubling things going on.

Pharmaceutical Industries Grubby "BIG PAWS"

Why is it that I feel like most all of us know this but just are so lost that we can't formulate the truth and take action? Let me explain!

Have you ever seen a commercial for a new drug that shows the person enjoying life and smiling whether they're walking through the park with a loved one or their family with some wonderful scenery behind them? The beginning of the commercial explains how you can have relief from your symptoms and live a better life. Now you get to the end of the commercial that begins to explain all of the possible side effects that are just as devastating as the symptoms or illnesses themselves. Many of the drug commercials disclaimers will even tell you that the medication that could help may also cause your symptoms to worsen or even may cause death. Ouch! Then the last part of the commercial states: "Contact your doctor to see if this is right for you." Fortunately, most of us are beginning to wake up and smell the coffee. But, what about those people that are truly suffering or are in chronic discomfort and or pain, what about them? Most that are in this state of mind and physical illness will pick up the phone and call their physician for an appointment, right? This is the hook that has pro- pelled western medicine into millions of homes across the world. Now, we all know that most pharmaceutical companies have a large number of over-the-counter medications or temporary pain killers that can be purchased without anyone's permission or with just a license and signature. The most lucrative of these medications must be pre- scribed by a legally licensed physician that is first being paid a minimal fee from you (co-pay), second, a moderate to large amount for your visit from your health insurance company, and third, the physician will be rewarded for pushing the drug by the pharmaceutical company in one way or another that will then demand a hefty amount of money from both the patient and the insurance company. This large sum of money is not a one-time thing; rather it becomes a monthly fee or a residual income that is divided among many parts of the healthcare industry's monopoly.

Now, on to the scary part. Most of the medications, although supposedly regulated and observed from government entities, are known to do one thing: "cause side effects". These side effects lead to other physical ailments that lead to more medications, which then place you in the loop. This loop I am speaking of allows the dirty part of healthcare and western medicine's big paws around your throat until you are sick enough to develop major ailments that require dras- tic measures such as surgeries, chemotherapies, dialysis, and so much more. In reality, once again, all of the drastic measures that I am referring to are tremendously expensive. They come with a large risk factor sometimes including percentages of death, which for the most part, could have been prevented if we would just learn to heal ourselves with preventative measures like good nutrition and exercise to begin with.

Here's an example of this! The American Heart Association esti- mates that nearly 73.6 million people in the USA; 1 in 3 adults, have high blood pressure not including 2 million children in the country as well. As a western culture, we are consistently being told to eat ani- mal protein daily for optimal health, which most of us know is the main culprit for clogged arteries. The well known risk factors for heart dis- ease are: bad diet and nutrition, lack of physical exercise or circula- tion, age, family history, ethnicity, gender, and let's not forget STRESS! However, one of the top 10 risk factors for high blood pressure is "OTHER MEDICATIONS." HMMM! That's something to think about... How many people are taking high blood pressure medications? Current statistics state that 51 million people in America take these medications daily. If we were to look at an average dollar figure, lets low ball it and say $10 per month for a prescription of medication x 51 million = $6,120,000,000.00 a year, just in the USA alone!! If you are having trouble with the zeros; that was 6 billion, 120 million annually as a low-ball figure, and this is just the payment on the side of the consumer. We should also not forget cholesterol-lowering drugs, also known as Statins, which grossed 12.5 billion dollars for the pharmaceutical industry recorded back in 2002. Although Statins are recommended by a lot of physicians in regards to preventing cardiovascular disease (this has never been proven in the medical industry today and is a huge myth). What is proven, however, is that the number of deaths per year in relation to cardiovascular disease has not really changed in 25 years with the massive influx of medications pumped into the public daily. Now, here's another statistic that I'm sure will floor you as it did me. Currently, 32 million Americans are taking more than 3 medications daily and this number continues to grow at record levels with new drugs that continue to hit the market adding to the thousands that already exist. This reality hits home for me personally, currently my stepfather takes 9 medications daily which totals 35% of his income, my father takes 11 medications totaling a 1/3 of his retirement income and I just recently found out that my mother-in-law spent twelve hundred dollars in one month alone on prescription medications. The sad truth is that most citizens are being dumped and herded like test rats through a cleverly developed, marketed and controlled system of health care that involves large powerful organizations to manipulate and control government regulators like puppets.

America's FDA, the Food and Drug Administration, has consistently protected and allowed the pharmaceutical industry, "Big Pharma," to quickly put drugs to market over and over again without thorough testing which have unnecessarily killed many, many people all while getting as little as a slap on the wrist. Although we have had proof for centuries through scientific studies of so many natural substances that heal, improve health, add longevity and quality of life, FDA regulations, namely the Dietary Supplement Health and Education Act, have and continue to protect the fat pockets of "Big Pharma" by not allowing manufacturers within the supplement industry to market nor claim that any natural supplement product will prevent, treat or cure any illness or disease. Instead, they are only allowed to make basic and general statements in regards to their products in which always requires a disclaimer that normally states that the product is not condoned or approved by the FDA. By allowing this regulation, the FDA creates confusion in the natural supplement industry by restricting these companies from placing important product information to help inform the public consumers of all of the true benefits of the natural products thereof. By not allowing this information to be stated, many people become confused and sometimes cynical about natural supplements because of the lack of information available and difficultly in finding time tested studies and scientific research.

This one-sided approach leads the majority of citizens that have been conditioned to believe that their doctors are gods and pretty much have all of the answers to protect their health. The truth is that many doctors are what I like to call "old school physicians" that have been so conditioned themselves by the pharmaceutical industry that they don't bother to even research the drugs that they push but rather push them because they have found a reliable tool that creates return visitors on a steady basis. Although I seriously doubt any western medical physician in the world would admit that, I really don't believe that the physicians' intentions are in these respects. The reality of the situation is that they are being duped as much as the public by a well-oiled machine of a massive industry that indirectly uses them as drug pushers.

However, to end this on a positive note, there are many young and old physicians in the world as well as the United States that are beginning to see and combine a more open view of the need for modern day medicine. Many physicians are waking up to smell the "herbal tea," if you will, and realizing that moderation and balance should be used in western and eastern medicine in taking unique approaches to help their patients. A new type of physician is evolving in many cultures that are referring to holistic medicinal approaches to treat the ailments of their patients. Thank God for this and lets all hope these physicians begin to rub off on the rest of the naysayers that they work next too.

My belief is that our government has to be less influenced by big money companies and more controlled by the people that have an interest in pursuing the truth. A balanced world of western medicine technology and natural medicine must be studied in combination to find healthy treatments and cures for everyone facing illnesses in the world. In all, nature and science need to come together in moderation to find less synthetic drugs with side effects that completely defeat the purpose and find more natural cures that treat and prevent illness to begin with. This starts with open accessible education to all that request it in relation to their well-being and health care concerns. No more lies or hidden truths from "Big Pharma" and no more drone doctors that follow their paths of greed for a steady paycheck. Doing the right thing should take precedence!

Imagine this for a moment: going to a physician that takes the time to sit down with you and find out why you are experiencing this illness and goes to the root of the cause. The physician then prescribes a natural treatment, which involves bettering your nutrition, creating a plan for improving your circulation and energy levels through exercise, or any other non-evasive, natural alternative treatment. Now imagine if these holistic treatments and natural supplements were paid with your insurance just as any other health insurance plan today. If these treatments don't work for you then you begin to shift into other more invasive alternatives and go from there. Why is it that our health care system doesn't do this today? Why is this not the norm? Why is it that we have to do this research ourselves? It is so skewed and confusing that many of us just give up due to confusion and fear and jump right back into the herd going in circles while paying the hefty price both financially and in the quality of life. These are the concerns that the people of the world should be asking and finding solutions to. We must step up to the plate and begin to ask our doctors to focus on our health from this perspective and take action. This is the only way that we will ever shift the awareness of the predominant health care systems and our government. Again, I urge you to talk with your healthcare professionals and when you are ill, ask questions, and put your health care professional in gear to find these answers for holistic nutrition, alternative therapies and medicines with little to no side effects. By doing this we will begin to set the premise for change and evolution in this ever-increasing industry and prompt big businesses focused on gluttony and greed to take a hike or get on the right path.

For those of you that are in the loop and on these residual medications, I challenge you to ask your physicians for a plan of action that will wean you from the medications. Do your research and work with your physician, ask as many questions as you can and let your doctor know that you want answers so that you can take control of your health and be less dependent on them and the medical system. Take Action!

Toxic Soup for Breakfast, Lunch and Dinner

Now that I have gotten that off my chest, let's talk about one of the main reasons that most of us are getting sick to begin with. However, before we do this, I must share with you some more scary information that most may know, and if not, hold on to your seat. The reason that I mentioned and gave the example of blood pressure medication to begin with was in correlation to the following information. Up until a few years ago, heart disease topped the list as the number one cause of death in America. Although today we have an epidemic of obese adults and children in this nation, with millions of clogged arteries per square mile, and the worst eating habits on record. Today, cancer is running neck and neck with heart disease for the number one spot. Why is it that so many people are developing cancer?

Statistics state that 1 in 3 men and 1 in 4 women in their lifetime will develop some type of cancer. Today there are over 200 types of cancers recorded. These include practically every organ in and on the body in which physicians are seeing more of everyday.

So the three important questions are:

1st) what is cancer and how does it begin?

2nd) what are the factors that cause cancer?

3rd) How can we prevent getting cancer?

First, cancer normally begins with a mutated gene or cell in the body's tissue that grows and multiplies.

Cancer, like most other illnesses except for infectious diseases, is considered to be multi-factorial. Multi-factorial is an easy way of saying that you can't blame it on one thing, you have to compile several things to cause the illness or cancer, so let's make a list and classify what our toxic soup is made of.

Let me give you an example that may give you a broader spectrum of the problems that most western and striving western cultures don't think about in our every day lives. Most of us wake up in the morning with common toxic hygienic and medicinal habits such as brushing our teeth, putting on deodorant, washing our hair and bodies with soap and shampoo, putting on make up, cologne or perfume, taking over the counter and prescription medications, drinking and eating our foods (Including Animal Proteins) with chemicals and byproducts that we have never heard of, and on top of that, we nuke them with our microwaves in plastics or cook them in pans made of metals like Teflon and more. These are just a few of a gazillion other things related to massive product consumption and use that we do throughout a typical day. Even if we have water and air purification systems in our homes, eat and use all organic products, it is still impossible to escape some of the most potent toxins on the earth today unless you live in an organic bubble for the rest of your life.

The second part of this toxic soup that I am referring to is not just the products, foods and medications that we consume and use each day but even worse, the environment that we work in for 8 hours or more a day to create these products and get them to market and on our shelves at home. Working, myself, in a profession for several years now that is designed to protect people's property and lives involves a heavy risk of ingestion of carcinogens and toxins that could kill you in one breath. Even being around a fire scene within what some would call a safe distance is still risky. In my career working in Fire and Rescue I have heard tragic stories and seen first hand accounts of cancer victims, some who lost their lives. Now, think of what you do or have done for a living and observe or recollect the surroundings that you work or worked in day after day. What are the toxins that may haunt you or others you work with? In almost every profession people are subjected to toxins, heavy metals and carcinogens that add more burdens to their immune system and risk towards weakening their health. Although the government has developed organizations to help regulate Big Industries and many of the toxins that we work and live with, it is still quite obvious again, that most of these government organizations desensitize and withhold important information from the public while providing a watch dog approach with minimal penalties in comparison to the profits these Big Industry giants make. Now let's revisit the top 10 list of killers in America. The National Center for Health Statistics, states on their current webpage the following information for 2005.

1. Heart disease: 652,091

2. Cancer: 559,312

3. Stroke (cerebrovascular diseases): 143,579

4. Chronic lower respiratory diseases: 130,933

5. Accidents (unintentional injuries): 117,809

6. Diabetes: 75,119

7. Alzheimer's disease: 71,599

8. Influenza/Pneumonia: 63,001

9. Nephritis, nephrotic syndrome, and nephrosis: 43,901

10. Septicemia: 34,136

The truth is that toxins and carcinogens whether purposely ingested or inhaled are becoming the tipping factor, not just in America but also in many parts of the world. This toxic soup is now being related to many illnesses and diseases everywhere. Scientist are now beginning to find that increased amounts of heavy metals commonly found in very small traces of our daily environment and necessary elements in sustaining good health, are now being found in compounded rates leading to toxicity. The seven heavy metals that are being studied by many scientists today: Lead, Mercury, Arsenic, Cadmium, Iron, Aluminum and Nickel are considered to be some of the most toxic when stored in the body tissue and circulated through the blood stream. There are many illnesses that are now being linked to these toxins. The International Occupational Safety and Health Information Centre "OSHIC" stated in 1999 that (Quote) many of these toxic metals may result in damaged or reduced mental and central nervous function, lower energy levels, damage blood composition, lungs, kidneys, liver, and other vital organs. Long-term exposure may result in slowly progressing physical, muscular, and neurological degenerative processes that mimic Alzheimer's disease, Parkinson's disease, Muscular Dystrophy, and Multiple Sclerosis. Allergies are not uncommon and repeated long-term contact with some metals or their compounds may even cause cancer. (End Quote) As a result of these studies a congressional mandate was established under the U.S. Department of Health and Human Services called the Agency for Toxic Substances and Disease Registry (ATSDR). This organization works closely with the Environmental Protection Agency (EPA) and the Food and Drug Administration (FDA) to observe, report and train on human health effects diminished quality of life associated with exposure to hazardous substances.

The FDA which regulates all Food, Drugs and other consumables along with the EPA, which regulates all toxicity involving industry and production, has been told by their own government controlled regulator, the OSHIC, to create an Agency to register toxic substances and diseases, the ATSDR. Why is it, that, I bet you, 99.9% of most Americans have never even heard of it? Perhaps this awareness in such toxicity would cause some big waves in a lot of industries that have carefully lobbied and bought their way into the system. Maybe these big organizations have invested so much money and time into controlling the masses that they are scared of change that may reach deep into their pockets. Maybe it's easier just to kill people and not think about it but rather write it off as the cost of consumerism. Again, the only way that we can change is to take action as an individual and lead the way by example.

A Different Way of Thinking about Supplements

The concept in many households and the general public's way of thinking when it comes to nutritional supplements absolutely floors me. I have had clients that will give me a health history that includes: chain smoking cigarettes, excessive alcohol drinking, fast and junk food consumption, all of the over the counter and prescribed doses of medications and lastly a multi vitamin and or number of other supplements from Vitamin A to Zinc. When I begin to explain to them that instead of spending their money on nutritional supplements they should probably use it to make a down payment on their burial plot and purchase a nice coffin they often laugh out loud. Although we all know that I am being facetious, think of it this way for a moment. If you are purposely polluting your body on a daily basis then do you think a few vitamins are going to really do anything for you? Not really! Nutritional supplements should not be used to counteract unhealthy abusive habits towards your body. Instead, they should be an additive to assist in developing good nutritional habits for only those that feel they cannot eat healthy on a daily basis. Unfortunately, most people living in a western culture society struggle with healthy daily nutrition. If this is you then I suggest that you once again focus first on eating healthy and then find a quality source of supplement(s) that fits well with your daily lifestyle. Because there are so many vitamin supplements out there today, I have provided you with a list of the top companies with the highest quality products.

www.generationawareness.org/vitaminsupplements

Although adding a carefully selected multivitamin to your daily grind may help to sustain your health, it is only a small part of good supplementation. The truth is we can add as many vitamins as we like to our bodies but the body will take what it needs and sometimes only what it can handle and the rest will be washed away. Learning to consistently detoxify the body is just as important than any ingestion of vitamins.

Detoxification is Key to Good Health

There are many ideas for detoxifying your body and many of them work well. Water & Juice Fasting are great sources for detoxing the body and restoring balance. As mentioned earlier when honoring your circadian rhythm daily this automatically promotes a positive source of nutrition and helps to eliminate waste and toxins properly.

Another common detoxification system that many people take advantage of today are colon cleaning supplements which help to clean the large and small intestines and improve the immune system. Another route that is more popular now a day is also colonic treatments. These treatments are a bit more invasive and actually require a licensed professional to clean you out from the other side. Although this type of treatment may seem rough most reviews and comments are positive. Many people state that they feel lighter, have better mental clarity, healthier skin, fewer headaches and can control their weight better.

Although these forms of detoxification can be used every so often I believe that all of us should focus on detoxing daily. In recent months I have found one of the most fascinating detoxification tools in the history of man, which I feel compelled to share with you. This product I believe is going to stir up western medicine as we know it today. It's truly unbelievable!

The Power of Zeolites

What's a Zeolite? A Zeolite in the simplest terms are unique groups of minerals that form crystals within volcanic rocks when lava reacts with alkaline and seawater. The molecules created within these crystals take on geometric shapes that interlock with each other into what is called tectosilicates. Imagine a four-sided honeycomb molecule. The Zeolite Molecules are negatively charged cages that attract positive charged metals and toxins.

Zeolites have been used for many years for many types of pollutions. Zeolites are considered "molecular sieves" which means that they are an incredible absorbent for all kinds of toxic gases and liquids that hold chemical toxic compounds.

In recent years one company has been doing some incredibly fascinating work with one particular type of Zeolite called "Clinoptilolite". This type of Zeolite has been used for over 30 years in the Livestock industries to withdraw microscopic parasites and molds from feed, which not only help to prevent the animals from getting sick but also allow an increased absorption rate for nutrients.

A team of scientists have found a unique way to use this particular Zeolite to improve human health by detoxifying the body in a major way. The patented processing of these Zeolites bends their molecular structure to clean them out while breaking them down small enough to travel into the blood stream to pull major toxins and metals from the body in a remarkable and effective way.

This organization is providing these Zeolites in something as simple as a dropper bottle. With a few drops on your tongue daily you will be detoxing in an incredible way. This stuff is no joke and is available online or through designated distributors within there company. So far they have published several different studies with fascinating results.

These controlled studies encompassed everything from testing employment related toxic exposures, serum electrolyte levels in healthy individuals, Post Workout Exercise Recovery, Ph Balances in healthy and health compromised individuals and present studies are being done on cancer, Alzheimer's and Autism patients. However amazing the test results are, proving to be what's more astounding are the real people that are giving first hand testimonies in the masses as to the power of this product. I have witnessed testimonials of relief and or recovery of so many illnesses, it truly blows me away.

Here are just of few of the illnesses that people are getting relief from: Acid Reflux, Allergies, Anemia, All types of Arthritis, Asthma, ADD, ADHD, Autism, Back & Neck Pain, Blood Sugar problems, Severe Burns, Several types of Cancers, Cholesterol, Chrohns Disease, Colitis, Cysts, Dental Issues, Depression, Diabetes, Ear aches, Emphazema, Eye Issues, Fibromyalgia, Chronic Fatigue Syndrome, Glycoma, Gout, Hay Fever, Headaches and Migraines, Herpes, High Blood Pressure, Hot Flashes, Insomnia, Irritable Bowel Syndrome, Joint problems, Knee Pain, Lupus, Memory issues, Menstrual Cramps, Multiple Sclerosis, Myopathy or Nerve Damage, Osteoporosis, Parkinson's Disease, Restless Leg Syndrome, Sinus Infections, Skin Disorders, Tendonitis, Thyroid issues, Ulcers, Viral Infections, Vision problems and too much more to name.

Here's a link if you would like to read these testimonies: http://www.testimonyinfo.com/index.htm

The facts are that this particular Liquid Zeolite product works in an absolutely incredible way. My self-study of this product has led to my own testimony as well. I have been taking this detoxification product for less then three months now and have seen amazing results. In recent months I went through a painful surgery, the recovery time was twice as fast, also the chronic hip and back pain that has bothered me for years has vanished into thin air. My sleep has improved and I noticed a more rested feeling in the morning. I have also noticed a dramatic improvement in my skin as well, not to mention my energy level, which was great, to begin with, has even improved. I have also noticed improvement in the recovery time with my strength training and yoga with more sustained energy during my exercise regimens. Even the lactic acid build up that would normally lead to a few days of discomfort after a new exercise regimen has dissipated tremendously. Incredibly exciting to me!

In my opinion, if there is such a thing as the fountain of youth or a wonder supplement, this could be it.

In a world of Toxic Soup that is virtually impossible to escape, we must realize that it's important to protect ourselves in every way possible. Now that science is finding more and more correlations with heavy metals and toxins in relations to cancers, autoimmune diseases and several other illnesses to date, it is all of our responsibilities to protect each other and our families from these situations.

No matter what approach you take it's important to find healthy ways to first form good eating habits and then if you need any supplementation find what works best for you. Most importantly don't forget to detox your body consistently. Read up on new science and do your homework on products before you take them.

If you would like more information on the Zeolite product mentioned above follow the link below.

www.generationawareness.com/NCD

Chapter 10

5. EXERCISE – The fifth source that perpetuates energy in life is physical exercise or resistance training, calisthenics, aerobic conditioning and so on. This chapter will cover several aspects and different types of exercise theories while providing a mini education of what you should know when it comes to exercise and all of the parts involved. It is my goal to make it as non-complicated as possible and to provide enough knowledge that will get you started on an exercise program as well. I will guide you through the basics of exercise and teach you step-by-step, the necessary keys in developing a well balanced and easy-to-follow program. I will help you get and stay in optimal health throughout the rest of your life and will give you a few options when it comes to exercise regimens.

When discussing any type of resistance of the body, there is first a word that must be defined and understood in basic terms. The word is **Homeostasis** - this is the body's way of maintaining balance and overcoming, defending and, most importantly, protecting against any environmental change. Homeostasis plays a role in all functions of the body from the endocrine system to the immune system. If challenged the body in most cases has the ability to miraculously find a way to fix and or adapt itself to many things. Exercise is a proven way to fine-tune the body and many of the functions thereof. When we push the body to limits of discomfort it will push back if given the proper energy to do so. This is why proper nutrition is so important to healthy living. Although time and age gradually work against us, exercise can slow down the deteriorating process of the human body. In the past 100 years, exercise science has been developed and has created many facets of exercise to determine the best ways to improve longevity both in mind and body.

By age 25 to 30 we are fully developed and begin to decline in life. Although minimal in early adulthood, by our mid 50 to 60's our bodies have certainly taken a beating in most cases. This is when we begin to experience difficulties whether internally, musculoskeletal or externally. Hormones are not produced as much as in earlier life and the metabolism of the body begins to really decline. It's estimated that after 25-30 years of age the average person gains ½ to 1 full pound of fat per year and looses the same in muscle mass. Our resting metabolism decreases significantly as well.

Here's the good news! It has been proven over and over again that proper resistance exercise, or strength training, along with healthy nutrition, can slow down the aging process. In many ways resistance exercises restore functions of the body, increasing the quality and quantity of our lives.

Basic Muscle Anatomy and Terminology

There are many benefits to adding resistance training to your lifestyle for good health. However, before we jump into this extremely fascinating new science, we must first learn the basics of the body's muscle anatomy and the terminology that goes with it. Remember, it is my goal to take the scientific mumbo jumbo out of all of this and just make it easy and understandable for everyone wanting to comprehend the basics.

Muscles are separated into three different categories: smooth muscles, cardiac muscles and skeletal muscles. Smooth muscles are considered to be involuntary muscles because they move in patterns or waves without our conscious mind controlling them. Great examples of smooth involuntary muscles are the stomach and pancreas. The stomach automatically moves food through its passages while secreting gastric enzymes to break down food. The pancreas is actually a solid organ that when signaled through the endocrine system contracts and squeezes insulin hormone throughout the body to regulate blood sugar. Although these smooth muscles play huge roles in daily living, we never really feel them.

The second type of involuntary muscle is the cardiac muscle. These muscles found only in the heart pump blood throughout the body. Although we can feel and hear our heartbeat, if necessary, there is still no known conscious thought involved. This is the first muscle that we will discuss in the section below and create a regimen for your cardiovascular system.

The third muscle group is called skeletal muscles, which are the body's most abundant tissue, comprising about 25% of a female's and about 45% of a male's body weight. These muscles are attached to bones by tendons and other tissues. They are voluntary, which means they can be moved through conscious thought and reflex actions. Each of these muscles is made of millions of tiny protein microfilaments striated and bundled appropriately together to produce all the extraordinary movements of the human body. More importantly, all of these muscles provide special links to the brain and spinal column making up the nervous system, which regulates and protects the body in many ways.

Muscles actually serve one purpose in general which is to pull or contract in order to allow the body to move, balance and coordinate through daily living. Although there are more than 600 muscles in the human body, for our purposes we will focus on only a few and group them in accordance to their patterns of motion and isolation in relation to exercise training.

Basic Anatomy Lesson on Muscle groups:

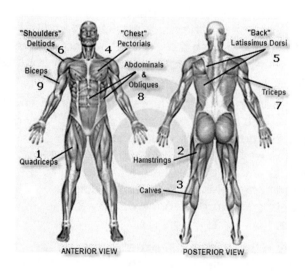

Resistance Training Defined

Resistance or strength training means using resistance in an exercise program that will help strengthen the musculoskeletal system. Whether using dumbbells, machines, elastic bands, stability balls or even using your own body weight, all of these forms of resistance will strengthen the muscles and the groups that they are composed of. Although resistance training has been around for quite sometime, it has been mastered and refined over the last 20 years and has several great benefits.

The three benefits of resistance or strength training are:

1.   Muscular strength, which will increase muscle size or mass to help the body increase its metabolic rate.
2.   Muscular endurance, the ability to develop more stamina with the muscles and their ability to endure longer under stressful conditions.
3.   Improved aerobic capacity. This one confuses most people, but you must understand that proper resistance training involves increased cardiovascular output.

Muscles are active tissues and need a lot of energy to function. One of the most beneficial functions with resistance training is an increase in our metabolism. The more muscle we produce, the more it will use excess fat for energy. This also means the more fat that's burned the more definition and shape the muscle takes on and the more proportionate you become. These three things are not the only benefits to resistance training; let's not forget all of the other important benefits for example:

- Strengthens bones, ligaments and tendons. This helps prevent all sorts of injuries.
- Prevents and helps all types of arthritis.
- Prevents and helps with neurological diseases.
- Prevents and helps regulate diabetes.
- Prevents and helps cardiovascular disease.
- Prevents and improves bone density for those with osteoporosis.

These are only a few things that exercise can do for you in any way, shape or form. But in order to understand the correct concept of exercise, it's first important to understand some fundamental principles.

Four fundamental principles of resistance training

1st INTENSITY – The only way to truly stimulate muscle growth and improvement of the body is through high intensity training. Now I'm not saying to join a gym of muscle heads and body builders and lift some monstrous dumbbells. I'm trying to emphasize that by slowly and consistently adding maximal amounts of stress to those specific muscle groups, the body will find a way to adapt to the stress demands placed on it. However, again, it is important to remind you that if the body lacks proper resources such as good nutrition and sufficient recovery periods, it will not adapt in the manner that you wish. The idea is to get the most out of the intensity so remembering to feed and rest the muscles at optimal levels is extremely important. You will know that you have reached peak levels of intensity when the muscles are completely exhausted. This will trigger the body to switch to it's reserve capacity and when this is done the body will begin the growth process and start to adapt to protect itself from future damage, thus homeostasis in resistance training.

2nd **PROGRESSIVE RESISTANCE** – As the body adapts to stress then more stress on the muscle groups must be applied for new muscle growth. Basically, the stronger you become the more weight you should try to lift with each exercise. Progressing up in weight resistance is the most fundamental part to this type of training and the results in muscle growth should be expected. This is the part of training that most lack mental discipline and fail to get to and maintain the body type and lowered body fat that they desire. Again, push the muscle, work on increasing the weight load and the body will respond and fight back.

3rd **DURATION** – This is defined as the number of exercises, sets and repetitions per muscle group. Duration is the most controversial part of resistance training today. There are more theories and programs designed as there are personal trainers in gyms and health clubs out there, few are based off of controlled scientific studies. The important thing to remember when it comes to duration of an exercise, is that everyone's goal should be to build and sustain a healthy amount of muscle mass throughout life. Whether it's a 12-repetition set or a max load test of 1 repetition it's important to endure to the last drop of energy that you can expend.

4th **FREQUENCY** - This means the number of times a muscle group is trained per training regimen. I believe the most optimal frequency of training days are 2 to 3 per week with 2 and 4 days of recovery time. Age has a lot to do with frequency of workouts and should be a major consideration when it comes to weekly exercise regimens. For example, I recommend to most of my clients 50 years of age and older that resistance training with weights should be limited to no more than twice a week for optimal health. Even other activities that involve high aerobic conditioning should be limited so that the body can regroup and regenerate itself.

2 Common Myths about Weight Training

Before we go any further into exercise and the recommended work-outs, I want to first clear up some common myths that people have when it comes to exercise regimens.

(Female) I don't want to bulk up!

The main misconception most women have about resistance or strength training is that it will build muscle, and create a bulky, body-building look. Yet some of us may have heard people say that women don't have the capacity to build large muscle because they don't have enough testosterone. While this statement has some truth to it, it's important to remember that not everyone responds to exercise in the same way. What resistance training does do is shape up and tone muscle. Including endurance activities into your exercise program also helps to burn away more fat.

I'm too old to work out!

At approximately age 70, loss of muscle strength can be significant enough to limit the kinds of activities a person can do.

For some seniors, that loss of strength may mean an inability to move a piece of furniture or to carry heavy grocery bags. Loss of muscle strength can reach the point where a person has trouble moving fast enough to cross a street or even getting out of bed. Loss of strength is also associated with an increased likelihood of falling.

Improved strength with weight training can help seniors by preventing many of the problems associated with loss of muscle strength. While not a perfect fountain of youth, a vigorous strength-training program can improve muscle strength in a 70-year-old to the equivalent of an average 40-year-old.

According to researchers at the Medical College of Pennsylvania in Philadelphia, lifting heavy weights stimulates muscles to grow and increases their size and strength. Their studies have shown this to be true even in a group of 90-year-olds!

Of course it's important to contact a doctor if you are older and get clearance before proceeding with an exercise regimen. I love to work with the senior crowd because most are always so willing to learn. When they come to me, they've decided to work with a trainer and are committed and have the time to really focus on all of the things that need to be done. What's even better is when they start seeing results in a short amount of time, and then the gloves are off and they're gung ho! If you are interested in finding a trainer after reading this book go to you know where and I'll find a qualified trainer in your town that I will personally recommend. www. generationawareness.com/directory/pt/local

Arthritis and Exercise

As mentioned earlier there are many potential benefits to exercising, including better heart and lung function, greater strength, improved mobility and independence, and a longer life.

Millions of Americans, especially among the elderly, do not exercise because they have arthritis, which limits their mobility. However, it's a fact that rheumatoid arthritis (RA), the most common type of inflammatory arthritis, and the second most common type overall, also leads to loss of muscle mass because of the metabolic changes caused by inflammation. The feasibility of exercise in this population, then, offers the most rigorous test of how practical exercise regimens can be for those suffering with arthritis. In recent years a study that included adults with RA and healthy younger subjects were trained for 12 weeks with intensive strength training or "sham" exercises (stretching and brief swimming only). The strength-trained adults all improved their strength significantly, with the greatest improvement occurring in the RA group (up 57%), compared to 44% in the young and 36% in the elderly, and 9% in the stretching/swimming controls. There were important improvements in joint pain, fatigue, walking time, balance, and gait among the arthritic group. These results demonstrate that strength training is feasible even in adults that suffer from severe RA. The lesson learned from this study was that those who suffer from arthritis should not be without a supervised exercise program and can really improve their lives by holding true to a steady strength training program.

Whether you have arthritis or any other illness, a steady exercise regimen can work wonders for most everyone. Now let's talk about the main reason that most people start and never stay persistent or outright quit, and never go back to exercise.

The Real Reason People Don't Exercise

Most people that begin exercising whether in a local gym or in their house really have no idea of the basics to a healthy strength-training program. They begin either watching someone else at the gym and mimic their movement or they purchase a video that throws them right into a fast pace program with no real explanation of the exercises. Some people will actually hire a personal trainer to help them become familiar with and guide them through an exercise rou-tine. The sad truth is that even most trainers nowadays don't even have a clue as to the basic components of exercise. So they may help in certain aspects but end up hurting in others. The end result is that the individual follows what they believe to be the correct procedure and ends up hurting themselves. Whether a wrenched back or neck muscle, strained tendon or sprained ligament, they quickly become leery of the whole exercise thing and associate it with a bad or uncom-fortable source of pain and discomfort. The following part of this chap-ter will eliminate the worry of any of this and help prevent you from hurting yourself when exercising. In this section you will learn the four basic components to any strength training exercise, which will teach you how to protect and allow your body to become extremely efficient so that when you do exercise, you get complete optimal results. No ifs, ands, or butts!!!

You may want to read this information over a few times and take the book to the gym with you, if needed. This is also a great way to find out if your personal trainer knows his or her stuff.

The Four Basic Components to any Exercise

1st) Posture - Before you begin any exercise routine, it's important to understand the significance of proper posture and balance. You may have heard that a strong mind leads to a strong body. As discussed in the earlier section of this book your body posture can also change your mental state. **As a child you probably heard "stand up straight, sit straight, don't slump your shoulders, pull your shoulders back or walk tall." Although your peers probably didn't understand the complete relevance of proper posture, they had the right idea.** Posture is portrayed in every day society as many things. A person walking with good posture is seen as more attractive, stronger and certainly more confident. The question is why do we see people that walk tall and straight as sexier, stronger, more intelligent people? This impression is almost second nature. Most of us look right through it or forget to consciously notice it. But our subconscious always picks this up. If you become aware of other's postures, then you'll also notice their posture fits their facial expressions and their attitudes. Now, adjust your posture if you haven't already; be cognitive to how your posture can actually change your mood, attitude or personality. It works, doesn't it? Even simple facial postures can attribute to these emotional changes. A great example is to simply smile as mentioned before. Something as simple as this facial gesture can change your whole outlook and posture from head to toe.

Now that you see the importance of posture, let's talk about what proper posture really is.

What is proper posture: Proper posture is very simple to understand and maintain. The only difficult part of posture is breaking bad postural habits with good ones.

Correct Standing Posture: The easiest way to achieve correct posture in a standing position is to stand with your feet shoulder-width apart. Pull your shoulders back slightly to straighten the spine and pull your chin in to balance the weight of your head on your neck. Roll your body weight slightly toward the ball of your feet. Slowly lean back towards the heel of your feet leaving the majority of the weight balanced between the balls of your feet and your heels. Shift your sternum (the center bone on the front rib cage) slightly forward to expand your chest. Also be sure to have a tiny bend in the knee so that you can take the resistance off of the lower lumbar. This will also prevent you from hyperextension of the knee joints.

Correct Sitting Posture: Good sitting posture is easily maintained when first making sure that you have good ergonomic support on the lower lumbar area of the chair. If the chair does not have this support then make sure that you are sitting briefly. A chair with no lower lumbar support, when sit in often or for long periods of time, can really cause a lot of stress to anyone's back.

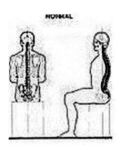

When first sitting in a chair, position your lower back flat against the seat. If the chair arches the opposite of your spine then position your gluts against the bottom corner of the chair. Next, make sure that your feet can reach flat on the floor. Position your feet at shoulder-width and pull your shoulders back. Make sure to pull your chin back as well. If the chair has arms and you are working at a computer, make sure that the arms are positioned evenly with the desk where your mouse is. This will prevent any discomfort in your back or shoulders from continual use of the mouse. Make sure that when typing, your keyboard is 3-5 inches above your knees. This will prevent your upper back muscles from strain. Also, make sure that when typing, you have some type of cushion or ergonomic device in front of your keyboard to rest your wrist on while typing. This will help prevent Carpal Tunnel Syndrome. Just a quick note about another posture problem: laptops! They are quickly becoming a serious problem with many people's backs and necks. So if you own one, make sure if you're using a laptop for a long time to sit properly at a table or in a chair that supports your back sufficiently with stable arm rests to prevent strain. It's also important to take frequent breaks so that you can move and keep your circulation going.

What consistent body alignment means - Now that you understand proper standing and sitting postures, let me explain why this is so important. When you develop better body posture it is much easier to live a normal healthy life. Why, you may ask? The answer is really pretty simple; let's go a little further into this research and talk about the physical effects of good versus bad postural habits. Good posture development not only improves your mental state, but also avoids physical misalignments in your body. This prevents you from having overly strained muscles. A person who has developed bad postural habits may tend to experience back, neck and shoulder pains. This could possibly cause overly strained leg and/or glut muscles as well, leading to problems like sciatica nerve damage or pain, which happens to be a major problem for millions of people every year.

When becoming aware of posture you may notice that you or others tend to either rub their neck as to relieve a pain, or possibly reposition their body when standing or sitting. This may lead to chronic aches or back pains when standing, sitting or sleeping. These are signs of discomfort due to strain on muscles in the body. Now, just for a moment, go back to your own posture and notice how you are sitting! When you stand do you normally shift all of your weight to one side of the body? Do you reposition your arms often to shift your upper torso when your back or shoulders are tired? When you sit do you tend to place your leg up on to the chair or cross them back and forth continually for comfort? All of these signs are habits of bad posture. These shifts for comfort or relief are known as posture shifting. When posture shifting, the body is trying to avoid any aches, pains or discomforts (normally due to a weak back.) Correcting this postural deviation can actually help you to realign your back and strengthen areas to improve posture.

The Posture Game

Exercise: Now that you understand the reasons for bad posture, let me show you a great way to steadily improve your posture day by day. I call this the posture game because if I called it a habit you probably would see it differently. The game is simple and easy to play. Find correct posture at the start of the day. Take a couple minutes out of your morning and position yourself correctly standing upright in a perfect posture position as you finish count # 1. Stand this way for a few minutes focusing just on posture. Next, throughout the day catch yourself 25 times in either a seated posture shift or a standing posture shift and correct yourself to correct posture. Count as # 2 and as you catch yourself again count # 3 and so on throughout the day. Trust me that you will, if doing this consistently throughout the day, find yourself more than 25 times with bad posture. However, by playing the posture game you will eventually break these bad habits of postural deviations with good up right posture. Remember, this will protect you and strengthen your back as well, not to mention improve your quality of life.

Posture and Exercise

Now that you understand the importance of posture in every day living, let's get to the specifics on posture and exercise. As mentioned earlier, back injuries are the number one reason that people stop exercising and never go back to the health club or gym. When exercising you are placing added force to the body in many latitudes and directions, the added force is always compensated by back and abdominal (CORE) muscles since they are the main support for our bodies. Because of this it is extremely important to be aware of protective postures when exercising.

5 Exercise Postures

1. ***A. Upper Body Exercise Standing Posture*** – This posture also known as a straddle stance is accomplished by standing in an upright regular standing posture. Feet flat, heals to the ground with ball of the feet flat as well. Very small bend in the knees, abdominals contracted for support with the shoulders pulled back in good alignment and the chin tucked in. The only differ-

ence during exercise is that you move one foot up (3 to 6 inches) one quarter to half of your shoe length. This small movement of the feet allows for the body to stabilize the back from any arching or bending motions and also allows you to perform any standing exercise with better isolation.

FOCUS POINT: One foot 3 to 6 inches back from the other!

B. Lower Body Standing Exercise Posture – When doing a standing exercise movement involving the lower extremities (legs) there are two standard exercises: a standing squat and a lunge.

In a standing squat, it is important to consistently place the legs in an even position. It is also important as well to place the feet in a outward position with the toes pointing slightly away from the body. Standing squats can be modified to place more isolation on specific muscles of the legs by adjusting the position of both the legs and the feet. The key is to keep symmetry and equal placement in both legs consistently.

Although there are many different variations of lunges from walking, alternating and stationary lunges all of them have two basic postural rules for protecting your body. First, always make sure that when in the down position the forward knee never extends beyond the toes. You can remember this easier by watching that the forward legs shin and calf muscles stay in a straight vertical position (straight up and down). The second rule in correct posture for a lunge is one in the same with the spine. When lunging through the lunge always make sure the spine stays upright and that the body doesn't shift forward too much. Although, when the body gets tired you may tend to shift your upper body weight forward for leverage and inertia through the movement, it is important not to over emphasize the movement. Another simple fix that I like to teach in educating a client as to proper lunges when exercising is to teach them to make a box or a small "h" with their bodies. By creating a box with the legs from foot to knee you can protect yourself and get the most out of this exercise.

Lying Posture (Supine) – This posture is quite simple in relation to exercises when lying on a bench. This posture should focus on preventing any arching in the lower lumbar but still allow full movement through the upper extremities. Lying flat on the bench with the head resting comfortably in a neutral centered position with the neck and spine even. Lift both feet up to the bench placing your feet completely flat on the bench as close to shoulder-width apart as the bench allows. Softly position your lower back at a comfortable position against the bench and make sure to push down with the feet flat while contracting the abdominal muscles when performing any exercises. This will automatically make your lower lumber compress against the bench and protect your back from any arching motion.

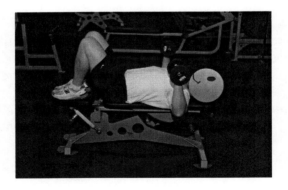

FOCUS POINT: Feet are always on the bench!

Seated Posture with Back Support – This posture is the same example as a common sitting posture. Starting from the bottom up, feet are shoulder width apart, making sure that the outside of the foot is even with the outside of the shoulder. Second, part of this exercise posture is making sure that the legs are boxed out by aligning the heels with the back or pits of the knees, this parallel positioning of the legs will allow you to use the legs to push the back flat which is the focus point of this posture. Thirdly, engage abdominals in order to keep the back muscles tight while doing any lifting exercise and lastly pull the shoulders back and balance the head or tuck the chin in. It's important to remember when balancing your head in a seated position that some people have thicker backs than others. Although some of us can place the back of our heads on the bench and keep good alignment, others may need to keep their head balanced by staying a few inches from the bench, while keeping the neck in alignment with the rest of the spine.

FOCUS POINT: Although it's only natural to have a small curve in your lower lumbar spine, make sure to use the knees to push the back flat and keep the abdominals engaged!

Seated Posture with NO Back Support – In this seated posture when having no back support, the focus will be mainly on proper alignment from the waist up with a complete focus on abdominal contraction through exercise movements. You must first remember to align your feet shoulder width apart and align your heels with the back of the knees. Although you will not have anything to push the back against, it is still important to maintain the leg and feet position forward and parallel so that there is no arch in the back. This posture is more advanced in that you are using more core muscles, so preventing hyperflexion or excess pressure on the back or spine is of major importance. One of the biggest mistakes that I see people do when in this posture is flip their feet back a little and balance on the ball of their feet and toes. This is very dangerous because of the natural flexion it causes in the back.

FOCUS POINT: Abdominals stay engaged!

Facedown Postures (Prone) – The face down postures involved in these exercises will be a little more advanced and a little more strenuous on your back than most exercises. Therefore, proper posture is very important. Although there are a few different postures the only one I consider safe is a standing unilateral movement, which uses one side of the body at a time. Place one knee at the edge of the bench and the standing foot to the outside of the shoulder. Make sure that the standing foot is even with the knee that is on the bench and that the toes are even with the top of the knee on the bench. Next, position the back straight and extend the hand of the same knee on the bench forward as you bend the torso from the waist. This should make a box from the hand on the bench to the knee on the bench, with the balance of the body towards the center of the back with the abdominals contracted for proper support. The last prone posture is when leaning forward onto a bench face down on an incline. When doing this you should make sure that your neck is supported properly and that the feet are flat and forward with a strong contraction on the abdominals.   Remember that these exercises are much more advanced and should only be attempted with assistance from a professional that may help you with proper technique and form.

FOCUS POINT: Abs engaged with balance between center of box. Do not shift back into hip or up into shoulder. Slight bend on both standing knee and benched elbow.

Other Rules to follow when establishing proper exercise postures:

PADS OVER LEGS - In some pulling exercise movements you will actually have padding to hold your legs in place. In these instances with no back support, make sure to place the legs under the pads in a box position from your hip to the heel of the feet. Always make sure that the pad is beyond your knees whether pushing or pulling. When using pulling leg exercises (ex: Seated Leg Curl) with back support most of the time you will have support bars to hold onto. Make sure that when these are available you use them to push your back flat instead of pulling and arching the back.

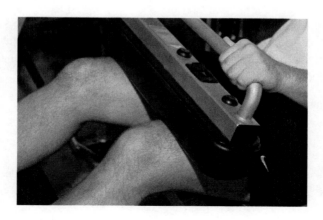

WHEN IN DOUBT, AB IT OUT – Whenever doing an exercise that involves a posture learned and you're uncertain how to position yourself, always go to the core or abdominals and engage. When contracting the abs the back acts as the antagonist muscle group for support and stays nice and tight for proper resistance and protection. Just make sure not to over strain but rather keep moderate to mild resistance in your core.

REMEMBER THE BASICS – Always start your exercise postures from the bottom up.

     1ˢᵗ   ***Feet always shoulder width apart***

     2ⁿᵈ   ***(Standing) Slight bend on knees or soft knees. (Seated) Knees boxed with heels aligned with back of knees***

     3ʳᵈ   ***Abs engaged (keeps back contracted)***

     4ᵗʰ   ***Shoulders back***

     5ᵗʰ   ***Head balanced***

Remember, this first component can provide you with the safety and assurance to protect your back, spine or neck from serious injury. Practice these postures in all exercises, be aware of your daily postures and practice good posture whenever you can.

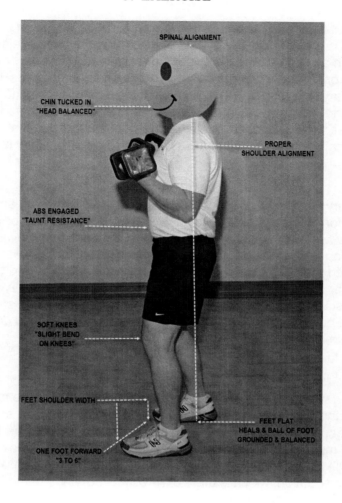

SPINAL ALIGNMENT

CHIN TUCKED IN
"HEAD BALANCED"

PROPER
SHOULDER ALIGNMENT

ABS ENGAGED
"TAUNT RESISTANCE"

SOFT KNEES
"SLIGHT BEND
ON KNEES"

FEET SHOULDER WIDTH

FEET FLAT
HEALS & BALL OF FOOT
GROUNDED & BALANCED

ONE FOOT FORWARD
"3 TO 6"

POSTURE PROTECTS NOT ONLY THE BACK, BUT THE WHOLE BODY!

2nd) Controlled range of motion and isolation   The second major component of any exercise is control through the range of motion and isolation. Before getting into the exercise part of this component, I'd like to hit on the concept of control in our daily living just as we did with posture. Having control of our lives whether financially, emotionally, mentally or spiritually is a key part of our existence. Control in daily living provides us with balance and symmetry and leads us to pro-ductive and successful (results-oriented) living.

To simplify and make it extremely easy, those people that you see in a gym or health club that speed race through an exercise, jerking up and down as fast as possible to get it over with and get onto something else, not only have a great potential in seriously injuring themselves, but will get very little results, if any, from all of the exercises they do. On the other hand, you are going to learn that understanding a moderate to slow, steady and focused quality movement throughout the range of motion that each exercise has will allow you to reap excellent results.

Every exercise that you will do always has a beginning and finishing position. This starting position is always point A. Remember that there are two movements to each exercise a (concentric movement) or contraction and an (eccentric movement) or extension. Earlier we had mentioned that all muscles really have only one function and that is to shorten or contract. So taking that into consideration, it's easy to see that our starting point will always be with our resistance exercises beginning at a point of extension. This will always be point A when doing any exercise movement!

Now we know that our plan is to have control and we've found our starting and ending point; the next question should be: How should we manage control? Developing a counting system for both parts of the exercise movement easily does this. There are many theories on counting repetitions for control, however all of the studies done basically relate the same equation, which is this, "Slow controlled range of motion leads to faster and greater results". Slow to moderate training throughout a range of motion that is consistent, will yield more micro tears in muscle fibers and allow greater recovery. The following analogy will help you to understand the concept of controlled range of motion and the benefits. I use this example when training most of my clients because for some reason they relate better to a car than anything else.

If you've ever driven a stick shift vehicle you know that there are normally five to six gears to shift through when achieving optimal speed and mobility (Results are achieved). The gear that is used for a moderate pace or speed is 3rd gear. It is third gear that we will begin this analogy. Imagine and compare yourself when doing a set of repetitions to be in your car on top of a slippery hill on your way down. Starting in third gear at a moderate pace you begin to go down the hill with steady control. As you begin to go through your reps you should begin with the same moderate pace as well. As we get half way down the hill we begin to build up momentum and need to down shift into second gear to maintain good control and balance of the car. On a set of 12 repetitions, half way down the hill would be at rep number 6. When shifting into an even slower pace, as we continue down the hill we will begin to slow even more as we reach the bottom of the hill. At the bottom of the hill we should shift into 1st gear to have complete control of the car or muscles. During the last 2 to 3 reps in first gear is the time to feel the burn and keep it. This is when you are getting the most out of the exercise and want to slow all the way down. On the last rep of the set it's time to put the brakes on, imagine in the analogy you are at the bottom of the hill and need to place the foot on the brakes and squeeze nice and tight. Hold the contraction and keep the muscles shortened for 5 to 10 seconds. Slowly release the brake and roll to a stop at the bottom of the hill. That means on the last rep when you've squeezed every last bit of energy out of it then slowly control the negative until finished. So, third gear, second gear, first gear, apply the brakes and roll to a stop. Moderate pace until half way through set, then just a little slower until the last 2 to 3 reps turns to super slow. Finally, on the last rep hold the push or pull and gently control the negative until finished. In relation to most people's exercise control, what I'm trying to do is train you to do the opposite.

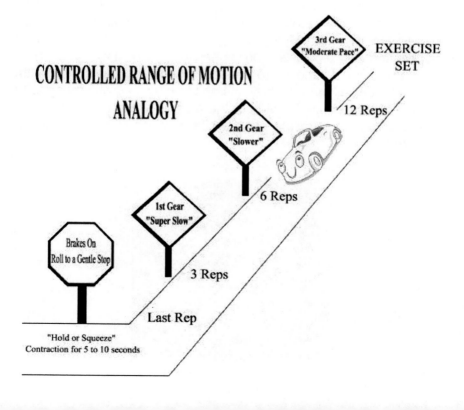

THE SLOWER YOU GO, THE FASTER YOU

GET THE RESULTS! ISOLATION EQUALS RESULTS!

Instead of speeding up to finish, it's more important to always go moderate to slow, to super slow then hold and release just as slow. Although this takes much more discipline it provides results much quicker. Although this analogy works for many, some people just don't have the physical or mental strength to maintain this technique throughout the whole exercise. The key point here is to stay conscious during your exercise sets and maintain a moderate to slow range of motion. This alone will get you the results your body needs.

Another part of controlled range of motion includes isolation on the muscle. If you are working with machines then always make sure that the plates never touch during the set of repetitions until completed. Over the years I've seen a large amount of people do this continuously while working out. It's like starting over each time and no results will ever be achieved. If using free weights it's important to always be aware of the pivot point on the joints being moved to do the specific exercise. It's important to position yourself properly in order to get as much isolation as possible on the muscle group being worked. For example, if you are doing a lying flat bench chest press to work the chest and your elbows are positioned in alignment with your shoulders you will be placing more stress on your shoulders verses the chest and receive less direct results on the muscle group trying to be worked. The correct positioning of the elbows would be in alignment with the center point of the chest while going through the exercise movement.

3rd) **Breathing Technique**

Breath is the most basic essential action and companion for our existence as human beings. Our breath shows truth in everything. Our breathing pattern and rhythms are in direct correlation to our nervous system. Our flow of breath almost always will interpret our physical and mental states. If a person is breathing rapidly or shallow this could be induced by many things good or bad. In all cases breath is the control center for our emotional state of mind. Although we talk of this direct link between the breath and your emotions, feelings and so on, most of us tend to forget about our breath and always take it for granted in all instances. Because our breath is part of our autonomic nervous system we tend to forget about the enormous power we have by controlling our breath. At the same time we tend to forget the power our breath has to our human existence.

When it comes to exercise and the breath we are looking for two things: control and power. Understanding first of all that controlling the rhythm of your breathing pattern during exercise is what allows us to continue to push ourselves to maximal results. Now let's separate breath into its two functions:

Exhaling – (Power breath) Blowing out while exerting effort is a natural autonomic movement in anything that we do which gives us power. We see this used in several sports when powerful force is needed. Some great examples are a boxer as he throws a punch, a tennis player as she serves a ball into play or a football player breaking through the line. All of these movements require controlled exerted effort and when focusing on the exhale provide 10 times the power in comparison to a regular breath. An easy way to remember when to exhale is to notice that each exercise being done with isotonic resistance (free weights or machines) only allows you to push or pull. You cannot do both, only one or the other! Evaluating the exercise before attempting it will allow you to figure out if it is a pulling or a pushing movement. The key to remember is that the exhale or power breath can only be used on a pushing or pulling motion.

For example, when doing a leg curl or bicep curl the movement is pulling so we would exhale or use our power breath on the pull as we are contracting the weight or resistance towards the body, an example of a pushing exercise would be a push-up or chest press, this movement would tell us that the exhale or power breath should be as we're pushing ourselves or the weight away from the body. An example of a pulling exercise could be a pull up. As we pull our body weight up to the bar we should exhale to give ourselves momentum and power to complete the task.

Inhaling – (Muscle Oxygenation) Just as important as creating power through the movement of an exercise, breathing in or inhaling is a must. Without providing oxygen to the muscles being worked we will fatigue quickly. Oxygen is our main source of energy for any movement and without it we will deteriorate quickly in every way. When exercising, we must also focus on providing a steady flow of oxygen back to the lungs. Although the objective of resistance training is to develop an anaerobic state to the muscles being trained, the idea is to make them last as long as possible by providing oxygen during resistance until anaerobic metabolism is achieved for each muscle group. This is called failure or exhaustion and is the way that muscles build a better memory to fight back for the next workout by building more strength and endurance. NOTE: It is important to remember during exercise not to exaggerate the inhalation. This could cause hyperventilation.

4th) Mind to Muscle

The fourth component to any exercise and is sometimes the one thing that is overlooked the most. Most people think of the old saying, "mind over matter" when they think of focused effort on doing something that seems extremely tedious or difficult to do, but as you practice even difficult things become much easier and less stressful. This is true when doing an exercise as well, therefore, I have changed the word matter to muscle since we're relating to exercise. Mind to muscle basically means using all of the first three components to the best of your ability but also adding isolated focus on the muscle group being worked. Look at it from this perspective, let's say for example that you are beginning to do a flat bench chest press exercise. First you should approach the exercise with your first component "Posture." The correct posture for this exercise is a lying down position with feet on the bench, spine in alignment of the center of the bench, and the back of the head not hanging off of the bench. The second component would be controlled range of motion. When beginning the exercise and throughout the range of motion, you should control the movement at a moderate pace slowing down as you move through to the end of the set of repetitions. Thirdly, you should find the proper breathing technique, finding the correct inhale for oxygenation and the correct exhale for power while going through your range of movement. Last but not least, mind to muscle is making sure as you go through all of the previous components, that you keep your blinders on and focus specifically on the muscle group being worked. This encompasses many common sense things like form and technique of the exercise, making sure that you have proper isolation and alignment to get the most resistance out of your progression through the exercise.

In conclusion to this Mind to Muscle concept, I urge you to apply this to each exercise. Put your blinders on and stay focused and disciplined, place your awareness to the specific muscle group being worked and feel the results as you slowly work through the burn. If you can do this Mind to Muscle concept and form these habits consistently with proper nutrition, then truly the sky is the limit and results are pretty much guaranteed.

Exercise has a few more important parts to consider which relate to these four components:

Exercise Form and Technique – Having proper form is the core of all four components above. Using the correct techniques when performing any type of exercise, stretch or movement will assure growth and improvement in your body in many ways.

Importance of Isolation – Understanding the importance of isolation on each specific muscle group when in action is the key to proper development of form and technique for each movement. For example, if doing a movement for biceps, allowing the arms to come behind the lateral seam of the shirt while not extending the elbow properly takes away from the isolation on the bicep muscle and will shift to the shoulder muscles. Therefore, it is important to remember that if you can't feel it right where you are trying to, you're probably doing something wrong.

Box method – The box method is a concept that I created to help people with isolation and posture for several exercises.

First, when working with legs in a seated position the box method is used to create correct posture and alignment of the spine. When doing certain standing leg exercises like lunges it is important to remember to use a box method. Focus on keeping the forward knee in line with the ankle and the back leg, when bent vertically, parallel with the spine. This creates a box with the legs and helps to balance and distribute the weight of the body with the least amount of joint compression on the ankles, knees, hips and spine.

Box Method
"LEGS"

The same is true when performing upper extremity exercises that involve pushing or pulling for the back, chest and shoulders. When performing a flat bench chest press, the beginning position should be in a box position balancing the weights from the elbow to the wrist, making sure not to flex the wrist, but keep them even with the rest of the forearm. The elbows should be just below the chest as well, beginning the movement with a box position and noticing the isolation on the chest muscles mostly. When following through and shortening the muscle on the extension, the arms, fist and dumbbells should stay even with the center or the chest. (I have marked all of the exercises that apply to this method accordingly.)

Pivot points in exercise techniques - While performing many exercises it is important to also remember that the body will adapt to the same exact movement over and over again. When technique is mastered on one generalized movement, it is not only necessary to find different exercises but also to adjust or modify standard exercises by adjusting the position of the joints of the body. When modifying and pivoting the joints of the body the points of isolation will stress different areas of the muscle groups worked. Again, a great example of this is the bicep curl. When changing the pivot point of the exercise whether rotating the hands in a hammer position or rotating the shoulders in a lateral position the stress on the muscles varies from one area to another although impacting the whole muscle. There are many pivot points that can be examined and worked with to help the body to become more responsive and prevent adaptation of muscles when progressing in a workout. (I have marked all of the exercises that apply to this method accordingly.)

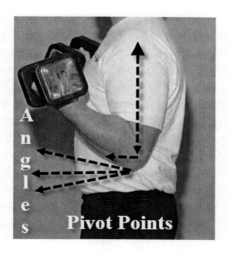

Now that we've covered the basic aspects of strength training let's start to put this training regimen together so that you can begin feeling and looking better. First things first, cardiovascular exercise is where we will start.

Resistance Training for the HEART

Cardiovascular resistance training or as it's well known cardio fitness is and should always be a part of your weekly exercise regimen and should be the first part of a strength training regimen. It seems though that most people are a bit confused about this important part of your fitness. While training people over the past 20 years I've found that most people are uncertain about 3 things:

1.   How much cardio should I do? Is more cardio better?
2.   How do I know I'm doing it right?
3.   What's the best type of cardio for me?

With these questions in mind, let's explore cardiovascular fitness to make it easy and simple for you.

First, the heart is an amazing muscle with some really fascinating features. It beats from the time that it is developed in the womb and never stops until you're dead. It is the workhorse of the body's muscles that keeps pressure and rhythm in our bodies for survival. Did you know that the heart actually has its own circulatory system within it? So when it comes to how much exercise we need to give it, it's important to remember not only how strong it is normally but also what stresses it out. Let's look at the heart as a machine pump to create an analogy for a minute. We all know that excess fat on the body increases the plague in the arteries, which narrows the passageways of this ingenious pumping system. Whenever an artery in the heart gets clogged, it creates more pressure in the lines, also known as blood pressure, making the pump work harder until something eventually gives. A heart attack is caused when an internal part of the pump is clogged and the flow of blood stops. A stroke is caused when one of the passageways gets clogged and backs up and re-routes pressure to another passage. Essentially that's all the heart is, an amazingly brilliant, long lasting pumping system that when maintained with proper lubricants, good sediment control and pressure testing a few times a week, will help keep it strong and steady throughout your life.

By staying conscious of your hand to mouth exercise and proper willpower, you will improve your eating habits to prevent this pumping system from getting clogged with sediments and allow healthy lubrication to exist throughout the pipes. (Less Plaque) (Lowered Cholesterol) (Low LDL's)

A healthy body fat percentage can equate to a healthy heart in most cases. If your body fat is above what is recommended in the BMI (Body Mass Index) equation then you should consider lowering it for your heart's sake. In most cases people with a high body fat percentage should consider changing their nutritional habits and adding a 4 to 5 day cardiovascular program weekly. Those of you that have an average body fat percentage on the BMI scale should consider no more than 3 to 4 cardiovascular sessions weekly. If you are below your body fat scale then more than likely you'll get enough cardiovascular fitness with a good strength-training program.

- High Body Fat % = 4 to 5 cardio sessions weekly
- Average Body Fat % = 3 to 4 cardio sessions weekly
- Low Body Fat % = 2 to 3 Strength Training program.
  (This could include 15 to 20 mins of Cardio)

Now that you have an idea of how many times weekly, what about the duration of time per cardio workout. It's obvious to say that everyone is different, we all come in all different shapes and sizes, not to mention, genetic dispositions. What works for one person may not work for another, so here's an easy way to cut through the science and make the most of it. Start slow and work your way up! It's that simple..... Test yourself with a simple cardio exercise and see how you do. If you can only do a few minutes then that's where you'll start. However, with each cardio session push yourself a little more, maybe 15, 30 seconds or a minute more. Eventually this will get easier and easier until the movement or the exercise and your cardio output becomes normal. Maximize your cardio sessions to no more than 20 to 40 minutes and make sure to warm up and cool down as well.

- Don't overdo it
- Progress at your own pace
- Maximize Cardio Session 20 to 45 mins

Overdoing cardiovascular exercise is not a good thing. It can lead to dehydration, low blood sugar, and affect your body's response system for losing weight. This leads in to the next commonly asked question: "How do I know I'm doing it right?"

The Karvonan formula is an equation that most people have heard of but do not understand exactly. So, let's make it easy. Dr. Karvonan was a cardiologist that came up with an equation that he believed would allow people to exercise within a range of aerobic capacity to be safe and effective for strengthening the heart while aging. The Karvonan formula is based off of two parts, aerobic capacity and anaerobic capacity. The word aerobic basically means activity with sufficient oxygen levels. Anaerobic is the opposite activity with insufficient oxygen levels. The idea is that if the body is to run effectively to strengthen the heart, we must have enough oxygen while taxing the heart. Too little oxygen over taxes the heart, doesn't supply correct oxygen and carbon dioxide exchange, which becomes toxic to the body. Here's the formula:

220 – Your Age = 100% of your Maximum Heart Rate

Anything above 85% to 100% Heart Rate would be Anaerobic and is not suggested to maintain for a long time.

85% to 55% is considered sufficient oxygen supply and is healthy aerobic conditioning levels.

How to take your Heart Rate

Although some people suggest sticking strictly with this equation, I have found that as you become healthier and learn to read your body more, you may notice that you can maintain closer to 90% without compromising your cardio workout. This will come in time and for some may never happen. Just be cautious and learn to read your body.

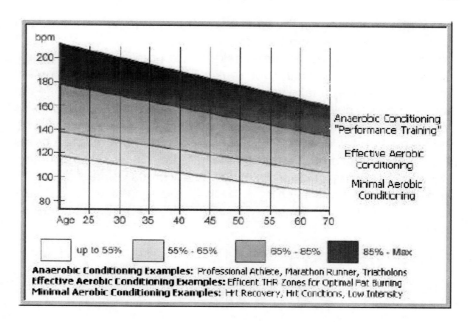

Now that we understand the basics of this cardio formula here comes the fun part. Taking your pulse! I mean how can you really use this chart if you can't plug in your heart rate? Taking your heart rate is not as difficult as most people think so don't be intimidated. All you need is your index and middle finger; curl the other two fingers in to the center of your palm with your thumb together. The two best places to find your pulse are first on the Carotid Artery on the side of the neck and on the wrist in the radial artery.

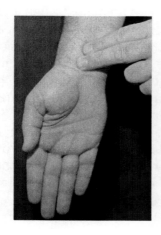
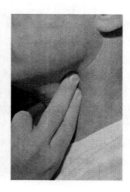

Place your hand on the wrist or neck gently without pushing too hard, close your eyes and feel for your pulse now. If you can't get it the first time don't give up, it may take a little practice but you'll get it soon enough. Once you find your pulse now it's time to start counting the beats. When you take your pulse while doing cardio exercise the idea is to check quickly without giving your heart much opportunity to slow down so for that reason I recommend a 6 or 15 second count. The idea when taking a pulse is to count the number of heart beats that the heart would beat within a 1-minute period. So when counting a 15 second pulse you must count how many beats you feel during 15 seconds and then multiply it by 4. 15 x 4 = 60 seconds. For a 6 second count feel for the number of beats within a 6 second time frame and multiply by 10. 6 x 10 = 60.

Example:

20 beats within 15 secs = 20x4=80 beats per min

20 beats within 6 secs = 20x10=200 beats per min

By learning to take your own heart rate while doing your cardiovascular exercise, you are ten times more effective and will become extremely efficient with your time and efforts.

Perceived Exertion

For those of you that feel a little intimidated by the whole heart rate thing, there is another way to track your progression with your cardio workout. Although not as effective, it can help most when it comes to beginning a cardio regimen. The perceived exertion method is one that simplifies target heart rate zones with a 10 to 1 scale ratio. Imagine that on a scale of one to ten the number ten is 100% maximum heartbeat. In this state you would be compromising your heart by going too fast, in this state of ten you probably would be panting and breathing very heavy, almost trying to catch your breath. So if ten has put you into this state then the target rate would be eight. In this rate you can easily tell if you are on target because although you are working hard, you may still be able to carry on a conversation without gasping for breaths. Anything between 8 to 5 would be considered target heart rate on this perceived exertion scale.

1_____5_____8_____10

{ Relaxed Heart rate zone } { Target Hrtrate} {Anaerobic}

But remember even if you use this scale, at first try to be persistent with practicing taking your pulse or heart rate. This is by far the most effective way to stay accurate with the Karvonan formula and cardiovascular fitness.

There are many different types of cardiovascular exercise regimens that you can adopt whether taking an aerobics class, going for a power walk or getting on a piece of cardio equipment at your local gym. All of these activities can be considered cardio workouts. However, when doing these exercises make sure to be efficient with your time and get the most out of your cardio workout. What I mean by this is sweat, push yourself and don't give up. If you're going to go for a walk don't take a leisure walk through the park, put your cardio shoes on and use them with the right intention to workout. If you're taking a cardio class then set your mind to get in the front of the class and learn the steps or moves and show people that you are not scared or shy when it comes to your goals on fitness. Don't give up!

Here's an important note: if you are using a piece of cardio equipment in your gym then get on it, put your mp3 player on and go for it. Remember not to get caught up in the gimmicks that most of these machines offer with special programs to work your gluts or thighs. That's not the objective when it comes to these machines. The idea is to strengthen the most important muscle of your body, your heart.

Use all of the machines even if you don't like them, one of the most important things to do when it comes to cardiovascular fitness is variety. Don't think that just a couple machines will work. NO WAY! The body is extremely intelligent and will adapt to most anything that you throw at it. Change things up and keep the heart and body guessing. You'll learn more about this when we get deeper into strength training as well. A great example of shocking the heart when it comes to cardiovascular fitness is a client that I trained in home; she had all the right equipment and even a treadmill for cardio, as we began to evaluate her training regimen she told me that she was religious at working on her treadmill 5 nights weekly after work. After observing for a few weeks I noticed some weak links in her exercise habits. I quickly suggested that the treadmill was doing her more harm than good and convinced her to purchase an elliptical machine. I explained to her that treadmills simulated walking, which is a very normal part of daily life. Therefore our bodies adapt quickly to this machine. Since part of her history had involved knee surgery and eventually replacement, I explained that the elliptical is an evolution of treadmills and prevents joint compression all the way from the ankles, knees and hips to the back and neck. Immediately after the implementation of the elliptical, her cardiovascular system improved, she began to lose more weight, which motivated her to strength train harder until the results came. So remember, if you are in a gym and have access to many pieces switch it up. If you are in your home don't keep the same machine forever until it becomes so boring it turns into a piece of furniture, or more than likely, a temporary clothes hanger.

Here are a few more things that you should remember when doing your cardiovascular exercise:

1. Take water with you and drink plenty before during and after any exercise.
2. Take your pulse at least 3 times during your cardio workout.
3. Remember to warm-up between 5 to 10 minutes before getting up to your target heart rate zones.
4. Be patient with yourself, but be firm and push yourself into a sweat. If you didn't sweat you didn't do enough.
5. Don't get stuck on one machine, use a variety of cardio exercises to change it up and shock the body into results.

Three Cardio Training Regimens:

1st) Stabilized Cardio – This is the first part of cardio. Finding your target heart rate after a 5 to 10 minute warm-up and maintaining it until you have reached 20 to 35 minutes and declining back to a cool down period to finish. Use this in a variety of fashions. Whether going from treadmill to elliptical to recumbent bike and so on.

2nd) Interval Cardio Training – This is a more advanced state of cardio that several cardio machines will incorporate into their programs. In this type of training, you will simulate hills and valleys with the speed, resistance and or incline according to what machine you are working on. This will allow you to shock your heart by elevating and lowering the heartbeat sporadically. This workout is normally done on one machine but can be divided among others during your training time.

3rd) Pyramid Training – This cardio workout simulates a long hill whether peaking in the center or later in the cardio workout and slowly decreasing into a cool down period until done. This workout is normally done just on one machine during your training time.

It's important to understand that all of the cardio exercises are nothing more than tools to get you to the final results. First, to strengthen the heart, and second, to burn excess calories. The following are worksheet tools that should be used to develop and track your cardio workouts.

Cardio Training Form

220 - <u>Age</u> = 100% Max Heart Rate _____BPM
85% Target Heart Rate _____BPM

Warm-up 5-10 min.
Training 20-35min.
Cool Down 5-10 min.   {--------------------}
Perceived Exertion Test   **1**   **2**   **3**   **4**   5   6   7   8)   **9**   **10**

Elliptical
Start Date: /   /   Incline _____ workload _____ strides per min. _____

1st mo Date: /   /   Incline _____ workload _____ strides per min. _____

2nd mo Date: /   /   Incline _____ workload _____ strides per min. _____

3rd mo Date: /   /   Incline _____ workload _____ strides per min. _____

6th mo Date: /   /   Incline _____ workload _____ strides per min. _____

Treadmill
Start Date: /   /   Grade/Incline _____   Speed _____ mph

1st mo Date: /   /   Grade/Incline _____   Speed _____ mph

2nd mo Date: /   /   Grade/Incline _____   Speed _____ mph

3rd mo Date: /   /   Grade/Incline _____   Speed _____ mph

6th mo Date: /   /   Grade/Incline _____   Speed _____ mph

Rec. Bike
Start Date: /   /   Level _____   RPMs _____

1st mo Date: /   /   Level _____   RPMs _____

2nd mo Date: /   /   Level _____   RPMs _____

3rd mo Date: /   /   Level _____   RPMs _____

6th mo Date: /   /   Level _____   RPMs _____

Upright Bike
Start Date: /   /   Level _____   RPMs _____

1st mo Date: /   /   Level _____   RPMs _____

2nd mo Date: /   /   Level _____   RPMs _____

3rd mo Date: /   /   Level _____   RPMs _____

6th mo Date: /   /   Level _____   RPMs _____

Go to: www.generationawareness.org/forms/printable

Monthly Cardio Schedule		
DATE	**TYPE**	**TIME**
1.		
2.		
3.		
4.		
5.		
6.		
7.		
8.		
9.		
10.		
11.		
12.		
13.		
14.		
15.		
16.		
17.		
18.		
19.		
20.		
21.		
22.		
23.		
24.		
25.		
26.		
27.		
28.		
29.		
30.		
31.		

Go to: www.generationawareness.org/forms/printable

It's time to put it all together now in the last part of this chapter. I will give you 5 simple workout programs in phases. Each one will be an interlinked advancement of another. But first, we need to understand a few more concepts of exercise. We will take a look at finding, setting up and plugging in the right weight for the exercises that you will be doing. Next, we will talk briefly about the correct order of training muscle groups and lastly we will discuss the number of times weekly you should train with this exercise regimen.

Let's begin!

How to find the right, "LBS."

One of the main reasons that people start out confused when getting into a strength training program is the misunderstanding of how to properly find the number of lbs to lift. Most people kind of guess what amount of weight to begin at and do a few of these or those. They have no set path outlined for progression and eventually they lose track and the regimen falls apart quickly.

As mentioned previously in this chapter, progressive resistance is the key to results when it comes to strength training. So a large part of that is tracking progression to see that adequate results are being achieved.

There have been several ideas on how to find a comfortable starting weight for an exercise but the most effective for me has been what I like to call, "The Slow 1/10 Method". This is a simple way of finding a healthy but challenging way to begin a workout regimen of any kind.

Here's how it works:

1st)   Before even testing your maximum load of resistance, familiarize yourself with the exercise and the proper form and movement. Use a moderately comfortable weight just to get your body used to the range of motion and natural feel to the exercise. Even if you have used the exercise before, take a moment to really focus on the four basic components that were taught to you previously. Posture, controlled range of motion, proper breathing technique and mind to muscle. Do 10 slow controlled repetitions and take a break. If you cannot complete 10 slow controlled repetitions, that's ok! Just remember the amount that you completed and the weight that was used. Example: 40lbs / 8 reps

Remember to use the analogy provided in the 4 basic components in the above section for controlled range of motion on all of your sets.

2nd) After completing the warm-up set and resting for approximately 1 to 2 minutes, revisit the exercise. Now we are going to use a 1 to 10 scale. If 1 is super easy then 10 is so difficult that you may only be able to lift (with good form) one or two good repetitions.

Your goal for this set is to find your true starting weight. Based on your first set's results, adjust the weight so that you may lift, pull, push or press 10 repetitions with slow control.

(1 TO 10 DIFFICULTY SCALE)

1   2   3   4   5   6   7   8   9   10

lbs— —25— —-20— —15— —12— —10— —8— —6— —4— —2— —1— —

Reps   Reps   Reps

3rd) Based on the form of the exercise and the number of repetitions you completed you will now be able to find your true starting weight. Going back to the 1 to 10 scale of difficulty, find your reps and place your weight in the appropriate %. This is where you will find your fitness goals that you may progress towards.

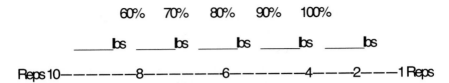

(1 to 10 DIFFICULTY SCALE)

60%   70%   80%   90%   100%

_____ lbs _____ lbs _____ lbs _____ lbs _____ lbs

Reps 10——————8———————6———————4————2———1 Reps

NOTE: Weights or lbs. can be increased from 10, 5, 2.5,
even 1 lbs increments.

Proper Order to Train Muscle Groups

Now that we've established a simple way to find a starting weight for your exercise routine, we must first talk about another important part of any good exercise regimen: proper order of training.

Knowing the proper order of training is a simple concept that most people overlook when beginning to exercise. If you are one of those people that have concocted your own idea of working with one machine before another and kind of switching everything up as you go along you are making a big mistake. Muscles when worked need to always train from largest to smallest.

Why? Because although our objective when using machines is to isolate individual muscle groups so that you may get precise results, it is impossible to use just one muscle let alone one muscle group. The body works as a pulley system when one muscle contracts or shortens an opposite extends or lengthens. When conducting many exercises that involve more than one joint to move this are called compound movements that require several muscle groups to work in coordination with one another to get the job done correctly for the specific isolation on the muscle group that the machine was designed for.

The reason that working larger muscles before smaller is important is that first, larger muscle groups have much more energy reserve because of their size, and smaller muscles being much less dense and smaller in size would be wiped out if trained with progressive intensity before the larger muscles. This would affect your training by not allowing the larger muscles to have complete assistance when needed.

Although there are many exercise training theories, in this specific method we will use a very common order for these regimens.

Muscle Group Training Order: 1. Quadriceps 2. Hamstrings 3. Calves 4. Chest 5. Back 6. Shoulders 7. Triceps 8. Abdominals & Oblique's 9. Biceps

(Picture on page 113 provides the proper order of the muscle groups.)

In this exercise program you will be dividing the body into three sections: legs, upper body, and arms and abdominals together. This is done in such a manner to allow your body to complete the movements with the lower extremities starting with largest and finishing with smallest which are the calves. It then proceeds to large muscle groups in the upper body starting off with chest and shifting to back and then into a mid size muscle shoulders. Although the chest muscle is a smaller muscle group, it goes before back because of the many muscles, both large and small, that work to coordinate basic postural movement and functionality in all of the exercises you will be doing. In other words all of the back muscles have to work to help us maintain posture while doing any exercise. The third section is arms and abdominals combined. I've found that because of the major assistance that is needed by these muscles to balance and isolate the larger muscle groups in the upper body, they will still fatigue fast. So, allowing abdominals to be trained in between the two arm muscles allows just enough of a break to make the training efficient for these smaller muscle groups to attain just as much of an intense workout as the rest.

Just to mention one other thing about abdominal training: I've found that abdominals are normally the last muscle group for people to do because they dislike them so much, and needless to say, is the one section that is avoided the most. Most people when they get to the last exercise, if it's abdominals, they will find every excuse in the book not to do them or put them off until next workout. For some unknown reason placing this muscle group second to last really works for most of my clients, this has been a trial and error game that I have played over countless years and this method seems to work best.

In all, this training order for muscle groups works great when doing a full body workout and will allow you to achieve optimum results fast without zapping all of the energy out of you.

How many days a week should I train?

This is another issue that most people have or are uncertain about when it comes to strength training programs: "Just how many times a week should a person workout with an exercise regimen?" First of all, strength training has no age limit; there are scientific studies that have proven that 90 year old people can get results off of a steady regimented workout program. The key to this however, is the distance of time in between training sessions that allows recovery of the muscles being worked to be rejuvenated and rebuilt by the body. Although we will go deeper into this as you progress in this book, for now, it is important to understand that strength training for the purpose of this chapter should be based off of your own personal fitness level.

If you have attained sufficient results including:

- Decreased your body fat to a healthy level
- If you have increased enough muscle mass to sustain a healthy body and have strong bones
- When you have achieved optimal muscular endurance in all muscles including cardiac.
- If you consider yourself in peak fitness

Then you should not have to strength train no more than once weekly. However when you are at this state you will understand that the intensity of this training session will be an all out muscle bearing progression because you will be lifting and training with a considerable amount of weight and really struggling to get beyond results that you have maintained for a long time. There should never really be such thing as maintenance. You should be pushing yourself as far as can be pushed.

Now, for most of us we do not have that type of discipline, so maybe strength training twice weekly will be sufficient. Starting out at three works well too, considering there are many other parts to fitness than just strength training involved.

How long should I rest between sets?

Resting periods when performing exercises or maximum load testing is typically the same in most instances. The suggested amount of rest in between exercises should be on average 1 to 2 minutes total of recovery time. This time frame allows optimal recovery before the next set of repetitions performed.

NOTE: For those with limited time for cardio training, by decreasing the rest period to 45 to 30 Second intervals during strength training regimens you will improve your cardiovascular while training. (Make sure to check your Heart Rate promptly after exercises and or sets for target ranges.)

Phase I

Machine Weight Training (Stack and Plate loaded)

In the early 1970's with Arthur Jones' first Nautilus piece, the concept of weight machines became a new and continuing trend clear up to the present day. The idea is to have a complete line of equipment that all major muscle groups can be worked with. These machines work with a pulley system that isolates a specific muscle group through balanced weight stacks. The two parallel bars that are vertically placed through the weight stack prevent any movement through a controlled range of motion. Plate loaded machines are similar. Some machines involve parallel bars for balance, others are single loaded bars with no pulley systems. Although one can achieve having a great amount of isolation with these machines, the person lifting the weight will be limited to developing coordination and balance. This type of strength training is the easiest type of exercise movements that you can do and should be a starting point for anyone starting a strength-training program for the first time.

If you belong to a local gym, you should be able to find this equipment. Most health clubs or gyms will have a line of commercial exercise machines that you can use. However, if you are someone that doesn't feel comfortable exercising in front of or around others there are some more affordable home versions of equipment that can fit in a corner of a room in your house. If you need or have an interest in finding equipment for your home or a local gym in your neighborhood, which we endorse, please feel free to contact us. I want to take as much guess work out of all of this stuff as possible for you. So I've done the research for you and have found what I believe to be the best facilities and or equipment for the money invested. www.generationawareness.com/facilitiesandequip.

The following is a unique Strength Training program that can be used for most anyone. Follow this program, step by step according to the days and repetitions. Make sure to place your pounds for each exercise in the necessary place provided for each one and start at a moderate weight but not too heavy or light.

This exercise program transitions into each Phase with five (5) week periods.

IMPORTANT NOTE: If you are starting out for the first time on an exercise regimen you should first go to your physician to get a complete physical checkup. After your physician clears you and tells you it's OK for you to begin an exercise program you can begin. However when starting an exercise program start out slowly and progress cautiously. Begin your first week doing only one set of exercises, then if you feel confident enough add

another set in the next week or two. Eventually you will be able to work up to completing all of the sets required. The important thing is to take your time progressing, get comfortable with the movement of the exercise and all of the four components that you have learned.

This strength-training regimen that I have provided for you in this book transitions into the next phase as you reach the fourth (4th Set) of each exercise. This means that as you progress with each muscle group being worked you will need to begin to familiarize yourself with the next phase of exercises provided.

EXAMPLE: The first exercise in Phase I (Machine Weight Training) is *Quadriceps Seated Leg Extension*. As you build your strength after a few weeks to begin adding a fourth set, you will use the Phase II (Body Bench Training) exercise for quadriceps , which is *Squats.* All of the exercises will progress to the 4th set of transition exercises there after.

The last part of the fourth set is what are called Rep-outs. A Rep-out basically means that you are not counting the number of repetitions but rather focusing on the movement and observing the muscle group. When doing a Rep-out set you are also trying to fatigue the muscle by feeling for the anaerobic metabolism or the burn. Once you feel this sensation you should try to endure through this for a minimum of 3 seconds. **This feeling is called results!**

It is your goal to steadily and persistently track your progression. So, I challenge you to keep with the program and track every single part and watch yourself grow and strengthen like you never have in all aspects of physical health and mental discipline.

Seated Leg Extension

Phase I Machine Training:

Four Basic Components

1. Seated Posture w/ Back Support

2. Controlled Range of Motion 3 – 4 Second Count

3. Breathing Technique – Exhale on the Push

4. Mind to Muscle – Focus on Quadriceps

TIPS

- Be sure to keep the pit of your knees close to the pad for less resistance in the knee joint
- Although this is a Seated Posture w/ Back Support it is important to note that when working legs the focus should

Seated Leg Curl

always be on engaging Abdominals since feet can not be used to push back flat. Remember when in doubt Ab it out!

Four Basic Components

1. Seated Posture w/ Back Support

2. Controlled Range of Motion 3 – 4 Second Count

3. Breathing Technique – Exhale on the Pull

4. Mind to Muscle – Focus on Hamstrings

TIPS

• Seated Posture w/ Back Support with legs off the ground. Remember when in doubt Ab it out!

Seated Calf Raise

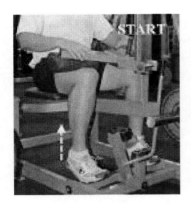 

• Keep elbows face down and push back flat with hands against support bar

Four Basic Components

1. Seated Posture NO Back Support

2. Controlled Range of Motion 3 – 4 Second Count

3. Breathing Technique – Exhale on the Push

4. Mind to Muscle – Focus on Calves

TIPS

• Be sure to keep pads at least 3 to 5 inches beyond your knees

Seated Chest Press

- Remember to place the ball of the foot in the center position of the foot pad

<u>Four Basic Components</u>

1. Seated Posture w/ Back Support

2. Controlled Range of Motion 3 – 4 Second Count

3. Breathing Technique – Exhale on the Push

4. Mind to Muscle – Focus on Pectorals (Chest)

TIPS

- Keep wrist in alignment w/ elbows for better isolation
- Remember to shift elbow down for better pivot point

Lat Pulldown

 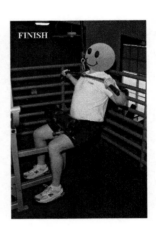

<u>Four Basic Components</u>

1. Seated NO Back Support

2. Controlled Range of Motion 3 – 4 Second Count

3. Breathing Technique – Exhale on the Pull

4. Mind to Muscle – Focus on Latissimus Dorsi (Back)

TIPS

· Make sure to pull bar to center of chest

Seated Shoulder Press

- Caution slamming bar against sternum
- Focus on retracting shoulder blades together

<u>Four Basic Components</u>

1. Seated w/ Back Support

2. Controlled Range of Motion 3 – 4 Second Count

3. Breathing Technique – Exhale on the Push

4. Mind to Muscle – Focus on Deltoids (Shoulders)

TIPS

- Box Method "Legs"
- Use knees to push back against pad

Seated Tricep Pushdown

- Make sure to grip center of Dumbbells

Four Basic Components

1. Seated w/ Back Support

2. Controlled Range of Motion 3 – 4 Second Count

3. Breathing Technique – Exhale on the Push

4. Mind to Muscle – Focus on Triceps

TIPS

- Box Method "Legs"
- Use knees to push back against pad

Ab Crunch Machine

- Keep elbows inside

Four Basic Components

1. Seated w/ Back Support

2. Controlled Range of Motion 3 – 4 Second Count

3. Breathing Technique – Exhale on the Pull

4. Mind to Muscle – Focus on Abdominals

TIPS

- Remember all Ab machines serve same purpose
- Focus on isolating Abdominals while protecting lower lumbar

Seated Bicep Curls

<u>Four Basic Components</u>

1. Seated w/ Ab Support

2. Controlled Range of Motion 3 – 4 Second Count

3. Breathing Technique – Exhale on the Pull

4. Mind to Muscle – Focus on Biceps

TIPS

Max Load 1/10 Slow Method
(Machine Training)

Quadriceps (Seated Leg Extension)

60%	70%	80%	90%	100%
_____lbs	_____lbs	_____lbs	_____lbs	_____lbs

Reps 10------------8-------------6------------4-------2------1 Reps

Hamstrings (Seated Leg Curl)

60%	70%	80%	90%	100%
_____lbs	_____lbs	_____lbs	_____lbs	_____lbs

Reps 10------------8-------------6------------4-------2------1 Reps

Calves (Seated Calf Raise or Press)

60%	70%	80%	90%	100%
_____lbs	_____lbs	_____lbs	_____lbs	_____lbs

Reps 10------------8-------------6------------4-------2------1 Reps

Chest (Press or Fly)

60%	70%	80%	90%	100%
_____lbs	_____lbs	_____lbs	_____lbs	_____lbs

Reps 10------------8-------------6------------4-------2------1 Reps

Back (Lat Pulldown)

60%	70%	80%	90%	100%
_____lbs	_____lbs	_____lbs	_____lbs	_____lbs

Reps 10------------8-------------6------------4-------2------1 Reps

Shoulders (Seated Shoulder Press)

60%	70%	80%	90%	100%
_____lbs	_____lbs	_____lbs	_____lbs	_____lbs

Reps 10------------8-------------6------------4-------2------1 Reps

Tricep (Seated Tricep Pushdown)

60%	70%	80%	90%	100%
_____lbs	_____lbs	_____lbs	_____lbs	_____lbs

Reps 10------------8-------------6------------4-------2------1 Reps

Abdominals (Ab Machine)

60%	70%	80%	90%	100%
_____lbs	_____lbs	_____lbs	_____lbs	_____lbs

Reps 10------------8-------------6------------4-------2------1 Reps

Biceps (Seated Bicep Curl)

60%	70%	80%	90%	100%
_____lbs	_____lbs	_____lbs	_____lbs	_____lbs

Reps 10------------8-------------6------------4-------2------1 Reps

---

Phase I Training Program

Cardio Warm-up Date _____	Time:			Transition Exercises / set 4 Week: 1-60% 3-70% 5 -80%
Quadriceps	SET 1	SET 2	SET 3	Transition Exercise
Seated Leg Ext.	LBS	LBS	LBS	LBS
	12 REPS	10 REPS	8 REPS	Rep-outs
Hamstrings				Transition Exercise
Seated Leg Curl	LBS	LBS	LBS	LBS
	12 REPS	10 REPS	8 REPS	Rep-outs
Calves				Transition Exercise
Seated Calf Raise	LBS	LBS	LBS	LBS
	12 REPS	10 REPS	8 REPS	Rep-outs
Chest				Transition Exercise
Seated Chest Press	LBS	LBS	LBS	LBS
	12 REPS	10 REPS	8 REPS	Rep-outs
Back				Transition Exercise
Lat Pull Down	LBS	LBS	LBS	LBS
	12 REPS	10 REPS	8 REPS	Rep-outs
Deltoids				Transition Exercise
Shoulder Press	LBS	LBS	LBS	LBS
	12 REPS	10 REPS	8 REPS	Rep-outs
Triceps				Transition Exercise
Pushdowns	LBS	LBS	LBS	LBS
	12 REPS	10 REPS	8 REPS	Rep-outs
Abdominals				Transition Exercise
Ab machine	LBS	LBS	LBS	LBS
	12 REPS	10 REPS	8 REPS	Rep-outs
Biceps				Transition Exercise
Seated curl	LBS	LBS	LBS	LBS
	12 REPS	10 REPS	8 REPS	Rep-outs

- Make sure to keep feet flat on floor
- Keep back straight and arm pits against pad
- Make sure triceps stay on pad while doing exercise

Phase II

Body Bench Training (Free Weights)

Now that you are beginning to understand the idea of proper strength training and how natural progression of the human body works, let's begin the second phase of your strength-training program..

As the body improves and muscles develop in these basic movements it's only normal to gain strength and endurance. Now it's time to go to the next level of strength training by starting to develop two other essential parts of natural healthy living: balance and coordination!

Body bench training is a basic concept that I've created over many years of study, critique and examination of myself and my clientele and their results. I will be the first to tell you that the format of this program, although it may be new to some, is really taken from some basic training methods that have been around for many years. I am not trying to recreate the wheel here, but more so educate and give you a detailed outline to guide you.

The difference in Phase I Machine Weights and Phase II Body Bench training, which uses just free weights, a bench and your own body is this:

Free weights when lifted must be balanced throughout a specific range of motion to focus on each muscle group being worked. This balancing act requires quite a bit of coordination from many other parts of the body to maintain proper alignment throughout the exercise. Although the bench is stabilized, most all of the movements, because of the free weight being balanced, require exact precision to achieve optimum results. Again, this second phase does not require a complete line of equipment but rather just an exercise bench that allows a full range from decline position all the way up to a seated position with back support. I recommend dumbbells with the newer technology that allow you not only to save space but to use a wide range of poundage that can be adjusted accordingly for each exercise. Again, I have taken the guesswork out of finding the better products on the market. If you want to go to my website I'll give you more info on benches and dumbbells for your convenience. If you have a health club membership you'll be able to find this equipment in the free weight section of the facility. Some gyms and health clubs have classes that use this equipment as well.

Phase II Body Bench Training

Squats

Four Basic Components

1. Standing Leg Exercise (Feet are even)

2. Controlled Range of Motion 3 – 4 Second Count

3. Breathing Technique – Exhale on the Push

4. Mind to Muscle – Focus on Legs (Quadriceps)

TIPS

- Keep feet at least shoulder width apart
- Make sure that heels and Ball of foot stay planted flat on the ground throughout the set

Stationary Lunges

- Make sure to grip center of Dumbells and balance on shoulders if possible
- Remember to work up to advanced squats with safety in mind and find a spotter if needed

<u>Four Basic Components</u>

1. Standing Leg Exercise "Box Method"

2. Controlled Range of Motion 3 – 4 Second Count

3. Breathing Technique – Exhale on the Push

4. Mind to Muscle – Focus on Legs (Hamstrings)

TIPS

- Always make sure that knee stays behind toes in this movement
- Make sure that forward heel and ball of foot stay planted flat on the ground throughout the set
- Keep center grip on Dumbells and balance in a hanging position with the arms straight towards the floor

Standing Calf Raises

- Keep back straight, shoulders aligned and head upright while going through each repetition
- Remember back knee comes down to create the box but stays ½ inch from ground

<u>Four Basic Components</u>

1. Standing Leg Exercise (Feet are even)

2. Controlled Range of Motion 3 – 4 Second Count

3. Breathing Technique – Exhale on the Push

4. Mind to Muscle – Focus on Legs (Calves)

TIPS

- Keep feet aligned with balls of feet on pad
- Make sure to control the flexion and extension of the foot
- Keep Abdominals engaged to prevent excess back joint compression
- Remember that when using dumbbells to hold them even in the hands balanced properly

Flat Bench Chest Press

<u>Four Basic Components</u>

1. Lying Posture w/ Knees elevated

2. Controlled Range of Motion 3 – 4 Second Count

3. Breathing Technique – Exhale on the Push

4. Mind to Muscle – Focus on Chest (Pectorals)

TIPS

- Place feet on bench if possible
- Upper Body "Box Method" – Place elbows in alignment with center of chest
- Keep dumbbells balanced in hand from wrist to elbow
- Observe Pivot Point adjustment for more isolation on the muscle group being work
- Make sure that your head and spine are aligned properly on bench before beginning

Bent "Back" Rows

<u>Four Basic Components</u>

1. Prone Posture (Knees are even)

2. Controlled Range of Motion 3 – 4 Second Count

3. Breathing Technique – Exhale on the Pull

4. Mind to Muscle – Focus on Back (Lattisimus Dorsi)

TIPS

- Unique "Box Method" Creating the box with the upper extremities and torso for proper alignment
- Back stays straight and Abdominals are engaged
- Prevent hyper flexion of standing knee and supporting elbow on bench with a small bend
- Remember that changing the pivot point in this range of motion will isolate different areas and muscles in the back

Seated Shoulder Press

<u>Four Basic Components</u>

1. Seated Posture w/ Back Support

2. Controlled Range of Motion 3 – 4 Second Count

3. Breathing Technique – Exhale on the Push

4. Mind to Muscle – Focus on Shoulders (Deltoids)

TIPS

- Keep feet at shoulder width
- Use knees to push back flat against pad
- Make sure to grip center of dumbbells

Tricep Kickbacks

- Remember to keep a small bend in the elbows as you raise the dumbbells even with shoulders

Four Basic Components

1. Prone Posture (Knees are even)

2. Controlled Range of Motion 3 – 4 Second Count

3. Breathing Technique – Exhale on the Push (Kick)

4. Mind to Muscle – Focus on Tricep (one at a time)

TIPS

- Unique "Box Method" Creating the box with the upper extremities and torso for proper alignment
- Back stays straight and Abdominals are engaged
- Prevent hyper flexion of standing knee and supporting elbow on bench with a small bend
- Remember to keep the working arms elbow even or above the back for better isolation

Ab Bench Crunches

- Be sure to focus on extending from the elbow and not moving the rest of the arm

Four Basic Components

1. Lying Posture w/ Knees elevated

2. Controlled Range of Motion 3 – 4 Second Count

3. Breathing Technique – Exhale on the Push

4. Mind to Muscle – Focus on Abdominals

TIPS

- Many variations of this exercise exist with feet on bench or elevated in a "Box Method" postion for more advanced isolation
- Make sure to keep spine in alignment with the bench
- Use the analogy of holding your head up with your finger tips like a bowling ball at the back of the skull, then relax your neck and rest the weight of your head on your finger tips for more isolation

Standing Bicep Curls

- Observe elbows for Pivot Point adjustment to create more isolation on the abdominals and obliques

Four Basic Components

1. Standing Posture (Straddle Stance)

2. Controlled Range of Motion 3 – 4 Second Count

3. Breathing Technique – Exhale on the Pull

4. Mind to Muscle – Focus on Biceps

TIPS

- Make sure to keep feet flat on floor
- Place one foot 3 to 6 inches in front of the other for more stabilized balance

Max Load 1/10 Slow Method
(Body Bench Training)

Quadriceps (Squats) DB's

| 60% | 70% | 80% | 90% | 100% |

_____lbs _____lbs _____lbs _____lbs _____lbs
Reps 10------------8-------------6------------4-------2------1 Reps

Hamstrings (Stationary Lunges) DB's

| 60% | 70% | 80% | 90% | 100% |

_____lbs _____lbs _____lbs _____lbs _____lbs
Reps 10------------8-------------6------------4-------2------1 Reps

Calves (Standing Raise) DB's

| 60% | 70% | 80% | 90% | 100% |

_____lbs _____lbs _____lbs _____lbs _____lbs
Reps 10------------8-------------6------------4-------2------1 Reps

Chest (Flat Bench Chest Press) DB's

| 60% | 70% | 80% | 90% | 100% |

_____lbs _____lbs _____lbs _____lbs _____lbs
Reps 10------------8-------------6------------4-------2------1 Reps

Back (Bent Row) DB's

| 60% | 70% | 80% | 90% | 100% |

_____lbs _____lbs _____lbs _____lbs _____lbs
Reps 10------------8-------------6------------4-------2------1 Reps

Shoulders (Lateral Raise) DB's

| 60% | 70% | 80% | 90% | 100% |

_____lbs _____lbs _____lbs _____lbs _____lbs
Reps 10------------8-------------6------------4-------2------1 Reps

Triceps (Kick backs) DB's

| 60% | 70% | 80% | 90% | 100% |

_____lbs _____lbs _____lbs _____lbs _____lbs
Reps 10------------8-------------6------------4-------2------1 Reps

Abdominals (Bench Crunches) DB's

| 60% | 70% | 80% | 90% | 100% |

_____lbs _____lbs _____lbs _____lbs _____lbs
Reps 10------------8-------------6------------4-------2------1 Reps

Biceps (Standing Curl) DB's

| 60% | 70% | 80% | 90% | 100% |

_____lbs _____lbs _____lbs _____lbs _____lbs
Reps 10------------8-------------6------------4-------2------1 Reps

Phase II Training Program

Cardio Warm-up Date _____	Time:			Transition Exercises / set 4 Week: 6-60% 8-70% 10 -80%
Quadriceps	SET 1	SET 2	SET 3	Transition Exercise
Squats	LBS	LBS	LBS	LBS
	12 REPS	10 REPS	8 REPS	Rep-outs
Hamstrings				Transition Exercise
Stationary Lunges	LBS	LBS	LBS	LBS
	12 REPS	10 REPS	8 REPS	Rep-outs
Calves				Transition Exercise
Standing Calf Raise	LBS	LBS	LBS	LBS
	12 REPS	10 REPS	8 REPS	Rep-outs
Chest				Transition Exercise
Flat Bench Chest Press	LBS	LBS	LBS	LBS
	12 REPS	10 REPS	8 REPS	Rep-outs
Back				Transition Exercise
Bent Row	LBS	LBS	LBS	LBS
	12 REPS	10 REPS	8 REPS	Rep-outs
Deltoids				Transition Exercise
Lateral Raise	LBS	LBS	LBS	LBS
	12 REPS	10 REPS	8 REPS	Rep-outs
Triceps				Transition Exercise
Kickbacks	LBS	LBS	LBS	LBS
	12 REPS	10 REPS	8 REPS	Rep-outs
Abdominals				Transition Exercise
Bench Crunches	LBS	LBS	LBS	LBS
	12 REPS	10 REPS	8 REPS	Rep-outs
Biceps				Transition Exercise
Standing curl	LBS	LBS	LBS	LBS
	12 REPS	10 REPS	8 REPS	Rep-outs

- Keep back straight and elbows even with or slightly in front of the center of the shoulders
- Make sure not to swing through out the range of motion and control the negative on the way down

Phase III

Body Ball Training

Now comes part three of this method, Body Ball Training. I hope you're starting to see the bigger picture of this system now. As mentioned in the second phase of this program, balance and coordination are essential parts of good physical health. When using free weights, we now know that these two parts have a big part of building strength and endurance for our bodies. So, let's advance even further into this concept.

A stability ball or core training has been around for several years now but is just now starting to be understood in modern exercise realms as an important part of strength training. If you're not with me yet I'm talking about those big bouncy rubber or PVC balls that kind of remind you of the bouncing horses that were popular back in the 70's. I know this because I had one as well. The one thing that I remember the most about these balls were not only the fun I had on them as a kid, but how you really had to balance yourself well while trying to bounce or you were going to fall right on your head. As a kid I didn't think much of this as exercise, but rather found it more fun and playful. What I didn't realize is that I was actually training my muscles to work together as I bounced across the room and this is what is so incredible about this exercise theory. If you are balancing yourself on a bench with free weights in hand, using all of your upper body muscles to coordinate a movement to isolate one specific muscle group, then what do you think is going to happen on a stability ball? If you said 'use more muscles' then you were absolutely right. Specifically, use more "CORE" muscles. The word core represents the several groups of muscle around your mid section including abdominals, inner and outer oblique muscles, hip flexors and lower back muscles. These groups of muscles create the band that encompasses your whole torso from the belly around to the back. This core area is really what gives us the ability to support our upright position and posture.

By using a stability ball, free weights and your own body, you have the perfect equation for complete coordination in all of the body while strength training. Think of it this way, while you're working your biceps you have to balance your body on the ball, this takes your legs, your abs, back, and shoulders just to achieve this movement. However, let me warn you that if you do not feel comfortable with all of the exercises, it's best to have a person to spot you or help you balance while practicing the movements.

NOTE: If you've noticed all of the exercises continually have all four basic components included as part of the explanations. Make sure that you form the habits to always use these components when doing any exercise, not only for your form and faster results, but most importantly, for your safety. Please remember that sometimes it's worth hiring a trained professional to help you get started and not hurt

Ball Wall Squats

yourself. No need to be a weekend warrior!

Phase III Body Ball Training

Four Basic Components

1. Standing Leg Exercise (Feet are even)

2. Controlled Range of Motion 3 – 4 Second Count

3. Breathing Technique – Exhale on the Push

4. Mind to Muscle – Focus on Legs (Quadriceps)

TIPS

- Lower Body "Box Method" Keep feet at least shoulder width or wider while extending feet forward to create range of motion in the box method fashion
- "Box Method Continued" Be sure to be on a surface that has a good grip surface on the floor. When coming down through the exercise movement make sure that the knees stay behind the toes and imagine the back of the box being your spine continuing down towards the floor. Make the box and gradually push back up while keeping the isolation on the quadriceps
- Remember to place the Stability ball towards the lower back so that as you roll through the exercise movement, you will finish with the ball towards the center or mid back while keeping the abdominals engaged and the spine perpendicular with your shins or calves
- Make sure that heels and Ball of foot stay planted flat on the ground throughout the set
- When using dumbbells make sure placement whether balanced on shoulders or hanging downward with arms extended will allow you to finish exercise and carefully place dumbbells to the ground or in the rack
- Remember to work up to advanced squats with safety in mind and find a spotter if needed

Overhead Ball Alternating Lunges

Four Basic Components

1. Standing Leg Exercise "Box Method"

2. Controlled Range of Motion 3 – 4 Second Count

3. Breathing Technique – Exhale on the Push

4. Mind to Muscle – Focus on Legs (Hamstrings)

TIPS

- As you rotate forward in this exercise movement always make sure that knee stays behind toes in this movement and focus on creating a box with the legs.
- Make sure that forward heel and ball of foot stay planted flat on the ground when going through the range of motion.
- When alternating to the opposite side make sure to push off with the forward leg while controlling the balance of the movement and centering both feet before continuing to the opposite side.
- Keep even grip on Stability Ball and make sure to rotate over your head while extending the arms straight into your forward movement.
- Keep back straight, shoulders aligned and head upright while going through each repetition
- Remember back knee comes down to create the box but stays ½ inch from ground

Seated Ball Calf Raises

Four Basic Components

1. Seated Posture NO Back Support (Feet are even)

2. Controlled Range of Motion 3 – 4 Second Count

3. Breathing Technique – Exhale on the Push

4. Mind to Muscle – Focus on Legs (Calves)

TIPS

- Keep feet aligned while **NOT** allowing the heels to touch the ground throughout the set
- Make sure to control the flexion and extension of the foot
- Be sure that you are setting on the top center of the ball before beginning
- Remember that when using dumbbells hold them even in the hands while balanced properly over the knees

NOTE: This may take some practice before finding isolation suffi- cient on the calves but watch out when you do.

Balance Ball Chest Press

Four Basic Components

1. Lying Posture w/ Feet grounded Shoulder width or wider

2. Controlled Range of Motion 3 – 4 Second Count

3. Breathing Technique – Exhale on the Push

4. Mind to Muscle – Focus on Chest (Pectorals)

TIPS

- When doing this exercise for the first time make sure to place your feet straight forward and wider then your average shoulder width for more stability
- Begin in a seated position and gracefully roll back placing the shoulder blades on the top of the ball while placing the dumbbells in the chest press position.
- Upper Body "Box Method" – Place elbows in alignment with center of chest
- Keep dumbbells balanced in hand from wrist to elbow
- Observe Pivot Point adjustment for more isolation on the muscle group
- Make sure that you are aligned properly on the ball before beginning
- In this exercise you will need to maintain proper alignment with the spine by balancing and stabilizing your neck during the movement. If you feel to much strain you can shift or roll down on the ball for comfort into an incline position which will support the neck and work the chest as well.

Ball Bent Rows

Four Basic Components

1. Prone Posture (Knees are even)

2. Controlled Range of Motion 3 – 4 Second Count

3. Breathing Technique – Exhale on the Pull

4. Mind to Muscle – Focus on Back (Lattisimus Dorsi)

TIPS

- Unique "Box Method" Creating the box with the upper extremities and torso for proper alignment
- Back stays straight and Abdominals are engaged
- Prevent hyper flexion of standing knee and supporting elbow on Stability Ball with a small bend
- Remember that changing the pivot point in this range of motion will isolate different areas and muscles in the back

NOTE: This exercise can be tricky at first but with practice you will find good balance and coordination

Seated Ball Shoulder Press

Four Basic Components

1. Seated Posture NO Back Support

2. Controlled Range of Motion 3 – 4 Second Count

3. Breathing Technique – Exhale on the Push

4. Mind to Muscle – Focus on Shoulders (Deltoids)

TIPS

- Keep feet at shoulder width use "Box Method" for Legs
- Keep Abdominals engaged for balance
- Make sure to grip center of Dumbbells
- Remember to keep Dumbbells centered as you press evenly over your head

Overhead Tricep Extension

Four Basic Components

1. Seated Posture NO Back Support

2. Controlled Range of Motion 3 – 4 Second Count

3. Breathing Technique – Exhale on the Push

4. Mind to Muscle – Focus on Triceps

TIPS

- Use "Box Method" for legs to stabilize the body on the Stability Ball
- Back stays straight and Abdominals are engaged
- Place both hands in a cupped position over one end of the Dumbbell and gracefully bring the weight over your head with the arms extended
- Remember to keep the elbows pointed straight up toward the ceiling
- Be sure to focus on extending from the elbow and not moving the rest of the arm

Ab Ball Crunches

Four Basic Components

1. Lying Posture w/ Feet just beyond shoulder width

2. Controlled Range of Motion 3 – 4 Second Count

3. Breathing Technique – Exhale on the Push

4. Mind to Muscle – Focus on Abdominals

TIPS

- Isolation can be achieved by rolling back further on the ball
- Make sure to keep spine in alignment with the center of the ball
- Use the analogy of holding your head up with your finger tips like a bowling ball at the back of the skull, then relax your neck and rest the weight of your head on your finger tips for more isolation
- Observe elbows for Pivot Point adjustment to create more isolation on the abdominals and oblique's

NOTE: Make sure that your stability ball is not over inflated so that you can sink into a comfortable position

Seated Ball Bicep Curls

<u>Four Basic Components</u>

1. Seated Posture NO Back Support

2. Controlled Range of Motion 3 – 4 Second Count

3. Breathing Technique – Exhale on the Pull

4. Mind to Muscle – Focus on Biceps

TIPS

- Make sure to keep feet flat on floor use "Box Method" for legs
- Remember Abs engaged for balance and Coordination
- Keep back straight and elbows even with slightly in front of the center of the shoulders
- Make sure not to swing through out the range of motion and control the negative on the way down

Max Load 1/10 Slow Method
(Body Ball Training)

Quadriceps (Ball Wall Squats)

60%	70%	80%	90%	100%

_____lbs _____lbs _____lbs _____lbs _____lbs

Reps 10------------8-------------6------------4-------2------1 Reps

Hamstrings (Over Head Ball Alternating Lunges)

60%	70%	80%	90%	100%

_____lbs _____lbs _____lbs _____lbs _____lbs

Reps 10------------8-------------6------------4-------2------1 Reps

Calves (Standing Raise) DB's

60%	70%	80%	90%	100%

_____lbs _____lbs _____lbs _____lbs _____lbs

Reps 10------------8-------------6------------4-------2------1 Reps

Chest (Balance Chest Press) DB's

60%	70%	80%	90%	100%

_____lbs _____lbs _____lbs _____lbs _____lbs

Reps 10------------8-------------6------------4-------2------1 Reps

Back (Ball Bent Row) DB's

60%	70%	80%	90%	100%

_____lbs _____lbs _____lbs _____lbs _____lbs

Reps 10------------8-------------6------------4-------2------1 Reps

Shoulders (Seated Ball Shoulder Press) DB's

60%	70%	80%	90%	100%

_____lbs _____lbs _____lbs _____lbs _____lbs

Reps 10------------8-------------6------------4-------2------1 Reps

Triceps (Seated OverHead Extension) DB

60%	70%	80%	90%	100%

_____lbs _____lbs _____lbs _____lbs _____lbs

Reps 10------------8-------------6------------4-------2------1 Reps

Abdominals (Ball Crunches) DB's

60%	70%	80%	90%	100%

_____lbs _____lbs _____lbs _____lbs _____lbs

Reps 10------------8-------------6------------4-------2------1 Reps

Biceps (Seated Ball Bicep Curl) DB's

60%	70%	80%	90%	100%

_____lbs _____lbs _____lbs _____lbs _____lbs

Reps 10------------8-------------6------------4-------2------1 Reps

Phase III Training Program

Cardio Warm-up Date _____	Time:		Transition Exercises / set 4 Week: 11-60% 13-70% 15 -80%	
Quadriceps	SET 1	SET 2	SET 3	Transition Exercise
Ball wall Squats	LBS	LBS	LBS	LBS
	12 REPS	10 REPS	8 REPS	Rep-outs
Hamstrings				Transition Exercise
Overhead Ball Alternating Lunges	LBS	LBS	LBS	LBS
	12 REPS	10 REPS	8 REPS	Rep-outs
Calves				Transition Exercise
Seated dumbbell Raises	LBS	LBS	LBS	LBS
	12 REPS	10 REPS	8 REPS	Rep-outs
Chest				Transition Exercise
Balance Ball Chest Press	LBS	LBS	LBS	LBS
	12 REPS	10 REPS	8 REPS	Rep-outs
Back				Transition Exercise
Ball Bent Row	LBS	LBS	LBS	LBS
	12 REPS	10 REPS	8 REPS	Rep-outs
Deltoids				Transition Exercise
Seated Ball Shoulder Press	LBS	LBS	LBS	LBS
	12 REPS	10 REPS	8 REPS	Rep-outs
Triceps				Transition Exercise
Seated Ball Overhead Extension	LBS	LBS	LBS	LBS
	12 REPS	10 REPS	8 REPS	Rep-outs
Abdominals				Transition Exercise
Ball Crunches	LBS	LBS	LBS	LBS
	12 REPS	10 REPS	8 REPS	Rep-outs
Biceps				Transition Exercise
Seated Ball Bicep curls	LBS	LBS	LBS	LBS
	12 REPS	10 REPS	8 REPS	Rep-outs

Phase IV

Natural Fitness (Body weight Resistance training)

If you have been following this system then you may be ready to start advancing into more natural moves. Don't worry. Natural fitness doesn't mean you'll be working out in your birthday suit or anything crazy like that. What it does mean is that when you have progressed through this fourth phase, you should very well be strong enough now to start progressing into more natural movements that involve your own body weight. Any movement to protect and sustain the body in life can be considered a natural movement, so in fitness what would this mean?

Let's imagine that you are driving down the road minding your own business. You have taken a simple day-to-day movement earlier to put your seat belt on and BOOM! Someone smashes into your car hurling you 50 feet off of the road into a canal. As your car begins to sink you regain consciousness only to notice the car filling up with water from the inside as the car continues to sink into the muddy water. What are you going to do? First you go for your seatbelt, although you're still somewhat dazed you manage to release it, next you begin to try and open the door but then notice that the door is blocked by the pressure of the water against the door. You begin to push, and then try to break the window, nothing works and you struggle to think what else you can do. As you continually push against the doors in the car your body wears out and you eventually drown to death. Why, because you didn't have enough strength to open the door or break the window.

Here's another example: Let's say you're an overweight, out-of-shape, older man or woman who because of chronically disregarding your health has developed some serious physical problems. You have developed Stage II diabetes and have problems with swollen feet and legs because of it. As you're going to the kitchen to get your insulin shot, you fall down and do not have the strength to pick yourself up in order to take your medications before going into a diabetic coma. You are found a few days later by relatives after not hearing from you for a couple of days.

And one more example: You're awakened in the middle of the night with thick black smoke choking you. You realize immediately that your house is on fire. You wake up your wife in a scream of terror as you both run for the kids' room. As you reach their room you grab your 5 year old boy and carry him outside to safety. You then see your daughter has already made it out and is standing in the driveway. Once you see her you remember that your wife was going to her room to get her. You tell your kids to stay put and quickly dash into the house to find your wife. You have not been burned but have inhaled a bit of smoke, so you rush back into the house to find your wife. You are already breathing heavy and because of your present health do not have much stamina and strength. When you find your wife she is unconscious and limp. As you attempt to pick her up you cannot do so because you are too winded and weak so you decide to drag her but because the smoke is getting thicker and falling closer to the ground you can only do so at a half crawling position. The coroner quotes in the paper that they found you in the living room 10 feet from the front door. You and your wife both died because you lacked the physical strength to pull her and yourself to safety. Let's not forget about all of the other countless things that could happen in the norm of life. Your car breaks down and you're stranded several miles away from the nearest gas station to get help, can you walk that far? Your boat breaks down and you are a half-mile from shore drifting out to sea, can you swim to the shore?

This may sound somewhat farfetched or unheard of, but I will be the first to testify to you that these types of things happen every day around the world and you never know where and when. These examples are actually pretty mild and tamed down in comparison to what I've seen so far in my other career as a Fire Fighter. I really hope that you are beginning to understand the value of natural fitness in all aspects of life.

Natural fitness is the ability to sustain your own or someone else's life when threatened. To naturally perform movements that will help you as an individual lift, push, pull or extricate yourself from harm and toward safety.

Natural fitness is sometimes referred to as functional training or strength training movements that involve every day movements simulated in life. There are several exercises that you could consider functional such as pushups, pull-ups, some that you've already been doing like squats and lunges. All of these movements involve sustaining your own body resistance in one direction or another. The following transition will show you specific movements that will help you begin to have the power and strength to sustain your weight and possibly another person as well.

Phase IV Natural Fitness Training

Power Squats

Basic Components

1. Standing Leg Exercise (preferably wider stance)

2. Controlled Range of Motion 4 – 6 Second Count

3. Breathing Technique – Exhale on the Push

4. Mind to Muscle – Focus on Legs (Quadriceps)

TIPS

- The main difference with a normal Squat vs a Power Squat is the amount of weight and how deep you go into the squat.
- Be cautious when performing this specific exercise and make sure that you have the appropriate weight so you do not injury yourself.
- Remember the range of motion is typically deeper and about 2 seconds slower on the negative movement downward.
- Make sure that heels and ball of foot stay planted flat on the ground throughout the set
- Before Beginning make sure that you have a spotter, all loaded plates are correctly locked on bar and your body is positioned even on bar.
- If using dumbbells make sure placement whether balanced on shoulders or hanging downward with arms extended will allow you to finish exercise and carefully place dumbbells to the ground or in the rack
- Remember to work up to advanced squats with safety in mind, once again, find a person to help or spot you with this exercise

<u>Four Basic Components</u>

1. Standing Leg Exercise

2. Controlled Range of Motion 4 – 6 Second Count

3. Breathing Technique – Exhale on the Push

4. Mind to Muscle – Focus on Legs (Hamstrings)

TIPS

- Once again this exercise is meant to be performed with heavier weights as you progress through the exercise program. Make sure to choose the appropriate weights so that you do not injure yourself. Be cautious!
- As you rotate forward in this exercise movement always make sure that knee stays behind toes in this movement and focus on creating a box with the legs.
- Make sure that forward heel and ball of foot stay planted flat on the ground when going through the range of motion.
- When alternating to the opposite side make sure to push off with the forward leg while controlling the balance of the movement and centering both feet before continuing to the opposite side.
- Keep even grip on Dumbbells and make sure to control the range of motion throughout the whole movement.
- Keep back straight, shoulders aligned and head upright while going through each repetition
- Remember back knee comes down to create the box but stays ½ inch from ground

Standing Dumbbell Calf Raise

<u>Four Basic Components</u>

1. Standing Posture for Legs (Feet are even)

2. Controlled Range of Motion 4 – 6 Second Count

3. Breathing Technique – Exhale on the Push

4. Mind to Muscle – Focus on Legs (Calves)

TIPS

- Keep feet aligned while **NOT** allowing the heels to touch the ground throughout the set
- Make sure to control the flexion and extension of the foot
- Be sure to keep your Abs engaged and your back straight
- Remember that when using dumbbells hold them even in the hands

Push-ups

 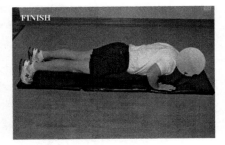

Modified Push-ups

 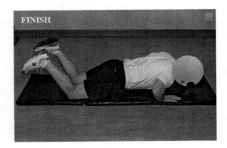

Four Basic Components

1. Prone Posture (Balancing on Hands and Feet or Knees)

2. Controlled Range of Motion 4 – 6 Second Count

3. Breathing Technique – Exhale on the Push

4. Mind to Muscle – Focus on Chest (Pectorals)

TIPS

- Make sure to maintain complete alignment from the back of the head through the spine down to the heels. If you are doing a modified version then again align the back of head to the pit of the knees
- Be sure not to sag or slump your body as you perform this movement
- Keep the head straight and remember not to reach with the neck as you come down through the exercise movement
- Using a pad for the modified push up will be more comfortable for your knees
- Observe Pivot Point adjustment for more isolation on the muscle group being work.   This can be achieved by hand placement whether close, midline or wide positioning.

- Ladies, if you are big chested make sure to wear a sports bra so that you can go through the correct range of motion. (No Cheating)

Chin-ups or Pull-ups

<u>Four Basic Components</u>

1. Up-Right Hanging Posture (My be Modified w/ machines)

2. Controlled Range of Motion 4 – 6 Second Count

3. Breathing Technique – Exhale on the Pull

4. Mind to Muscle – Focus on Back (Lattisimus Dorsi)

TIPS

- Although this is a difficult exercise it is not impossible and takes persistent repetition so don't give up.
- Position hands with a good grip on inside or outside grip on Pull-Up Bar or Machine.
- Starting at the lower position slowly pull your self up with your chin even with your hands.
- Remember that changing the pivot point or the hand positions in this range of motion will isolate different areas and muscles in the back

NOTE: This exercise is no joke and many people need to have a lot of assistance at first with this exercise so find a spotter to help you finish your set or find an assisted Pull-Up Machine.
Most local Gyms have them!

Starting Dumbbell Lateral Raise

<u>Four Basic Components</u>

1. Standing Posture (Straddle Stance)

2. Controlled Range of Motion 4 – 6 Second Count

3. Breathing Technique – Exhale on the Pull

4. Mind to Muscle – Focus on Shoulders (Deltoids)

TIPS

- Keep feet at shoulder width and Abdominals engaged for balance
- Make sure to grip center of Dumbbells
- Remember to keep knuckles even with the center of the shoulder as you raise the Dumbbells to the top of the shoulders
- Keep a small bend on the elbows during the exercise to take resistance off of the upper trapezius (Upper Neck) muscles and help to isolate the deltoids better

Tricep Dips

Four Basic Components

1. Seated Hanging Posture NO Back or Leg Support

2. Controlled Range of Motion 4 – 6 Second Count

3. Breathing Technique – Exhale on the Push

4. Mind to Muscle – Focus on Triceps

TIPS

- This is another exception to the basic postures that provides no back or leg support but specifically depends on and isolates your arms
- Back stays straight and Abdominals are engaged
- Place both hands next to your sides as you move your butt off the bench
- Remember to keep the elbows pointed straight behind you for this exercise movement and find a reasonably comfortable position for your hands on the bench
- Be sure that when extending down in the exercise movement you continue to keep your back straight and as close to the bench as possible (barely touching if possible)
- Remember when the back is to far away from the bench you are placing more resistance on your shoulders and taking the isolation off of the triceps
- Make sure that you come down in a position no further than both triceps in an even horizontal position. Any further than this could cause a hyper flexion in the shoulders

- As you advance in this exercise you will learn that the more you extend the legs the more weight you are placing on the Triceps. Eventually you will be able to place dead weight or dumbbell weight between your legs for more resistance.

Advanced Double Crunches

Four Basic Components

1. Lying Posture w/ Knees bent and Feet flat on ground

2. Controlled Range of Motion 4 – 6 Second Count

3. Breathing Technique – Exhale on the Push

4. Mind to Muscle – Focus on Abdominals

TIPS

- This is a much more advanced version of a typical abdominal crunch. Control is the key component throughout the movement.
- Find a pad or yoga mat to perform this exercise while protecting your spine
- When performing this Abdominal exercise clasp your fingers together and place them behind your head towards the top of the neck
- Bend your knees at a 90 degree angle and begin crunching as you simultaneously bringing your knees towards your chest
- Make sure to lift your shoulders off of the floor and focus on coming together balanced at the top while slowly rotating back to the starting position

NOTE: Make sure to maintain the isolation throughout the entire set with no breaks in between

Standing Alternating Bicep Curls

Four Basic Components

1. Standing Posture (Straddle Stance)

2. Controlled Range of Motion 4 – 6 Second Count

3. Breathing Technique – Exhale on the Pull

4. Mind to Muscle – Focus on Biceps

TIPS

- Although this is a standard bicep movement in this section it is intended to be done with a reasonable amount of resistance
- Make sure to place one foot 3 to 6 inches in front of the other for proper balance
- Remember Abs engaged for balance and Coordination
- Keep back straight and elbows even slightly in front of the center of the shoulders
- Make sure not to swing through out the range of motion and control the negative on the way down

Max Load 1/10 Slow Method
(Natural Fitness Training)

Quadriceps (Power Squats)

60%	70%	80%	90%	100%

_____lbs _____lbs _____lbs _____lbs _____lbs

Reps 10------------8--------------6-------------4-------2------1 Reps

Hamstrings (Alternating DB Lunges)

60%	70%	80%	90%	100%

_____lbs _____lbs _____lbs _____lbs _____lbs

Reps 10------------8--------------6-------------4-------2------1 Reps

Calves (Standing Calf Raise) DB's

60%	70%	80%	90%	100%

_____lbs _____lbs _____lbs _____lbs _____lbs

Reps 10------------8--------------6-------------4-------2------1 Reps

Chest (Push-ups or Modified Push-ups)

60%	70%	80%	90%	100%

_____lbs _____lbs _____lbs _____lbs _____lbs

Reps 10------------8--------------6-------------4-------2------1 Reps

Back (Chin-Ups or Modified Chin-ups w/ equipment)

60%	70%	80%	90%	100%

_____lbs _____lbs _____lbs _____lbs _____lbs

Reps 10------------8--------------6-------------4-------2------1 Reps

Shoulders (Standing Lateral Raises) DB's

60%	70%	80%	90%	100%

_____lbs _____lbs _____lbs _____lbs _____lbs

Reps 10------------8--------------6-------------4-------2------1 Reps

Triceps (Dips "Straight Leg or Bent Knee")

60%	70%	80%	90%	100%

_____lbs _____lbs _____lbs _____lbs _____lbs

Reps 10------------8--------------6-------------4-------2------1 Reps

Abdominals (Double Crunches)

60%	70%	80%	90%	100%

_____lbs _____lbs _____lbs _____lbs _____lbs

Reps 10------------8--------------6-------------4-------2------1 Reps

Biceps (Standing Alternating Bicep Curl) DB's

60%	70%	80%	90%	100%

_____lbs _____lbs _____lbs _____lbs _____lbs

Reps 10------------8--------------6-------------4-------2------1 Reps

Phase IV Training Program

Cardio Warm-up Date _____	Time:		Transition Exercises / set 4 Week: 16-60% 18-70% 20 -80%	
Quadriceps	SET 1	SET 2	SET 3	Transition Exercise
Power Squats	LBS	LBS	LBS	LBS
	12 REPS	10 REPS	8 REPS	Rep-outs
Hamstrings				Transition Exercise
Alternating DB Lunges	LBS	LBS	LBS	LBS
	12 REPS	10 REPS	8 REPS	Rep-outs
Calves				Transition Exercise
Standing DB Calf Raises	LBS	LBS	LBS	LBS
	12 REPS	10 REPS	8 REPS	Rep-outs
Chest				Transition Exercise
Push-ups				
	_____ REPS	_____ REPS	_____ REPS	Rep-outs
Back				Transition Exercise
Chin-Ups				
	_____ REPS	_____ REPS	_____ REPS	Rep-outs
Deltoids				Transition Exercise
Standing Lateral Raises	LBS	LBS	LBS	LBS
	12 REPS	10 REPS	8 REPS	Rep-outs
Triceps				Transition Exercise
Dips	LBS	LBS	LBS	LBS
	12 REPS	10 REPS	8 REPS	Rep-outs
Abdominals				Transition Exercise
Advanced Double Crunches	LBS	LBS	LBS	LBS
	12 REPS	10 REPS	8 REPS	Rep-outs
Biceps				Transition Exercise
Standing Alt. Bicep curls	LBS	LBS	LBS	LBS
	12 REPS	10 REPS	8 REPS	Rep-outs

Conclusion

The great thing, however, with the outline of this method is that all of the exercises transition into the next phase. For example, as you've seen in the first phase, after the first month of machine training you have learned an additional exercise to finish your routine with. This exercise will now be your primary movement for the next phase of the program until all of the phases have been completed. **After all five phases are completed you will have a library of routines and exercises to mix and match in order to prevent not only boredom but most importantly stagnation of results.** This means that you will continue to keep the body guessing and therefore it will continue to grow. Variety in exercise is very important and should always be thought about in accordance with exercise routines. Remember to keep the body and muscles guessing! After you have completed this whole exercise program from beginning to end, then you can really start to become creative with your routines, mixing and or alternating phases and exercises to make it interesting all the while tracking your results. In all, this program will allow exercise to become not only a challenge of the old mundane traditional workout you may have gone through before, but also a challenge of the mind. To design your routines with your library of exercises, track your progressions and have the ability to prevent adaptation of muscle as much as possible.

Please note that the exercises that I have given you in this program are just a few in relation to hundreds of modifications and different exercises in general. Although some of the exercises are basic movements, others may be a bit more advanced for you and may need to be modified as well. Please feel free to visit the website to learn more about all of the different exercises and routines that may be used with this training method. Who knows, maybe you have something that you can share with everyone as well. www.generationawareness. com/trainers

Vanity and Fitness

In recent years of western culture influences in the health and fitness industry it has become quite obvious that vanity has taken over the role of what most people would consider healthy. Many generations are getting sucked into these concepts of the ego that have such great influence with such negative truths and harmful effects on our souls. Because of the influence of business, advertising, media and news, some believe that if they do not have six pack abs, rock hard buns of steel, a flat stomach, bulging biceps and super low body fat percentages, that they are somehow inadequate to the world and their peers. Although keeping you in good physical condition is an important part of life for longevity and comfortable living, the truth is that most people lack the discipline mentally and physically to have the socially accepted "perfect body." You know, like the ones on the covers of magazines all over newsstands!

When you exercise for good health, do it for the right reasons and leave the vanity out of it. Don't compare yourself to others and learn to be happy with any results that you have achieved. Remember, the body that you have been given is only temporary and is made to deteriorate to dust anyway, so do your best to take care of it like the temple that it is and be happy with who you are, the results that you have achieved and most importantly how you feel from the inside out. If you have children or plan on having children one day it's important to teach them these lessons and it sticks even more so when you are a great example!

Chapter 11

6. FLEXIBILITY

In general, stretching is a great way to condition any muscle. In Bill Anderson's book, Stretching, he mentions several benefits from daily stretching such as a reduction of muscle tension, increased coordination and range of motion, and helps to prevent injuries or strains. It also helps to make strenuous exercise easier by warming your muscles up and letting them know that they're about to be used. Stretching also promotes a greater amount of flexibility in each muscle and a sharper awareness of the body, and last but not least, it just feels good.

Remember a few things before diving into a stretching routine. Never, **ever** over-stretch a cold muscle. Although soft movements which lead into mild stretches may be ok, as you get older it is ever so advisable to make sure to heat your body core up with some type of increase in circulation and blood flow. Whether you decide to jump on a treadmill for a few minutes or walk around the block a couple of times warming up is mandatory to prevent yourself from injury. The second part of preventing injury from stretching is to be aware of too much force or resistance in a stretch. Although there are some types of stretching techniques that take you to the brink of pain, such as PNF (Proprioceptive Neuromuscular Facilitation) stretches, a normal stretch should be passive. This means to always stretch to a moderate comfort level. In other words, if you're just beginning a stretching routine, don't force the stretch. Let yourself go as far as your body will take you and breathe through the exhale to release the muscle a little more. This is the best way to stretch and can prevent you from tearing a muscle or straining a tendon. In some cases extreme over stretching can sprain a ligament as well. This is very painful and I don't wish this on anyone. Another type of stretch to avoid would be a dynamic stretch; a stretch through movement. In many cases dynamic stretching can cause injury if not done properly. However, if using this type of stretch make sure that your movement is very slow and controlled without any extra force at the end of the movement. In some therapies or exercises dynamic stretching can be great, but I suggest you always have a specialist educate you on this type of stretching beforehand. Stretching is a very important part of exercise and fitness, but everyone should realize that it is only effective when stretches are held for 10 to 20 seconds or more. Yoga has brought a beautiful meaning to stretching through controlled movement and should be practiced in a daily fashion. At the end of this chapter you will find your fifth phase of exercise which is a simple yoga routine that can be used and incorporated with a weekly regimen to help you improve your flexibility in many aspects. Remember that stretching can be done anywhere at any time and is a wonderful way to become more aware of your body.

In this section on flexibility, I am going to guide you through a couple concepts that have worked extremely well for me as well as my clients. The first is a simple morning stretch routine that will help to improve your mobility throughout the day. This routine includes a brisk walk and basic stretches for each part of the body. The second is Your Personal Yoga Program, which encompasses not just stretching but all aspects of fitness in one. Mind body and soul connection! So let's begin.

Simple Stretch Routine

As mentioned above, I really love waking up to this routine and it sets up my day to be a great one. First things first, start your morning with a brisk walk, which will allow the body to warm up and get your blood flowing. It's good to take your pulse while into your walk and make sure that you are within a minimal target heart rate. If you have forgotten this, revisit the section above on cardio fitness and find your target before you go in the morning. I should also mention that it's important to have good walking shoes that are specifically made for walking or running to support the feet and ankles correctly. Give yourself at least 10 to 20 minutes before beginning your stretches. Follow the routine below in accordance with the pictures and the amount of time the stretches are held. Remember not to overdo it. The objective is not to make yourself tired but more so refreshed and ready to start your day.

I also would like to mention that this is a great time to incorporate some of the mental skills exercises on pages 44 to 47 that you have learned in previous chapters, not only to save time and make your day more efficient, but to stretch your brain as well.

NOTE: Make sure to hold these stretches for a minimum of 10 seconds and a maximum of 30 seconds. Remember not to force the stretch. Use the exhale to release the muscles and focus on Mind to Muscle to get best results.

Your Yoga Program

This form of yoga is really a mix of many things including basic yoga poses that stretch many muscles in the body. This program also includes isolation techniques for strength and power. Your Yoga Program is set up to learn a series of asanas, (Yoga Poses) within a yoga routine including a lesson plan. The lessons or worksheets provide a series of questions or statements and encourage you, the student, to quiet your mind as well as journal your thoughts. At the end of each lesson is what is called five and five, which is a simple mental skills exercise including an easy meditation to quiet the mind after the yoga. These classes can be done at the beginning, middle or end of the day and work well any time. I've saved this routine for last because it is by far the most effective in relation to all aspects of life.

Please remember that any yoga is good yoga and with so many wonderful old and new concepts around today find the one that's right for you. Finding a knowledgeable instructor and someone that feels right for you is important as well. I encourage you to go out and explore your neighborhood's local yoga talent and stick with it. I believe yoga is just as, if not more, important of an exercise as strength training is or any other sort of physical activity. Just stay persistent and disciplined in a regular practice and you will see exactly what I am talking about. I hope you enjoy the classes that I've designed as much as I love to teach them... Namaste!

Mountain Pose

Standing with spine erect, feet parallel at shoulder width. Arms may be straight by sides or in prayer position. Focus on staying grounded to the earth with feet and toes spread apart.

Take nine deep breaths relaxing the body while standing tall.

Forward Fold Sun Salutations

Gently dive down with the hands into a standing forward fold, bending the upper torso toward the floor as the hands meet together. Take 3 deep breaths and begin to exhale as you open the arms wide from side to side and slowly rotate upward while stretching the fingers, elbows, arms and shoulders in both directions until reaching the top. Once you've reached the top, gently dive down once again making three in total rotations of this salutation movement.

Triangle

On the last movement gracefully bring the hands down extending the arms side to side in a perfect horizontal position while extending the feet. Extend your right foot in a 90 degree angle pointing the toe out to the side, while keeping the arms parallel rotate the hip and bring the left hand down to the big toe while raising the right hand straight over your head and looking up into the palm of the hand with your eyes.

Gracefully rotate back to center while alternating feet positions and rotating to the left side. Each pose can be held from 3 to 9 breaths based on your comfort level. Perform 3 rotations per side.

Counter Triangle

Using the same position of the feet gently rotate and extend the right arm straight up above the head while continuing to straighten the left arm parallel with the right, guiding the arm and hand down along the back leg towards the left calf. Once again holding for 3 to 9 breaths and rotating to center before shifting to the exact same pose on the other side with the same uniformity. 3 rotations per side.

Warrior I / Prayer Squat

In the same position rotate both arms up over the head and if necessary place the forward foot deeper into a lunge position. As arms are
positioned over head stretch fingers, elbows and arms from the shoulder and imagine holding a perfectly square box with the palms of your
hands. While doing this shift mildly deeper into a lunge position and
stay for 3 to 9 breaths. You can also look up to the hands by tilting the
head back if you choose to do so.

Before you rotate to the other side for the Warrior I, first rotate both
feet in a forward position while gently bringing down the hands into a
prayer position. Once you have done this begin to slowly shift down
into a seated position creating static isolation in the legs. Bend as
deep as comfortable and hold this isometric contraction for 3 to 9
breaths. Afterwards rotate to the opposite side to continue your 1 to 3
rotations of warrior ones with prayer squats in between

Warrior II / Prayer Squat

This Warrior II pose is similar to Warrior I except for first falling into a deeper lunge position and rotating the arms down into a perfect alignment with the shoulders in an even horizontal position while looking at the forward hand with both palms facing down towards the ground. Once again, rotate to the prayer squat holding for 3 to 9 breaths each time and shifting sides for 1 to 3 rotations.

Warrior III / Prayer Squat

The only variation with Warrior III is the deeper lunge position if possible and the palms up facing the opposite direction while turning the head to look back into the rear palm. I like to tell my students to imagine they have a glass in their hand that is full which they are trying to balance and not spill.

Forward Fold to Plank Pose

Transition from Warrior III by slowly dropping rear hand and allowing the body to follow back to the mountain pose once more. With a nice deep breath exhale down into a standing forward fold once more. Breathing in as you gently place the hands shoulder width even on the mat and walk the legs back into a beginning push up position or what's called a plank pose. If necessary you may modify this pose by falling to the knees. Hold this position for 2 to 3 breaths if possible before shifting to the next pose.

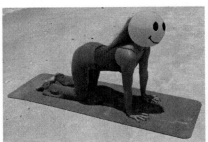 

Down Dog / Up Dog / Happy Cat / Scaredy Cat Poses

From the plank pose slowly exhale and push your body back while shifting your hips up into an inverted V position. Remember to keep your heels and hands pressed flat on the ground while retracting the shoulder blades and dropping the head between the arms if possible. Hold this pose for 1 to 3 breaths and exhale back to the plank position once again.

After 1 deep breath exhale again and drop the torso while arching the back gracefully. Gently squeeze your butt while rolling onto the tops of your feet and pulling the head back to look straight up.

Now rotate back to the plank pose once more and with one deep breath slowly bring your knees to the floor to create a box position with your thighs and arms. Make sure to have the arms positioned right under the shoulders and the knees just under the hips for correct alignment. With a deep breath exhale as you round the back up creating an arching position like a scaredy cat. Make sure to suck in the belly as you exhale. Next, exhale the spine into a happy cat position arching the back while rotating the head to look straight up to the sky or ceiling.

The Down Dog, Up Dog and Cat Poses can be rotated 1 to 9 rotations based off of your current fitness level. Please make sure to modify this movement if you need to.

Plank to King Pigeon (forward stretch option)

After finishing your last Cat Pose shift back to the plank for a deep breath. As you exhale, gently swing your right knee up between your two hands. Slide the left leg back as you rotate to the top of the foot and turn the right leg out to a slight angle. Lift your torso up with your arms and hold this deep hip stretch for 3 to 9 breaths.

 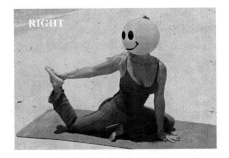

Pigeon II Pose

Gracefully rotate the right hand to the inside of the right knee and find your balance while you lift the left leg from the knee. Reach back with your left hand to grab the inside left ankle and hold this pose for 3 to 9 breaths.

Afterward release the back leg and gently rotate back to the plank pose before rotating to the opposite side for the same pose. 1 to 3 rotations can be performed for each side.

Cobra Pose

After shifting out of the last pigeon pose rotate for the last time back to the plank with one swift movement into a cobra pose by falling face down to the mat and taking a deep breath. Position the hands next to the chest and with a deep breath exhale while pushing up the torso with the arms and arching the back. Make sure to keep the shoulders in a downward position while arching the neck and looking straight up. After 3 to 9 deep breaths gently fall back to the ground. You may perform 1 to 3 of these rotations.

Extended Childs Pose

After falling out of your last Cobra pose take a relaxing breath and slowly push your body back with your hands while rotating to the top of your feet. Gracefully fold your body over your legs while relaxing the forehead on the mat and keeping the arms extended with elbows gently touching the mat as well. Hold this Pose for 3 to 9 breaths and relax.

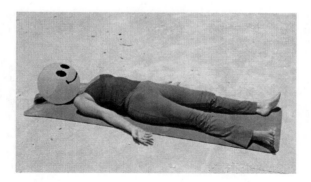

Corpse Pose

After holding the Extended Childs Pose for a relaxing amount of time slowly walk forward to an extended position on your belly and rotate to your back in a lying position with feet relaxed, palms facing up towards the sky or ceiling and spine extended and relaxed on the mat in a comfortable position.

This will conclude the Yoga portion of the class, before getting up take 3 to 5 minutes just to relax and breathe. Afterwards you may begin the remainder the yoga class by completing the following below. I hope you enjoy it!

Empowerment

Lesson #1

Your Definition of Empower:

Name 5 things that empower you?

1.

2.

3.

4.

5.

Explain how each of the five items listed above empower you?

1.

2.

3.

4.

5.

5and5

Mental Skills Exercise

For five minutes, sit and focus on all of the things that you have written in this lesson today. After this time is up, begin your writing meditation by allowing yourself to place the pen or pencil to the paper below and continue writing any thoughts that come to mind on the subject for five minutes to conclude the lesson.

Conclusion

Many people have asked me why I always emphasize the importance of a solid yoga practice over anything else. In all, yoga is one of the few systematic exercise programs that teaches physical and mental endurance while opening up to our spiritual essence. I believe that this is really the goal in our lives to become enlightened with the bigger picture of truth that although we are all different, in a bigger way, we are all still the same: souls trying to find our true purpose to make it to a higher state of consciousness. Yoga is such an incredible way to use the body to calm the mind, which in return allows you to tap into the collective universal spirit in which we are all a part of. I encourage everyone to take up the practice of yoga in your everyday life. It will certainly change your outlook on many things and not only keep your body strong and flexible but your mind as well. I believe yoga to be one of the best ways to keep you centered, grounded and purposeful. If you are interested in more classes they are available online at

www.generationawareness.org/body/yoga.

Chapter 12

7. RECOVERY

Just as exercise and nutrition are key essentials for a healthy body, so is relaxation and sleep. There are many different parts of recovery for the human body, mind and spirit. The first part to recovery is proper amounts of sleep. We spoke about circadian rhythms earlier in this book; the two rhythms that take place during our sleeping hours are the assimilation process and the beginning of the detoxification process. These two circadian rhythms when respected will always promote good internal health and allow the body to heal and purge toxins or poisons and possibly even prevent cell mutations from the body.

Unfortunately, as the human body ages, a good night's sleep sometimes becomes much more difficult to achieve for some reason. Some say its hormones, others may say that it's a void of not being stimulated with normal living habits that you were used to for years. Don't believe the hype on all of this. The truth is those people that exert more energy have more energy and in return recover much more effectively. It's also important to remember as well that using and stimulating the mind daily will help us to sleep and recover better. When it comes down to sleeping it's been proven over and over again that if you work hard you'll sleep well. Remember that exercise releases hormones called endorphins. These are the magic hormones that will keep you young and vibrant. Just be cautious of exercising too late in the day as these energy booster hormones can keep you revved up for hours.

The second part of recovery is relaxation. Now this doesn't mean sitting on a beach sipping pina-coladas all day. It's relaxation in the form of taking time out daily for just you. Finding a few minutes to calm and empty your mind and forget about all of the thoughts and situations that exist in your everyday life. This can also mean a quick catnap or a 5-minute break to lay your head down at your desk at work or while listening to your favorite music in your car. These small daily rituals allow us to defragment and release stress, which is the one thing that makes us old and tired. Finding a couple daily recovery rituals as well as exercising to get a good night sleep are the simple keys to recovery of the human body and mind as well.

Five simple things to help you sleep better

1. ***Focus on just breathing*** – When lying down in bed take several
    minutes to just focus on observing your breath. This is often
    done at the end of yoga classes and quiets the mind tremen-
    dously. Just allow yourself to stay focused on observing your
    breath as you breathe in and out. Notice the rise and fall of the
    belly or the feeling of the breath going in and out of your nose. If
    you notice that your mind wonders off into a thought, gently pull
    your awareness back to observing just the breath. Focus on just
    breathing alone! This seems to work very well with people that
    have initial problems falling asleep. We will talk more about this
    in the next section.

2. ***Avoid big meals and alcohol before bedtime*** – This is one of
    the most common causes of restlessness when trying to get to
    sleep at night. As mentioned excess food in your system not only
    makes you uncomfortable but keeps the body from shutting
    down like it should because of all the processes going on in order
    to break up the food in the digestive system. Although many
    people feel that alcohol relaxes them in the evening, too many
    people over do it. Remember that too much alcohol pollutes the
    body's systems, placing our bodies into overdrive to get back to
    normal either with blood sugar or mental functions that help us
    fall into a deeper sleep. It should also be noted to avoid caf-
    feinated beverages a few hours before sleep as this will create
    the same effects.

3. ***Avoid over stimulation of the mind*** – I believe this is probably
    the biggest problem with people in civilized countries getting a
    good night's sleep. It's called TELEVISION! I would bet that at
    least 80% of all Americans watch T.V. up until the time they go to
    bed. This amount of stimulation is completely draining. Between
    noises, constant pictures flipping back and forth, subject change
    from channel surfing and commercials that bombard the psyche,
    it's just overwhelming. However, because of the mind's ability to
    link visual images and compare them to our own conscious and
    subconscious thoughts it becomes sometimes difficult to shut
    this off after we turn the T.V. off. It amazes me how we can get
    sucked into a television and sit like a bug attracted to a bright
    light until we absolutely can't take it anymore. Let's not forget the
    new culprit on the scene, the INTERNET! This is the same thing,

too much information, that you just get lost and surf from one thing to another until absolutely exhausted. So here's a solution, turn the electronics off both T.V. and INTERNET about an hour before you go to bed. Read a book or a magazine listen to some soft relaxing music and just chill out. Be quiet and your mind will follow!

4. ***Get enough sleep each day*** – When we are younger sleep is something that seems to be irrelevant. We are just too busy having fun, but as we age things change. We need our sleep but just can't find enough time or are so stressed out that we can't get enough. Although eight hours is recommended for a good night's sleep, the truth is to sleep until you feel rested! If that is 4 hours at a time then just make sure that those four hours are productive deep sleep.

5.   Another one of the best things to do each day is to plan out a mid-day nap, whether you call it a cat nap, siesta or power nap doesn't really matter as long as you make it a habit to close your eyes for at least 10-30 minutes during the middle of the day. Believe it or not this will not only rejuvenate you for the rest of the busy day, but also helps you to sleep better at night. Studies have shown that a little siesta during the day makes people much more productive, helps to control stress hormones and aides in better sleep patterns at night.

Whether you're young or old, recovery of the body is important and will eventually play a role towards your health in life. So don't abuse your body and stay up late and fight a good night's sleep. If you are a baby boomer who is getting into the retirement age and you have plenty of time on your hands, take action and exercise, eat well, siesta for a little bit during the day, and this will help you to live longer and healthier. If you have problems sleeping, try the above methods and avoid getting caught up in the pharmaceutical traps and addictions. With a little common sense and effort you can sleep like a baby every night, it just may take some practice. Here are some natural suggestions for sleeping better.

www.generationawareness/recovery/sleepingsolutions

Chapter 13

8. TOUCH

The eighth concept of a healthy life is touch. Although the first seven fundamentals of life touch you externally and internally, it is the touch of a human that I would like to refer too. Being touched or touching another in a healthy positive fashion improves human life considerably. There have been many studies on the power of touch that have shown several interesting and sometimes tragic results. In the early 13th century an Italian Historian named Salimbene wrote of an experiment that German Emperor Frederick II conducted. The Emperor was on a quest to know what language these children would speak and how they would interact without hearing any language at all. So, he took several babies from their mothers and had them raised in complete isolation. In doing this experiment the conclusion was that they all died. Salimbene wrote, "they could not live without petting". Another study performed hundreds of years later published as a movie in 1952 called "Psychogenic Disease in Infancy" by Rene Spitz M.D. This study detailed the effects of maternal and emotional deprivation of attachment of infants. Dr. Spitz noted in his study that within the sixth and eighteenth month of an infants life when deprived of their mother without adequate substitution, the babies would develop systems of retardation and become increasingly unapproachable as well as weepy and irritable. As the experiment continued and these infants became deprived during the first year of life for more than five months they became lethargic, their weight and growth stopped and they were unable to sit, stand, walk or talk. This study concluded that 37.3% of these cases watched these infants progressively deteriorate mentally and physically through malnutrition which led to their death by the age of two. Although I believe these examples to be extremely inhumane studies, I look at many things in society and see several unrecognized versions being adopted in our developing world cultures today. I remember as a child being afraid to touch two people that where actually family members of mine. First my grandmother, she was old and just looking at the texture of her skin and appearance was almost scary to me, little did I know until I grew up and realized that I too would be this way one day did I see into her and beyond her flesh to see that she was brilliant, beautiful and had the mind and soul of an angel. I often wonder what would have happened if I would have just held her hand more often or just hugged her for 10 seconds longer. Hmm! I wonder if she would have lived healthier that day.

My second relative was Mark, my cousin; he had Muscular Dystrophy very badly and progressed into a contoured fragile structure over the years. Mark had this from birth and dealt with it quite well. Always chipper and happy although you could see the pain he was in sometimes. However, being the kid I was, and having no true knowledge of his disease, I brushed his painful grunts off as a child. When thinking deeper into those moments as a child I think that I felt them too, but for me it sparked something and I didn't know how to react. I wish that I wouldn't have been so scared of Mark and would have stayed in contact. But because of his differences I made myself unknown and unseen. I wonder if it would have made a difference holding his hand or hugging his little twisted shell of a body. I'm sorry Mark!

In our culture today we are becoming more and more distant and introverted from others. The generation of computers, the Internet and video games, with the 'keep up with the Jones' western societal ways, which are unfortunately rubbing off on many other countries and societies, we are now living in a world of unclear law and questionable human rights ethics that leave many of us on edge especially when touching someone. In some cases we're scared to hug our own children.

Several years ago while living in Miami, Florida, I had the privilege in participating in a couple of studies with Dr. Tiffany Fields at the University of Miami Touch Research Institute. The first study was the study of touch response, where we studied the results of Fibromyalgia and Chronic Fatigue syndrome. The study concluded that Touch (Massage therapy) worked just as good, if not better, than all other treatments. The second study became Dr. Fields prized work, which studied infant growth and development. This research entailed several parts, from premature babies to infant growth responses based on touch and stimulation. Toddlers intellectual development was also tested based on human touch. Again, the results of touch from a human hand proved to increase the growth rate of premature babies as well as improve the intellectual development of the infants and toddlers. Amazing! Just to add a quick note to those results, I was able to improve my own daughter's health as a 2 lbs premature baby by the touch of her daddy's hands.

So, touch and be touched whether a hug or pat on the head from a loved one, or a real hand shake and a pat on the back, it's important that we do not forget to communicate emotionally through the physical aspects of touch. It's really amazing what the power of touch can do to a person if done with sincerity.

Here are a few suggestions:

- Hug your wife or husband, kids, or partner every day. Try to keep hugging for more than 30 seconds. Take a few deep breathes with them and talk to them as you do.
- Shake hands like you mean it when you meet someone. People know a sincere hand shake when they get one.
- Hold hands with your family no matter how old they are. Tell them why you want to and what you've learned and pass the information on so that you can create a new family rule.
- Rub or massage your spouse's or partner's shoulders or feet just for the heck of it.
- Hug people that you meet for the first time and show them your true nature of caring for a stranger. They may end up being a dear friend from that initial contact.
- Guys! Don't be afraid to show affection to each other even if you have to do it in a manly way. At the fire department we do the old hand shake into a hug routine or even the side hug works well.
- Mothers, brush your daughter's hair and daughters do the same. This is for some reason a very passionate form of endearment for women. I know my daughters love it!
- Hug someone older then you! Like your grandparents or maybe someone else that could be like a grandparent. Stay with them and hold their hands in yours. This is an amazing thing and it seems that some sort of wisdom always comes with it.
- Be extra affectionate with mentally handicap people that may have deformities. Remember they are souls just like you and I. They need love, affection and touch even more than we do.

Be Touched Yourself

It is not only important to touch others and share in this human experience. The rewards that you receive are tenfold. It is also necessary to be touched by others as well. Most of the time a lack of touch in a relationship or friendship is due to a lack of communication on one or both people's part. Make sure you stay in a good line of communication with those people that you love and care for and tell them how you would like to be touched as well. Sometimes just opening up a direct line of communication on the subject can provide enough clarity to expand your relationship into an even deeper level. Maybe you'll find out that the reason the person doesn't want to be touched or doesn't express themselves that way is due to a past experience that you can help them with. Just don't give up on not only touching but being touched too.

I also suggest that you find other forms of touch such as massage therapy, going to the nail salon, the beauty parlor or barbershop. I've even studied touch response with personal training clients and found that just laying my hands on there's as they are struggling to complete a final repetition for an exercise, 99% of the time helps them to complete the set. Nothing like a helping hand!

To reach out and touch someone is a magical thing that has been proven time and time again to lift spirits, soften hearts, ease pain, bring about instant understanding and compassion, and most of all transform our lives into a loving state of mind and spirit.

TOUCH EXERCISE

Answer the following questions:

How were you raised as a child in relation to touch?

Do you remember a touch response from your parents while growing up as a child?
Example: mother or father kiss on the cheek, hugs, rubbing your head or tickling your ear.

Do you feel you have carried on that learned behavior?

Is there anyone that you feel that you don't touch enough? Why?

What could you do today to improve your fear or inadequacies in the touch department of life?

Touch Exercise continued...

Write your thoughts on the subject of touch:

Chapter 14

9. Belonging

Enjoying the social journey of life is one of the biggest problems we face in today's world. It's so easy to keep busy going through the rut of the everyday grind or hiding in front of the T.V., Internet or computer in the evenings as we wind down from a busy day. Heck, we even push our kids or grand kids in front of it now-a-days to get just a little more time to do our regular chores or just take a break.

But for those of you that can remember back to when you were a child and you played a sport in school, participated in band, choir, gym class, even played on the school chess team, or anything like this, **"It was great to belong." You were a part of something that worked together as a unified group.** This is what I'm talking about when I mention the word belonging. Finding common beliefs, whether hobbies, interest, skills, religion, spirituality, politics, humanitarians of human or world kind. I remember being a young kid when my mother would tell me either stay in or out of the house. Of course back then we all opted to stay out and play. Sometimes we'd sit on the porch, brothers, sisters, neighbor kids and whoever. We'd talk about the things that really mattered to us back then. I think unconsciously most of the time we were day dreaming together. Of course, until one of us would think up something new to play or do, then most of the time it was off to play hide and seek, capture the flag or some sport that was in season. We would play until we could play no more or it got dark outside. Didn't think anything of it, just played and laughed! That was all we knew back then, we were taken care of for the most part, didn't have to worry about all the stresses in life; we were kids. No responsibilities, just school work, chores, eating and sleeping. Our perception of the world was easy and simple. **"Unfortunately, as we get to be adults and our responsibilities become a bit more serious, we forget how important it is to just go outside and play."**

Sharing your thoughts and experiences with others is rewarding in so many ways you could not even imagine the return one human can receive from another. Because it is just that, "The communication skills, and the ability to grow in knowledge, not just any knowledge but one that allows you to rationalize your thoughts, except, distain, or compare." When you really think about it, it's the other people in your life that make you who you become. Do you remember when someone said, "Oh he's just like his father, mother, uncle, aunt, brother, sister, etc." Well you know what, they were right on, to an extent. Even if you didn't like who they were comparing you to or with, you are a piece of all of those who influence you directly or indirectly.   The conversations that sink and absorb into your conscious and help you to form opinions and ideas that eventually change your patterns of thought into belief and or faith make you who you are becoming every day that you continue to live.

It's important to belong, to your family, your group of friends, a club or anything uplifting and positive involving another human being that you can relate to. Belonging is the core essence of living a happy and healthy lifestyle and that is why I consider it to be the ninth source of energy for a lifestyle worth living. Don't let another day go by being cooped up in your own little shell of a life. If you aren't involved in a group or don't belong to an organization of some sort, find one and get truly involved. Most people don't realize how much they have to say or what they can teach others just by sharing their experiences and being a part of another person's life in one way or another. There are many facets of belonging; the first should be family and friends. Make the time to spend with your immediate family daily and weekly. Sit at the dinner table and talk or go for a nature walk and just enjoy each other's company. Parents, make sure that your kids feel a sense of belonging in your life. In this day and age, parents are so busy trying to work, pay the bills and do their own thing, that the kids often get left behind. Spend a special day with your children. Husbands and wives, go on a date once in a while and do things to show each other that you are a team that belong to one another. Invite your friends or co-workers over for dinner or a barbeque or something. Be involved in things that mean a lot to you, that make you feel happy, accomplished, and complete as a person. Whether it's a sports league, a group of friends hanging out or a community association that stimulates you intellectually. The important thing is to belong and be a part of something that you have a desire or passion for. Here are some examples of groups that you can belong to:

- Community Sports League
- Local Trades Union
- Community Association
- Group of Friends
- Motorcycle Club
- Book Club
- Debate Club
- Habitat for Humanity

- Volunteer for Non Profit
- Big Brother / Big Sister
- Community Park
- Bridge Club
- Bike Club
- Ski Club

Follow this link to find local groups organized with Generation Awareness.

www.generationawareness.org/directory/local/groups

Belonging Exercise:

1st Find 3 organizations that you would like to get involved in.

Name:
Address:
Contact person:
Phone #:
Meeting Times:
Cost if any?

Name:
Address:
Contact person:
Phone #:
Meeting Times:
Cost if any?

Name:
Address:
Contact person:
Phone #:
Meeting Times:
Cost if any?

2nd Make a Plan of Action.
Starting Date
What you will be able to contribute to this organization.

3rd Complete your first date and journal your results.

Be realistic with yourself and don't under or over extend yourself. If this organization is not right for you then find another that you may like better, but try not to jump around too much.
Journal Here:

Chapter 15

10. Balance

The last source of energy for our bodies is the idea of balance, not only physically, but emotionally as well. When we speak of balance in the physical, we talk of coordination to center one self. Whether standing on one leg or keeping a steady writing hand, balance is a necessity in our every day lives that can help us to live with a true quality of life. As in the mental and emotional world of our lives, balance in life is the ability to coordinate and maintain a steady keel on all of the positive and negative experiences in life so that we may be centered and focused on the real things that matter.

As we age as human beings, balance becomes more of an issue for most. In the physical realm of life, balance is a major concern for both men and women. Losing balance can mean a nasty fall that could lead to a broken ankle, hip or bone in general. Losing balance for anyone can mean an injury of some kind but with age paranoia becomes more relevant. We fear falling or lacking coordination due to diminished eyesight, loss of hearing or sometimes even calcium buildup in the ear can lead to a problem with our equilibrium. Many people as they age also develop problems with vertigo. Although age can be against us in these matters, it is possible to control and improve our balance in the physical. Physical balance daily can be achieved through simple yoga postures and balancing exercises that can be done day in and day out. Here are a couple examples of yoga poses and balance exercises that you can perform daily.

Yoga Poses:
- Straight leg circles
- Warrior pose transitions
- Tree Pose

Basic Balance exercises:
- Tip Toe to Heels- This simple exercise involves you standing next to the wall or some support. Stand arms length away and with only your fingertips, touch the wall. Flex up to your tiptoes and slowly take your fingers off the wall for as long as you can balance. Try to maintain balance on your tiptoes for as long as you can. When you can't hold it anymore then roll back to your

heals doing the same thing until you can't hold any longer and rotate forward to the tip toes again. The idea is to train the body and the muscles in the legs that it takes to coordinate this balance in the body. Try to do 3 to 5 rotations a day.

- Walk the Line – this exercise I use often with my clients that have balance issues. For this exercise get a rope of some kind; I use a jump rope with my clients. Place the rope in a straight line down the center of the floor. If you are by yourself you should place it a little less then arms length parallel with the wall. Start with both feet on one side of the rope. The exercise will consist of placing each foot on the opposite side of the rope. I normally will say GO! The client will place the outside foot on the opposite side of the rope and once done will not move until I call to GO again. Before the next foot crosses to the other side of the rope, the person must have both feet facing forward completely flat with the heals down flat to the floor with legs crossed, and feet on opposite sides of the rope. It's best when beginning this to stand next to a wall or table for extra support in case you lose your balance while doing the exercise.

Balance in Life

"Too much of a good thing is a bad thing!" This saying holds very true in life. If we over indulge in life then we pay the price one way or another. For example, a workaholic, a couch potato, a bulimic, a hypochondriac, any type of addict; all of these are forms of an unhealthy unbalanced life. I've even seen people that become extremely unhealthy by over-exercising! All of this over indulgence is nothing more than a void in a person's life. When we get confused or can't understand things, most of us will find something that we feel comfortable with and obsess over it to fill our misinterpretation of a specific void in our life. This glitch becomes such a repetitive comfort zone that once we adapt and form an unhealthy habit it becomes extremely hard to stop. Therefore, use moderation in all that you do, find a balance in work, family, friends and play. Coordinate your schedule and implement these 10 sources of energy into your daily life. Create these lessons and turn them into a lifestyle that will become second nature. Find positive healthy habits to fill the voids that you may have in life. More than anything, be good to yourself and treat your body and mind with respect and dignity by balancing all that you do in life and treating everyone that you meet and know with that same respect and love that you have for yourself.

Soul

Chapter 16

SPIRITUAL ENERGY

When understanding and realizing that we are so much more than just a body, that we are beings of creation with the same creative ability and infinite, celestial potential as our maker, this awareness will allow us to find complete liberty and freedom of our minds, bodies and souls.

The life force energy that exists within us is the purest and most powerful energy that links us to each other and everything of truth and goodness throughout this world and the universe. If we accept and learn from all the energies of life then we will grow and blossom into enlightened states of mind and spirit. This interconnectedness of mind, body and spirit will allow us to stay centered within our own lives moment-by-moment and lead by example.

In the last section of this book you will learn how to use your mind and body to connect to the third state of consciousness, which is your spirit. You will learn first how simple physical breathing techniques can induce an inner state of peace and serenity in the mind in order to allow you to tap into the universal energy from which you come from. You will also learn the solutions to any problem or worry is to acknowledge and accept these glitches or problems for what they are: thoughts in a continuous experience or journey, nothing more or nothing less. I will also teach you how you can use some of the life tools that you have created with this book as well as a few easy meditations and calming techniques that you can use daily to stay focused and purposeful. Lastly I will share with you my belief of a new rising world consciousness, that you will see after reading this book and using the exercises, you are a major part of.

Breathe

Before you read these chapters take a deep breath, in your nose and out your mouth. This is called a cleansing breath. Now take a few more... After you read this paragraph close your eyes and take a few more breaths, try to relax and feel your chest as you breathe. Feel your abdominal wall expand and fold as you breathe. Notice on the exhale whether your neck and shoulders begin to relax and fall slightly. As you read this chapter continue to breathe and focus on the most powerful physical tool of your life experience - your breath!

The word breathe in Latin is spirare while the word spirit is spiritus. This word in all cultures tends to translate to the same term; to the one thing that gives us life on this planet, our breath! In some eastern Indian philosophies breath is known as prana, when translated means the universal life force. The same interpretation in the Taoism or Chinese culture is known as "chi" as we mentioned at the beginning of this book and many times "qi". You may be more familiar with these words in context such as "Tai Chi" or "Qi Gong". These two powerful forms of Chinese exercise and energy movement incorporate special breathing techniques to energize the body and mind towards a higher spiritual and meditative state of being. Learning these masterful energy movements and breathing forms will change anyone's life forever.

www.GenerationAwareness.org/TaiChi
www.GenerationAwareness.org/Qigong

Breath is the most basic of essential actions and companions for our existence as human beings. Breath is the connection between the physical, mental body and the spiritual realm of our higher consciousness.

Our breath shows truth in everything. Our breathing pattern and rhythms are in direct correlation to our nervous system. Our flow of breath normally always interprets our physical and mental states. If a person is breathing rapidly this could be induced by fear or anger and on the other hand if a person is breathing shallow this could be a potential sign of insecurity or depression. In all cases breath is the control center for our emotional states of mind. Although we have spoken of this direct link between the breath and your emotions, feelings and so on, most of us tend to forget about our breath and always take it for granted in all instances. Because our breath is part of our autonomic nervous system, we tend to forget about the enormous power we have by controlling our breath. At the same time we tend to forget the power our breath has to our human existence. If you've ever been prevented from breathing you know what I mean. So, we continue to stay in the realm of unconscious breathing.

As a word in our language we use the word breathe in many dialects to express intense emotional expressions. For example: "It takes my breath away" is an idiom that we use to behold immense beauty and or excitement. "I'm breathless" is another example, expressing complete passion or love. "I had to catch my breath", is a meaning of telling someone that you need or had to slow down to rest or relax. Isn't it interesting that we use the same types of expressions in relation to the heart as well. "You took my heart or breath away"; "You have my heart". We've even taken these expressions down into single words. To be heartless, heartache, heartbreak, heartily, hearty, hearten, heartfelt and much more. In all, the physical and spiritual relationships are the same. We all know that in order for the heart to continue pumping blood through the circulatory system and throughout the body we must first have oxygen. This oxygen comes from every breath taken into the lungs. At the same time in the spiritual aspect we see that our breath is life, and by learning to consciously become aware of and control our breath, we in return will learn to control the emotions and feelings in our lives.

In all reality, it is important to understand that we are presently living in a mental realm or dimension of physical life in which our breath is the silver cord that connects our souls to this plain of existence or universal spirit. This allows in turn a greater respect for this journey that we are breathing through and experiencing from the first inhalation of life to the present at this moment.

The importance of breathe has been taught for thousands and thousands of years by many masters that have walked on this earth. In Helmut G. Sieczka's book "Charka Breathing," he mentions that several religious teachers have expressed in their teachings of the breath that the experience of conscious breathing leads one to the true experience of oneness with self and the universe.

Some would assume that all of these teachers would be of eastern or native religions and cultures, of which in this case would be correct including, Buddha, Sufis and one of the most famous eastern meditation teachers, Maharashi. However, what's most fascinating to me is to see that even in Christianity, Jesus Christ speaks of the sacredness of breath. In the Dead Sea scrolls he says: "We revere the holy breath which is beyond all creation. For behold, the eternal, highest realm of light, where the infinite stars reign, is the realm of air, which we inhale and exhale. In the moments between inhalation and exhalation, all the mysteries of the eternal garden are hidden. Angel of the air, holy messenger of the earth mother dive deeply into me, like a swallow dives from the sky, so that I may know the secret of the wind and the music of the stars."

The action of breath

The word inhale or inhalation is the physical action of taking in or breathing in oxygen. When interpreted into the mental and spiritual equivalent means to inspire or inspiration. In other words inspiration is the universal energy that stimulates our mind and soul into creation and creative thought, creating everything that we develop and experience in life. With that inspiration we exhale in the physical, which means to breathe forth, emanate, radiate or expire. Again in relation to the mental and spiritual realm we are in expiration, which means to release or pass forward. A great example is my personal quest for this knowledge to better myself and share this information with the world, which I inhale with every opportunity that inspires me to write this book. In return for the exhale to this inspiration is the creation of this book.

Breathing to Center Yourself

In day-to-day life simple breathing techniques can bring you to a state of relaxation and calmness. Learning how to use the breath as a conscious tool to draw yourself out of unhealthy or dysfunctional thought patterns can take you above these human states of mind and allow you to become the observer as mentioned in earlier chapters. Learning and training yourself to use these simple breathing tools will allow you to reconnect to your spirit and higher consciousness in times of stress or turmoil which will dissipate disillusioned thoughts of worry, anger, depression, sadness or any other unproductive, unhealthy state of mind and, or perception.

The following three breathing exercises are designed to be used daily and may be used in any particular order, fashion or at any particular time of the day. Most importantly you will learn that these simple breathing techniques can many times be used to begin meditations

Three Basic Breathing Exercises

1.   Relaxed Belly Breathing: If you have ever observed a young child when breathing, normally up to the age of four. You will notice that these little children breathe like all of us are naturally supposed to, from the belly. Expanding their bellies or diaphragm muscles and allowing their lungs to follow. Unfortunately, as we age we become more familiar with stress and anxiety and we forget to breathe naturally. Follow the step-by-step instructions below and remember most importantly not to try too hard. Breathe softly and relax your body and mind. Do not allow the thoughts that creep up into our mind to take you away from your breathing.

Step 1 - Posture: Find the most comfortable posture for you. Whether sitting in a chair upright, in a lotus or half lotus position on the floor or standing, put yourself in a posture that is going to allow you to stay still with less discomfort or body aches for at least 5 to 15 minutes. If you are most comfortable in a lying position, you may do this as well, although it is not recommended because of the relaxed state that this breathing exercise will place you in and it may make you go to sleep. Also, make sure to sit or stand upright straightening your spine and head so that you may use your diaphragm muscles efficiently. Pull your shoulders back slightly, this will help you lift your rib cage so that you can expand your belly easier.

Step 2 - Feel your Breath: Quiet your mind and begin relaxed breathing. Focusing on Exhaling for 3 to 4 seconds from the belly, allow the lungs to follow suit from the soft extension and retraction of the belly. Place one or both hands on the belly near your navel and observe the soft expansion of the belly as you begin to inhale. Now, notice the gentle release and fall of the belly as you begin to exhale again. Gently continue breathing while observing this natural phenomenon of life. Don't force the rate or rhythm of the breath just allow yourself to observe the rise and fall of the belly.

Step 3 - Release your thoughts: As you begin to breathe you may have thoughts enter your mind. As you become aware of them gently observe them and allow yourself to shift your awareness back to your belly breath. Shift your thought back to the gentle rise and fall or the subtle feeling of the breath as it touches the nostril or lips as you gently shift your awareness back to the breath.

Step 4 - Breathe into discomfort: If you find your thoughts shifting to an uncomfortable position that may be causing your body an ache or pain, take your breath to the area of discomfort and softly breathe into it. Allow the muscle to expand and release as the belly rises and falls until the discomfort goes away. If you need to posture shift a little for comfort do so gently and once again shift your awareness back to the belly breath.

Step 5 - Breathe Correctly: Make sure that your mouth is slightly opened with your jaw relaxed. The breath is inhaled through the nose and exhaled out of the mouth. Remember not to force your breathing, just allow your body to find its natural rhythm as you calm your mind and focus on the rise and fall of the belly.

NOTE: If you become light headed or dizzy then attempt to slow your breathing pattern, you may not realize you are breathing too hard or fast.

This simple breathing exercise has been used for eons as a tool for many types of yoga and is an easy meditation. Today's western culture medicine is using this simple breathing technique to help alleviate anxiety and stress disorders, lower blood pressure without taking medication and more. If you want to learn more about this go to the following link. www.generationawareness.com/alt/bp/control

2.   Breath Counts: This simple breathing technique taught as a basis of focused meditation by Zen masters over the centuries is very calming and powerful to relax the body and mind.

Step 1 - Posture: Again, find a comfortable position whether standing, sitting or laying. Make sure to keep the spine erect and begin the exercise with a few deep breaths to settle your body into a comfortable relaxed position.

Step 2 - Find your natural breathing rhythm: As you begin to breathe close your eyes softly and allow your breath to naturally flow in your nose and out your mouth with no force. Take your awareness to the breath as you take a few more breaths, just allowing your body to find its own steady relaxed flow.

Step 3 - Begin to Count: After a few breaths slowly shift your thought to counting each full breath while relaxing more and more. As you exhale out the mouth, gently begin your internal counting dialect by saying quietly in your mind, "1". Allow the word to last as long as your exhale lasts but make sure not to force the exhale. Now, as you inhale in the nose you may either stay silent or use the word "and", which will be naturally a shorter time frame. It is best to practice this counting breath in cycles of 3, 6 or 9 which are single syllables words and allow better concentration. Continue counting in whichever number you choose while focusing on the breath explained above.

Step 4 - 5 to 15 minutes of focused meditation: It is always easier to begin your practice of this breathing technique for a shorter duration and to work up to them. But make sure to track your progress in time and slowly improve on your breathing as you increase your time frame. Whether you use a timer or a stop watch most of the time it will be easy to gauge your progress just by viewing a clock or just allowing yourself to continue until you feel you are relaxed to the state that you wish to be in and are consciously ready to finish the exercise.

3. Bellows Breathing Exercise

This breathing technique is unique and promotes a crisp, alert energy source for anyone that uses it often. This breathing exercise, if done correctly, actually creates a chemical endorphin rush of feel good hormones in comparison to a caffeine rush that so many of us are use to by drinking caffeinated energy sodas, coffee or tea drinks. The benefit with this however is that it is completely free and natural not to mention it doesn't come with caffeine or sugar crashes afterwards and it allows you to avoid all of the nasty byproducts associated with some of these manmade addictions.

Step 1 - Posture: Use a sitting position only for this breathing exercise whether sitting on the floor or in a chair. Make sure to sit upright and expand your spine straight. Never stand during this exercise because as you start you may find yourself getting a bit dizzy or faint. Again, always sit down and make yourself comfortable.

Step 2 - Breathing like a Bellow: Close your mouth slightly without pressing your lips together hard. Begin to breathe evenly in and out of your nose at a moderately rapid pace (2 to 4 cycles per second). Although this breathing technique is meant to be exaggerated, keeping the inhale and exhale equal and continue for no more then 1 to 3 minutes total at first. This time frame can be added to in 1 minute intervals weekly until you reach a maximum of 20 minutes.

Step 3 - Resting Period: After you are finished with the exercise stay seated for a few minutes until your normal breathing pattern comes back and you feel no light-headedness. Be warned that although this breathing exercise can be very beneficial and promote great energy it sometimes can cause hyperventilation, which could cause a person to faint or lose consciousness for a moment. If you have high blood pressure or any other circulation problems make sure to do this with someone who knows what they're doing in relation to these breathing exercises.

Breathing Conclusion: All of the breathing exercises that you have just learned, although best to start your day in the morning, may be used any time that you feel the need to relax, de-stress or to get a quick energy boost.

The wonderful thing about these breathing techniques is that they are simple but yet with repetition in everyday life become a powerful tool to keep you grounded and centered as well as lead to a greater awareness of the emanate source of energy that comes from simple daily forms of meditation.

Chapter 17

Taking the Voodoo out of Meditation

What is meditation anyways? To study, contemplate, revolve, say to one self, reflect, view, consider, speculate or dream. I feel the better definition is to connect or tap into the life force energy or prana that everything derives from.

Although our western civilization has shown meditation to be a bit of a silly or hokey subject with an old oriental fellow or maybe even a monk sitting on top of a mountain as the sun rises. This ancient tool of wisdom has been studied for thousands and thousands of years, and every one does it in one way or another whether they realize it or not. Meditation comes in many different forms whether zoning out as you walk down the street or picking up an extracurricular activity that gives you some sort of stress release, many people meditate to music at home or in their cars.

In many religions, daily meditation rituals are commonly used to keep spiritual leaders close to their source of belief. Most all religions use chanting meditation rituals and prayers, from Buddhist Monks, Catholic Priests and Nuns, even Southern Baptist Ministers use words, phrases or songs that feel good enough to repeat at every sermon. The point is that no matter what you believe or how you do it, meditation brings us all closer to inner peace, calmness and our faiths in a higher power, God, our creator. Although some may see mystery in meditation or prayer it is quite obvious that its power is positive and has no negative or Voodoo negativity involved. It just gets us closer to maintaining an enlightened or positive state of existence and allows us to stay connected to our spiritual and eternal selves.

Meditation and Human Senses

All of the physical body's human senses are what act as a median to meditation, which allows us to connect to spirit. In this section we will explore visual, audio and touch senses. Afterwards I will give you a couple of individual meditations in each source and show you how you can combine them, if you wish to, for even better results.

However, it is worth mentioning two things. First, I will not give you or expect you to know any other language then your own when it comes to terminology of meditation. I have realized over the years that it frustrates most, including me, to try and pronounce words from another language that I have no formal schooling or knowledge in. I will not give you words, or sayings that you don't know how to read, rather I prefer to use a language that you are comfortable in. Secondly, it's important to realize that all of these forms of meditation use the breath to link you to the spiritual realm. Make sure to always practice breathing techniques. Make them a common practice and combine them with other daily habits. Breathing techniques shouldn't just be used in stressful situations or hectic moments in your life.

Practice breathing while you are out and about in your daily activities such as exercising, walking, sitting down for breakfast or lunch or even brushing your teeth or going to the restroom. Incorporate breathing techniques in as many habits that you can to keep your mind and body calm and relaxed. One such habit that I have combined my breathing practice with is catching myself in bad posture shifts. When I find that I am slouching and need to stand or set upright, I find that taking a few deep breathes allows me to gain focus and relax the muscles that are stressing my body. Use this, it works well for most.

Visual Meditation

Most everything that we do in life, for those of us that have not been blind from birth, is seen and or created in our minds as visual pictures or images. We view things with our eyes in every present moment while we are awake. We also view pictures or unconscious live video feeds with our minds even while we sleep (dreams or nightmares). From this powerful sense, we create visual images from our past as well as our future to create thoughts.

Unfortunately, most of us never take time out to just smell the roses and view them without thought. This is why I believe that visual meditations, although the easiest of simple meditation tools, can be the most difficult for many people. Most of us have a difficult time viewing something with our eyes open and not being distracted with a thought popping up in our minds that takes us down a wormhole of thoughts.

Although there are many great new concepts in visual meditation, I will introduce two very effective types of simple visual mediations that we will explore. The first, as a way of clearing or emptying the mind of thought, and the other of conscious gratitude that most all of us have experienced in life at one time or another.

V.M. Exercise I

First, visual meditation that allows you to lose thought, although tough at first, is a very rewarding and powerful tool that I like to use. It allows an individual to clear the clutter out of the mind and de-fragments, tames and rejuvenates the physical and spiritual mind and body.

1st) Find a quiet spot with no one to interrupt you. You should be able to sit quietly for at least 10 to 20 minutes in this sanctuary and not worry about being taken out of your meditation practice.

2nd) Find a visual object or point that has no true sentimental attachment, emotion or long drawn out past history of thoughts towards it. One example is a picture of your loved one or family, etc. Try to find an object of simplicity that is either still or has small natural flowing rhythmic patterns to it. Some great examples of things to use is a candle, a body of water, a tree, even a spot on a wall or ceiling works well. I do believe, however, that connecting with anything earthly such as fire, water, vegetation and the sky are the best sources.

3rd) Focus on your breath as you observe the object, releasing any thoughts that may come into the mind and gently shift your awareness to the breath. As you visualize the object you will begin to release the focus of the breath and notice the visual sense becoming enhanced. If thought floats back into the mind gently release it by shifting to the breath once more until your visual image takes hold again. Many people after practicing visual meditations can begin to see shades of lights or colors around objects. These are called Auras, which are sources of energy that emanate from objects, most everything has them. Just observe them without thinking about them.

4th) Continue to maintain your visual connection with the object and allow your mind to stay empty until you feel you are completely relaxed or ready to finish. Most people will begin with 3 to 5 minutes with this mediation and progress up through 10 to 20 minutes.

The best times to do this visual meditation are either first thing in the morning or last thing at night before retiring to bed. I use it as a precursor to my morning journaling and it works great!

V.M. Exercise II

Have you ever caught yourself admiring someone or something that gives you great joy, makes you warm inside and sometimes just makes you overwhelmed with love and compassion? This is a wonderful visual meditation that you can consciously use every day.

Whether it's our children, grandchildren, spouse, girlfriend, boyfriend, family pet, whoever or whatever, visual images of these people and sometimes things evoke past and present emotional states of mind and stimulate our spiritual minds as well. Most of the time when we are having these fine memories we are replaying a past event that connected or brought us in tune with this moment.

Finding visual images that create thoughts of gratitude, appreciation and thankfulness for someone or something intrinsically stimulate positive emotions and purposefully evokes these thoughts and memories, which can be used as a powerful tool for connecting to and maintaining a spiritual mindset daily.

1st) This Meditation can be used while driving, but works best when you are quietly sitting with no disturbances.

2nd) Use a visual image of the person or thing and sit quietly viewing the object and or visual thought while focusing on the breath for a few moments. Calm your body and settle the thoughts in your mind.

3rd) Begin thinking of and evoking thoughts from the visual image of love, compassion, respect and any other positive thought that comes to mind. Attempt to visualize past experiences that give you a greater appreciation for this person or thing and find as many things to be thankful for as possible.

4th) When finished, gently allow yourself to go back to the breath and begin shifting your awareness to the rise and fall of the belly until you are ready to end the meditation. This simple visual meditation is an absolutely wonderful mood adjustment or mood setter and can keep family, friends and or intimate relationships intact and sharp. If your focus of this meditation is towards a person I would also like to encourage you to do a live version. Teach them what you've learned in this book and sit face-to-face with them and share your appreciation and gratitude while you're eye to eye. I look forward to hearing about your experiences.

Auditory Meditation

The second sense that most all of us use and many of us take for granted is the ability to hear sounds. Many of us use this sense so much that we subconsciously and sometimes consciously block them out and avoid them as much as possible. In many ways we condition ourselves to the environments that we walk into day after day by having selective hearing. To block out the unnecessary clang and clatter of everyday life sounds and hone in on the necessary vibrations that we need to hear in order to get things accomplished. If we didn't do this we'd probably go crazy!

However, most all of us are drawn to and again condition ourselves to use other sounds and vibrations to drown out the background noise of our lives, which many times is not even real noise but internal dialogue or chatter from our minds.

The power of sound is the most powerful sense that we use in connection to our physical bodies and spiritual existence. Many of us overlook this connection. Think of it this way, we previously discussed the body's orchestra, which is the vibrations that all of the body resonates with consistently. When we really view the body like this we can quickly see that our bodies are a big tuning fork that can be tuned or pinged to resonate on higher frequencies or pitches of sound. Although these sounds may not be heard, science of the human body acknowledges that they are there. Many present studies are being done that show increased brain wave patterns with certain vibration sound waves. If we really want to find truth to this we can look thousands of years in the past and observe many of the types of sound meditations that were created as tools like singing bowls and even chanted or hummed by monks, priests, and even ceremonial rituals from ancient tribes.

Using sources of sound for meditations simply opens up our higher spiritual consciousness. Whether the sounds are just listened to from another median or produced by an individual themselves. Sound vibrations are a masterful tool to connect each of us to our inner self and come in many different ways.

Music

Music has always been a creative force in connecting human consciousness and spirit. Since ancient times music has been used in tribes, cultures, countries, nations and religions as a vibration tool within traditions and rituals. If you thought for a moment of the number of songs that are attached to cultural traditions you would think of many national anthems, rain dances for native Indians, wedding songs, religious songs, commercialized holiday songs and birthday songs as well. Many of these songs, when played, open our intrinsic emotions of love and compassion for the human spirit and elevate us in a higher more blissful state of mind.

The true and awesome power of music is undeniably one of the most powerful sources of meditation in today's modern world. With all of the different Genres from New age, Pop, Hip-Hop, Country, Classical and some Rock and Rap, these forms of music can inspire us and take us to new expressions of awareness in our daily lives.

Think about a song that gives you immense joy and lifts your spirit or improves your attitude or outlook on life. What is the name of that song? Write it here because we will use it later.

Song Title:

Artist:

Now, think about what part(s) of the song that you related to the most, was it the instruments or the words, possibly even both?

Answer:

The sound of music, as it is being made and created, comes from a higher form of intelligence and always resonates on a higher frequency. Whether opera or gangster rap, creating beats, tracks, instrumental combinations and rhythms, it is always certain that it all comes from intuitive inspiration.

Growing up as a child with parents that had a strong attraction and passion to a variety of music blessed me in many ways. I learned to appreciate and see the beauty in many genres and artists. The one thing that has always appealed to me is the artistic poetry that lives in music with lyrics. The lyrics to a heartfelt song are so powerful to most because of the empathetic or sympathetic value that they hold in a story or lesson learned in another human beings life journey. Although sometimes aggressive or hateful lyrics may come out of these songs, there is always a lesson to be learned. It is important to limit yourself from low energy music that creates thoughts of violence, anger or hatred towards anyone or anything. One thing that I love to point out to people is the concept of gangster rap music and the evolution of some of these now grown adults that were a heavy influence into this genre. When you dissect much of their music you hear the aggression that is placed on modern day racism in the world in which at the time they had an inspirational need to express. Although a lot of this rap included vulgarity and I'm sure came with and perpetuated violence, some of the end results restored our freedom of speech by defeating certain realms of censorship. The progression of a lot of this music has died down quite a bit and now we see these gentlemen and ladies as grown adults with healthy families that are thankful for their blessings, respect their creator and acknowledge their gratitude with every opportunity given in front of a camera or the media. You even see what used to be once "hard core gangster rappers" making Disney family movies. I love it! That's the power of all kinds of music. I think, though, if you would ask them what their favorite song in the whole wide world is, they would more than likely give you the name of a song that expressed love, intimacy, compassion and a soft, gentle beat!

No matter what type of music you enjoy, you should always make a habit of finding music that lifts you up and places you in a healthy, peaceful and happy mood. Find songs that you relate to intrinsically and keep them on a list of favorites that you can build and share with others over your lifetime. Sit quietly and listen to the instrumentals, vocals and or words and find your relation to the song or just feel the vibration of the music and observe where it takes you emotionally. Using music as a meditation tool is a great way to stay connected to inspiration and happier days of contentment.

Music Meditation Exercise:

Let's start by taking the first song that I had you list above.

Step 1

First, find the song that you wish to meditate on. If you have the song on your computer or on a compact disc, place it in the computer that you are reading this eBook on.

Step 2

Second, you should find a quite time and or place to listen to the song. Begin with a comfortable and relaxed posture.

Step 3

Next, you need to quiet your mind with simple breathing techniques. Calm your mind and relax your body. When you are relaxed and ready to begin, push play and begin.

Step 4

 Listen to the song from the observational point of view, non-judgment and non-resistance to the emotions or beauty of the words, sounds and vibrational rhythms. Try not to let the song take you into a chain of thoughts from past or imaginative future. Just observe the intrinsic waves of emotion and spirit that absorb your soul.

Step 5

Once the song is finished make sure to stop or pause the music so that you may sit quietly for a minute or two once more.

Step 6

Gently shift your awareness to a pen and a piece of paper or the page below and begin journaling your thoughts of inspiration. You may feel inspired to write a poem or a song yourself. You may just want to express your gratitude towards the musician or songwriter. You may want to interpret what you got out of the song and how it touched your life. Whatever you do don't skip this step. It is life changing when practiced.

Music Meditation

Share your thoughts; write a poem, song or a comment as to your inspiration from the song.

Song:

Artists:

Musician:

Song Writer:

Step 7

Share your inspirations with others by talking, blogging, emailing, or even better, sitting in person with another person or group of people that have the same passions and interests as you.

Mantras and Prayers

Mantras have direct vibration meaning and are to be compared to prayer. A prayer really is in the same context as a mantra whether a ritual that the masses or congregations use to assist or take part in during each sermon, communion or sacrament. A great example of a ritualistic Christian mantra for many is the Lords Prayer:

Our Father, who art in heaven,
hallowed be thy name.
Thy Kingdom come,
thy will be done,
on earth as it is in heaven
Give us this day our daily bread.
And forgive us our trespasses,
as we forgive those who trespass against us.
And lead us not into temptation,
but deliver us from evil.
Amen

It is important to note that sometimes these repetitive prayers quickly become ineffective and lack understanding and sincerity from the individual saying it aloud. I've spoken with several people in relation to this particular prayer and after having them repeat it in one version or the other, verbatim; I would ask them what it really means to them. Most of the people didn't really understand the prayer and admitted that they were just taught to memorize it as a child but almost all of them eventually returned to me remembering that this was a prayer that they turned to in moments of deep fear or extreme insecurity in their lives. The lesson here is that no matter what standard prayer rituals you adopt, it's always important to create a greater awareness and dissect them to make a deeper meaning to your life and your purposes that follow.

Many modern beliefs teach the concept of personalizing prayers into individual conversations with our higher power. Most still teach mantras to begin and finish the spiritual conversation. Here are some examples of these introductions of prayers.

Beginnings: Dear God, Our Heavenly Father, Our father who art in heaven or father.

Most all Christian based religions end with the word; "AMEN!" Amen in this context means, "So be it". However, the word amen really comes from one of the most famous Egyptian Kings that ruled over 1300 years before the birth of Jesus Christ. King Tutankhamun, or who we know as King Tut, translated to "Living Image of Amun". Amun, or as we say it today, Amen, was an Egyptian deity which was acknowledged as the father of all Gods.

The wonderful thing about this widely used ending mantra or closing to a prayer is its true expression. Amen is really the concluding affirmation of your spiritual gratitude. A universal ratification and acknowledgment of belief and unity in our higher power, our God! Again, the lesson of understanding the power of this affirmation has been numbed for centuries by repetition lying on spiritually deaf ears.

Affirmations

Affirmations when created by an individual with true spiritual intentions are extremely powerful. Affirmations normally are simple sentences, paragraphs and sometimes just a word that carry individual spiritual meaning that affirms beyond a positive belief or outcome into absolute knowingness. Unlike prayers that request assistance by our higher power into action, affirmations acknowledge and affirm that action is already being taken.

Developing and using your own mantra, prayer or affirmation is a wonderful foundation in the realm of sound meditations and should be developed and used throughout your daily life.

For this exercise we will create your choice of a personal mantra, prayer or affirmation or all of these. First, here are a couple of examples that I would like to share with you.

My Personal Mantra: I am open, intuitive and receptive to all goodness in my life and all of the abundance that follows.

My Personal Prayer: Dear Heavenly Father, I thank you for my family, my friends and all of those who touch my life each day. Father, please bless them all to keep them safe, healthy and in tune with divine purpose and spiritual wisdom. Amen.

My Personal Affirmation: I am Happy, Calm, Content, And Peaceful.

Interesting Tip: Have you ever noticed when most people say a prayer or mantra the majority of the time they close their eyes. This is for a good reason; taking away the visual sense of the body allows you to create more direct focus on your other senses. In other words, when you take away your vision your sense of hearing becomes more alert. However, don't close your eyes and let your eyeballs fall with your eyelids. Try this: when you close your eyes, do so softly with not a lot of pressure. Afterwards, gently raise your eyes up (while your eye lids are still closed) to look with both eyes right between your eyebrows. Try not to cross your eyes but just look up gently right in the middle point between your eyebrows. If your eyes become strained then use your breath to relax the muscles in the eyes and gently shift your awareness back to the breath. Making this a habit with any prayer or meditation is magical and allows you to go deeper and stay much more focused in your prayer or meditation practice.

Mantra – Prayer – Affirmation Exercise:

My Mantra: This doesn't have to have a title and can be a daily ritual that you can establish in your life to keep you centered and grounded in spirit.

My Mantra –

My Prayer: Whether you choose to use a prayer that you already feel deeply inspires you or create your own like I do. This can also be established as a daily habit and will keep you spiritually alert and healthy.

My Prayer –

My Affirmation: Again, no titles if you don't feel it necessary just words that you affirm to live by that help you stay centered, relaxed, focused, calm and at peace. Forming a daily habit to do this is a must, and is a simple and powerful form of staying connected with intention.

My Daily Affirmation –

Chants

Spiritual Chants are defined as repetitive rhythmic speaking of words or sounds that normally have simple melodies with limited notes. Once again, the Voodoo factor in many western cultures has stereotyped these sound meditations. However, Chants have been used as a spiritual tradition in many cultures from Roman Catholics, Lutheran, Eastern Orthodox, Judaism, African and American Natives. However, most popular in reference to chanting are eastern cultures such as Buddhist and Hindu beliefs. In any case, all of the above mentioned and many more all do chanting with one specific purpose in mind, to give individuals or groups of people a tool to evoke or help people to maintain or grow or tap into our higher consciousness. Chants may also sometimes be referred to as God Sounds; the two most popular of these sounds is "AUM" and sometimes just a "AH". In Hindu cultures, AUM is the sound of white light and purity representing universal energy or the alpha & omega of the cosmos. The sound of AH has been used in many cultures and tends to be considered an angelic sound in many types of spiritual music.

I have learned from Dr. Wayne Dyer in one of his many wonderful and inspirational books called, "Getting in the Gap" the concept and process of Japa meditation that involves the sound of AH. This god sound is used in his book to explain the importance of observing the gaps between thoughts to observe and create a conscious connection to life force energy that exists in everything.

In understanding the fundamentals of chanting as a sound meditation, first become aware that just because you chant AH or AUM does not mean that you are betraying your religion or cultural beliefs. It doesn't mean that you are practicing Buddhism or anything else either. It just means that you are finding another form of meditation to enjoy that will bring you closer to spirituality.

Follow the link below to find out more about these forms of meditation chants. www.GenerationAwareness.org/meditations/chants

As I have mentioned earlier, the true power of sound meditations are incredible and powerful. In the sound meditations that you interact with, whether prayers, mantras, affirmations or chants, using your own voice and creating your own vibrational frequency from within you stimulates your human body to connect to your inner light. I've noticed over the years in my own practices of sound meditations that once you find the sound that works best for you and once you've practiced often enough, the sounds that you use will take you into an almost immediate state of inner awareness and peace. I urge you to make this a daily habit, include it to be as much of a part of your daily rituals as eating. I guarantee you, if you do, life will never ever be the same.

Touch Meditations

Although there are many concepts on touch meditations in eastern cultures, the focus on this section of touch that I speak of is in relation to our true physical sense of touch and how these present and conscious actions transmute into spiritual touch.

In the earlier section of this book when speaking of the major sources of energy for the body, touch was a very important but largely overlooked source of energy in our human existence. When we are able to break away from the fear based boundaries or stigmas of physical touch that plague many cultures and societies today, we can see that the awesome power of touch is truly a wonderful tool that allows us to connect to each other in spirit through physical means. The truth is that we all have the ability to touch each other spiritually, whether through the power of a hand shake, hug, bow, or even a gesture as simple as a smile. What I mean by this is that most of the time we touch people not just physically but by the actions that we take towards them in acts of loving kindness, compassion, passion, tolerance, understanding, forgiveness and so much more.

One of the most powerful and productive ways to touch others is through finding forms of meditation that touch and inspire you. Finding your intrinsic talents and skills that bring passion to your life, along with these expressions and creations of love and self-realization that come from the heart. When these forms of meditation are nurtured, molded and articulated they eventually manifest themselves from your thoughts, hands and actions.

Once again, an example of this is my own passion for writing this book. Whether you're inspired to write a book yourself or create or perform poetry, music, acting, art, photography, dance, or anything else, find the time to indulge yourself into these inspirational gifts as much as possible. Make the time to focus on observing, developing and fine-tuning those talents that keep you connected to your higher purpose and tapped into your true self.

In all reality, if you see this as just finding a hobby or a past time to take your mind off of the hustle and bustle of life, so be it! (Amen) A growing trend of people in all ages and many countries around the world are beginning to shift their awareness in their present jobs and incomes today. We are beginning to see more and more individuals who are getting away from the reformed mindset of expected education as well as income levels. People are beginning to realize that having the biggest house on the block with the fanciest car and earning more money then the Jones' next door doesn't necessarily complete them or fill empty voids that haunt their lives. Many of us are awakening to the call of our higher purposes. Finding ways to use our God given talents to make an income that although lower than their previous jobs comes with much less stress and anxiety. People are beginning to realize that money isn't everything and are taking pay cuts or resigning from high paying positions to focus on talents and skills that get them excited to wake up each morning and begin another day. These new crowds run off of inspirational motivation that allows them to stay in sync with their intentions while following their intuition on a daily basis and connecting to success without even really trying to. This type of success is above money or any tangible item on this earth. This success is called spiritual currency.

Spiritual currency is any act of love that disregards and humbles the human ego while connecting spirit to spirit. A currency that as it is passed forward with no conditions grows stronger in us each time. Whether simple acts of kindness, gifts that we share with the world, concepts that are inspired to help one another or anything that is good in human and spiritual nature. Spiritual currency is a self-perpetuating currency that allows us unlimited abundance and wealth. The wealthiest of those on this earth today with this currency are those who practice giving, teaching, sharing and receiving unconditional love. The question is how much are you worth and can you find ways to increase this source of wealth. By finding your sources of inspiration that you can zone into, you can increase your spiritual currency and live a more fulfilled life than you ever imagined. Even though we can't all quit our jobs tomorrow and do whatever we please, we can still find ways to make a difference in ourselves and others by becoming in tune with and exploring our gifts and talents.

The lesson here is to take the time out to find the passions that elevate your spirit and dive into them as much as possible until you soar. Again, whether you consider this to be meditation or a hobby, don't pass up the chance to expand your life with the things that you love. Even if you don't directly share it with the world or anyone else you'll still pass it forward with your attitude, moods, words, expressions, actions and so forth.

Touch Meditation Exercise

Complete the following exercise by answering the questions first and then following the three steps that follow.

Question: What are your hobbies, talents and skills that give you the most joy in life?

Question: If more than one, which is the closest to your heart that brings out goodness in you?

Question: How often do you get to or take the time to participate in this particular joyful activity?

Question: How often would you like to participate?

Step 1: Create a weekly schedule for what you want to do.

A. Days and Time of the week

B. Supplies needed

C. Location

Step 2: Take the time to perform a 10 to 20 min meditation before beginning.

Step 3: Journal your thoughts at the end of your scheduled time.

www.generationawareness.org/meditation/ctm/exercise

Quick Note: If you feel that you have other hidden talents or skills but just are not sure what they are, use the above exercise to focus on what you might enjoy doing. Just use step 1 as a scheduling tool to focus on quieting your mind and journal your thoughts on the subject that arises.

Many traditional ancient meditation practices have used touch sensory to assist themselves and others into deeper meditations or prayers. Some practices have established mudras which are symbolic gestures that can be complete body postures, however, for the most part, mudras are hand signs that in Buddhist and Hindu beliefs represent energy flow to specific reflexes of the brain and are believed to complete circuits of meridian lines. The most popular meditation and prayer mudras are what are called Gyan mudra, prayer position and just lying hands in the lap.

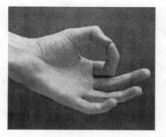

Gyan Mudra – is the placement of the index finger against the thumb. This hand position is mostly used by Buddhist and Hindu cultures and is said to elevate expansion of consciousness and spiritual knowledge.

Lying Hand Mudra – is the placement of hands into the lap with palms in an upward position. Placing the right hand into the left for men and the left hand into the right for women and touching the thumbs from tip to tip. This is the simplest and most common of all mudras that represents an open heart and spirit within unity as one.

Prayer Mudra - The prayer mudra is by far the most widely accepted hand position. Placing the palms of the hands together with fingers extended up towards the face and the head slightly bowed. This represents reverence, balance and peace and is believed to neutralize the right and left hemisphere of the brain representing male and female dominance. In ancient times, yogis would extend their thumbs towards the body and touch their sternum to stimulate the "nerve mind," which is believed to improve not only their higher consciousness, but also improved mental and physical clarity. The prayer mudra hand position is widely represented by Christian faith as seen in many depictions of Jesus Christ. In eastern cultures this mudra or hand position is also commonly used as a formal greeting.

Malas and Prayer Beads

Many traditions incorporate tools as well as mudras / hand signals to practice chanting and prayer meditations. Malas, or what are also known as prayer beads, are the most common touch sensory tools for many prayers or meditations and are used as a counting system for chanting and repetitive prayer mantras or affirmations. Other traditions like Taoism (Yin and Yang) have included touch sensory tools that were adopted by royalty as a precious tool used for calming and centering the mind that created a high-pitched sound when rubbed against each other in circular movements. Let's not forget Catholics use Rosary beads to count prayers as well.

In today's modern world views we still use touch sensory symbols to represent faith and hope in many aspects. In recent years many people have adopted wristbands with specific words and colors to represent unity in belief and prayer for the greater good of humankind. Whether these bands are purchased and worn to give or help with cures for a number of cancers or to support others in harms way, the concept and representation of faith in belief is the same.

The reason these touch sensory tools are the same, whether rosary prayer beads, mala japa beads or a colored wristband, is because of the purpose they all serve. When we wear and use something that touches us daily we form the habit of remembering, and with that comes awareness. This awareness may lead to a scheduled prayer, a moment of silence, a repetitive mantra or affirmation. Most importantly, it leads our minds from the physical touch of something in hand to a spiritual habit that keeps us connected to our inner truths and purpose. It really doesn't matter what you use to remind yourself of staying connected to your greater source, it could be a pebble or rock from the ground, a ring, a bracelet or necklace even a hand full of sand in your pocket. What matters most is making the connection from touch to spirit a habit.

Touch Meditation Exercise

Earlier in the chapter you had an opportunity to create a mantra, prayer or affirmation for yourself. In this exercise you will chose one of the following and find a touch sensory tool to connect with it. Remember the tool that you choose can be anything that you feel intrinsically connects you to the affirmation, mantra or prayer. As mentioned in earlier chapters, a business card can be a powerful touch sensory tool as well. If you feel that a more traditional approach is better, then follow the link to the touch sensory meditation tools below.

www.generationawareness.org/meditations/ts/tools

Step 1   Decide on the meditation that you will use. Mantra / Prayer / Affirmation

Step 2   Choose your touch sensory tool to link your meditation with and decide the count or number of repetitions that you will chant or repeat your mediation in. Some eastern cultures use 108 as a count, if this doesn't work with your daily life or schedule, then I suggest using a number that comes to you while in meditation.

Step 3   Find a simple way to remind yourself of your meditation practice and be consistent everyday. I like to use my cell phone alarm setting to do this, it works great for most people and most have cellular phones that provide several alarms so that you can practice more then once daily. If you don't have these conviences then make a valiant effort to remind yourself in another fashion daily.

Step 4   You can use any meditation you choose that feels right to you.   Whether you find a friend to share or trade the affirmations, mantras or prayers with, continue to observe your own and others. This is a very powerful habit that will benefit your daily life more then you could imagine.

Guided Meditations

Now that we have discovered the three major sensory meditations individually and understand the importance of visualization, sound and touch in meditation, lets combine them all into one with what is called guided meditations or creative visualization meditations. The concept of a guided meditation is just as it sounds, going into a meditative state with someone guiding you through voice. This is also called creative visualization because many times the guide or voice of the person taking you through the mediation will ask you to visualize with your imagination, observe sounds, and feel or sense internal or external movement of inside and outside forces like the wind, the breath, our heart beat or tingling sensations in your fingers and or toes. Guided Meditations are just as beneficial as all other types of meditations and are used to promote good health and balance in life. There are many guided meditations designed for many things. Guided meditations are a wonderful option for starting and developing easy meditation practices and should be considered when creating your own practice.

The following link will direct you to several guided meditations that you can try.   www.generationawareness.org/meditations/gm

Meditation has been a practicing belief for thousand and thousands of years with no questions as to the powerful results that follow from a simple practice. Fortunately, in the last 50 years, science has come around to acknowledge the physiological benefits as well. The number of systems of the body that are improved by meditation range from the endocrine, cardiovascular, nervous systems and so much more. Meditation has also been proven to improve a number of other things not limited to:

- Decreased Blood Pressure
- Coronary Artery Disease
- Depression and Anxiety Disorders
- Chemical Dependencies
- Skin Conditions
- Fibromialgia
- Pain disorders
- Improved T-Cell counts for HIV patients
- ADD and ADHD

Studies done on prayer have proven similar results as well. Prayer has been studied in science and found improved results for cardiac patients, improved blood pressure and more. Prayer studies have actually been done on plants, showing improvement in germination and improved growth as well.

The following web links will guide you to all of the research studies past and present. This page or section of the website when signed into will give you updates on new studies that have been completed and results that have been posted as well as interesting webpages and fascinating books on this particular subject. Share these with your friends and family.

www.generationawareness.com/scienceandmeditation

In the last three hundred years, the quest for tangible and physical proof of knowledge on many, many subjects has defined the human existence. Until recent years and with the improvement of communication many individuals have been left out of the loop. Today technology is providing us with more and more information at our fingertips in an instant, but even with such proof and human intellect, many of us still question so many things in our existence. As mentioned at the beginning of this book, why is it that we make our lives so complicated, complex and questionable? Why is it that we as a species have become accustomed to seeing then believing? A good friend of mine always had a saying, "Believe none of what you hear and half of what you see." After years of this quote, I realized that living by this creed is nothing more then living in a world of doubt and fear. Living with this perception in life that no one can be trusted and things are never as they seem tore at my soul for years. Until the day that I learned to sit quietly and still my mind, then things began to change. Life began to make more sense and I began to work on adjusting my perceptions to many things. The lessons in this book are my evolution in perception to this existence. Each day I begin to open up more and more as a spiritual being and see my path for humanity in this time of the world. I urge you to do the same, find purpose in your life and live it with assertive passion and commitment.

Final Chapter

Harmony in Life

Finding harmony in life may seem like a complex combination of skills that need to be performed daily in order to reach complete prosperity and happiness. In a way, this could be true and we've reviewed and studied several aspects of your life that will serve as tools that can help you to achieve balance and contentment. From changing and observing your attitudes and being aware of yourself in the moment physically, mentally and emotionally; you can certainly make a huge difference in your life and I'm sure that you have begun to discover this for yourself already. You've also discovered that one of the most important tools for a healthy existence is meditation and prayer. However you choose to see it, meditation and prayer are by all means the skill that takes us closest to our inner self, which many of us refer to as our spirit and our connection with our creator. This allows us to connect as we truly are, not just human beings but more importantly "spiritual beings, which are going through a human experience".

The realization of aligning yourself to live in a more harmonious state of consciousness instantly changes everything by providing you with purpose and meaning. You will begin to vibrate on a higher frequency of awareness that excludes the dependency of ego-minded thought processes. Greed, consumption of material life and judgment of your self and others will dissipate. Your resistance of the negative situations in life will fall to the way side as you realize the true power in each lesson that unfolds and how living in this higher consciousness allows you to stay reverent, humble and always in a state of gratitude. As you begin to vibrate higher on this path you'll understand from the inside out that learning to live happy is really learning that happiness is the ego-less state that shares, educates, gives and leads by example in unconditional love towards every one and every thing. You'll find yourself not looking for acceptance or acknowledgment for anything that your ego may want to attach to. Whether it's resisting to give your opinion or criticizing others, you will begin to see that life is not meant to be lived in seclusion and fear, but rather joy, passion, unity and freedom.

Religions Good and Bad

First off, I'm not going to bash any religion nor will I ever. Actually, the concept of structure and organization in unified belief can be a wonderful thing. Having the freedom to believe and say what we choose is a God given right and part of most all democratic unions to date, however, I will give you my view and what seems to be a new generational view that people are starting to share in this day and age.

Religion is a belief and worship of God(s). As our species began to evolve into tribes, clans, colonies, empires, countries and nations, the natural state of herds as a species for protection evolved into intelligent cultures of all kinds, rich with many unique and different traditions. However, as all cultures evolved and humans began to sharpen their skills of thinking and reasoning, they each shared the same quest for truth in a higher power. This quest for GOD has been recorded as far back as 3000 years before the birth of Jesus Christ. Many beliefs were reinterpreted in several ways and from that many religions were born. Each belief had developed their own organization, which preached their way of thinking and seeing what they believed as the truth. Within many of these interpreted beliefs were systems formed in order to create structure to these religions. As people began to adopt these beliefs and organized forms of structured religions, in some cases the consequences have been absolutely devastating. Why do I say this you may ask? Well let's look at what some formed religions have accomplished in the world.

A great example is the earlier civilizations of our so-called humanity when the church was the state and religion was the law. If you were caught gathering or stating your opinion or interpretation of anything different, you were punished, cast out and many times murdered for having a separate view or opinion. *(Jesus Christ is a great example of this tragedy.)*

To understand and conceive the slaughter and mutilation of millions upon millions of souls because of their differences of culture and opinion towards their faith and belief in religion is beyond many. *(Another example is Hitler and the Jews)* When you really sit and think about this for a moment, religion has a two-point prong at the end of it. Many people believe having a rigid or narrow structure of belief when it comes to our creator is wrong because it limits others and sets the scene for judgment in which some unconscious humans have developed an extreme and sometimes bloody thirst for. The second prong is that religion segregates us on many different levels from countries, communities, cultures and even socially. This segregation is not healthy in any way and prevents us from unifying this world and works against us by creating seeds of animosity, jealousy, envy and more. This leads to hate, which is the most profound force of negative energy that has created as well as destroyed many civilizations, as we know them today. A slew of judgmental separatists who hide behind governments, integrated in cultural traditions which continue to fight their holy wars, creating, stock piling and aiming nuclear weapons of mass destruction at one another all the while smiling, shaking hands and pretending to be civil towards one another.

Many of us today believe this is a grave mistake for humanity and the world. Millions and millions of men, women and sadly little children have lost their lives because of these segregated beliefs by human beings that are supposed to be of strict religious faith in every way towards the same God that we all share.

Although religion gives us unity in the intangible belief of our creator and many wonderful rituals and meditations that are important to have as we have just reviewed earlier in this chapter, today many believe that the business of religion and the undeniable greed and need of control of humankind or man has skewed these wonderful concepts of belief and unified faith.

I've often wondered what the power of unified churches could accomplish for humankind and the world. Imagine what could be done with the gross tithing of all organized religions on this earth in one year. I bet it could completely cure major diseases or save and educate millions of starving children.

"Something to think about, isn't it?"

I believe that a universal GOD does not command, condemn, judge or cast aside anything or anyone. Beware of those who judge others by claiming to be the only truth or light on this earth. Most importantly, beware of those religions based on fear, hate, acts of violence and condemnation for not believing every thing they say as the truth. I'll conclude this section with some fascinating quotes from some famous and influential people.

"Religion is a defense against the experience of God".
-Carl Jung

"As far as we can discern, the sole purpose of human existence is to kindle a light of meaning in the darkness of mere being."
-Carl Jung

"My religion consists of a humble admiration of the illimitable superior spirit who reveals himself in the slight details we are able to perceive with our frail and feeble minds."
-Albert Einstein

"I like the silent church before the service begins, better than any preaching."
- Ralph Waldo Emerson

"I believe in God, but not as one thing, not as an old man in the sky. I believe that what people call God is something in all of us. I believe that what Jesus and Mohammed and Buddha and all the rest said was right. It's just that the translations have gone wrong."
- John Lennon

"A cult is a religion with no political power."
- Tom Wolfe

"If you really want to make a lot of money, start your own religion."
- L. Ron Hubbard

A New way of thinking

Let's imagine for one moment that people congregated not just once a week in small masses from individual beliefs, but networked daily in large masses from all religions and beliefs. Let us imagine as well that no one pointed fingers or rolled their eyes at one another; that no one judged one another but just worshiped the same creator whether God, Yahweh, El Elyon, Jehovah, Heavenly Father, etc.; that we all gathered with compassion, understanding, true passion and concern for one another with a concept of open spirituality that taught you and everyone around you the value and importance of creating your own beliefs and interpreting things not as you view or hear them but more importantly how you feel them in your heart. Get your own positive lessons, not just out of scriptures or teachings, but also from spiritual relationships, friendships and the intuitive conversations and experiences that interpret goodness in your life.

Having the ultimate friend, companion, coach, teacher, and philosopher or interpreter, to put all of your trust, faith and belief into, from all of the actions that you create from the outside in and all of the thoughts that create you from the inside out, this is what I'm talking about. The age of a new personal belief that is not based off of fear but off of the understanding of one's self journey and relationship with our creator.

"En" Lighten Up

So, what does it mean to enlighten up, just that, lighten up! Don't allow yourself to be caught up in the guilt game of many fear-based religions and stereotypical cultural-based teachings that if you don't believe exactly what they preach in their way, that you will be cast into a burning lake of fire or forever live eternity in outer darkness. These are incorrect teachings that will do nothing but hinder you from growing spiritually. Allow yourself to find belief, in what you feel to be positive and true in your heart and spiritual mind, so much so that it enlightens your soul in knowingness and pure faith. Take the words of your spiritual friends, guides and or scriptures of your religions and apply them towards your life in a way that feels right to you. Use religious scriptures or parables as teachings and find your meaning and truth.

I know that many will say that this is an easy out without consequences for actions referring to sin and what many of us believe, called karma. Whatever your faith is, do so with an open and non-judgmental spiritual mindset that respects all creation and species alike.

I believe there is a movement of these common beliefs and faith that is growing rapidly in this informational day and age. People are becoming more informed and less fearful than their parents, grandparents and great grandparents. This generation is all about awareness of a higher truth.

Generation Awareness

Generation Awareness stands for many things. It stands for a generation of a new beginning, educating the world public no matter their age, cultural background or heritage. Generation Awareness stands for a generation that needs to go back to the ABC's and start looking at our lives from a more open perspective; an open generational view of our present situation as human beings that inhabit this earth. An understanding of where we are with ourselves as a collective race and why we are in the physical, mental, emotional, spiritual and environmental turmoil at this point in our existence. Most importantly, Generation Awareness stands for the conscious awareness that is clandestine and growing for the good of humankind throughout the world; a new view of common sense philosophy and change that is blooming and spreading in the hearts of many.

This collective thinking must spread in order to break the chains of those who continue to mislead the public into cultural and societal ruts, conforming to past views of tradition that knowingly hurt our species and the one earth that we all share. Teaching an enlightened view of capitalism and politics that neither swings to the right or left in shades of red or blue, but rather to the center with no prejudgments. Leading a global army of peaceful action from all ends of the world to come together and communicate the balance of governments and religion by providing true and sincere examples of our values and morals from within ourselves, our families, our communities, states and nations.

Generation Awareness is a new and universal societal view to provide proof to humankind of the power of open-minded spiritual thinking in unity. A new order of all races, countries, cultures, old and young men, women and children to save our present and future human race and the earth that we inhabit as well. Finally, Generation Awareness is about educating and helping each individual to realize that the only way we can really make a difference or improve humankind is to start from within ourselves. Learn to connect with the positive energy that thrives in each of us. Develop awareness of the beauty and intellect that each of us possesses while learning to let go of our egocentric ways that lead to greed and selfishness. In all, Generation Awareness is the "Effect" of conscious awareness of each person's inner and outer self and the action and power of natural goodness, purity, compassion and love, first for our selves and in doing so for the present and future of all humanity and our world.

Although this is an individual progression for each person, sharing my relationship with our creator and tapping into the unbelievable energy that excites my day, gives me extreme joy and happiness in myself and my life. It provides me with a better and growing consistent awareness of everything around me and helps me to have compassion, love, and understand myself and others. Most importantly this relationship allows me to feel complete and directed as to my true purpose and mission on this earth and in this life. If you haven't figured it out yet, this is it. By giving you these gifts of mind, body and spiritual intellect, I am fulfilling a big part of my purpose and I hope and pray that you will see the same and share this with as many people as possible. I believe this book and the exercises given within it are a powerful tool for life and may help to lead you down a path of greater understanding, peace, joy and happiness.

The greatest part about this is that when you open up your heart and soul just a little bit, when you really want it, it finds you needlessly. It becomes very simple and so very rewarding and floods your spirit with the most powerful knowingness that any sentient being can have, unconditional love, which you naturally share with every thing and every one that crosses, touches or walks with you on your path and journey of life.

Your journey as an Author, C.A. Human

I hope that as you have read and studied these concepts in this book you have been inspired to take action in your life and in others to make a difference.

It is my intention to give you a gift that no author has ever given, "my name and Authorship, C.A. Human" stands for Consciously Aware Human (Being), which is "YOU" and what we should all be striving for in this life experience. This book belongs to all of us and perpetuates egoless selfless living. As C.A. Human, the Author, I am allowing you now to write and share your life story. This book is extended to you so that you may share your own chapters, analogies, poetry, profound statements, expressions and anything else that you believe will inspire, excite, motivate, touch or enthuse people from all walks of life. It is my belief that this intention when shared with others will allow the world to shift in unity. Follow the concepts in this book and use, add to, share and compare your thoughts, experiences and insights with others. You are now the author of this book and have the power to add your own happy ending to make a lifestyle worth living.

4 rules below to help establish a better you in life

How to do this

Technology of the Internet and mobile phones are allowing people to communicate better than ever. Although I agree with many people that much of these savvy technological advances are hurting or impairing our humanity and causing large amounts of stress and anxiety on half the planet's daily lives. I also believe that moderation is once again the answer to living in this highly sophisticated world that we live in. Moderation equates to simplicity, which in this book refers to four easy-to-follow rules:

Rule 1: Use news and media websites as a tool only.

Chaos, chaos, chaos. This is what makes a misunderstood and hectic world go round. News, although sometimes with good intentions mostly thrives off of negativity. Most morning, noon and evening news shows equate to turmoil, gloom and doom as well as fear, more fear, disgust and anger. All of this negative energy bombards us and sabotages our spirit. In conversation with friends and family, I always like to make a point when conversation turns to media events, Hollywood gossip or Wall Street Stock market blunders. How much does it matter and how much do you watch? When you think about it, how much does it matter that a movie star said or did something inappropriate? How much does it matter that another country's foreign minister made acquisitions towards someone else? How much does it matter that the stock market went up and down 200 points in 5 hours? The truth is that it really doesn't matter at all. People say and do things inappropriately in all walks of life. Whether Hollywood or Government royalty, money is made and lost every second of the day. What does matter is that you waste your precious time and thoughts on this daily grind of bull. Here are a few rules to live by when it comes to News and Media.

a. Limit your Daily news to 10 minutes
b. Stay away from shows that gossip and criticize people in the
    spot lights personal lives.

c. Go back to the old fashion way of checking on your invest-
   ments. Read the newspaper or email in the morning once!
   Use technology to alert you if a necessary change in your
   stock portfolio is needed.
d. Find News shows or cable channels to watch that are not all
   negative but rather teach, motivate or inspire you.

If there is something on the news that is pressing your spirit then don't
just sit and watch it happen. Find a way to take action and do it
swiftly. For example, if you are from the USA and you believe that we
should pull our young men and women serving in the military out of
the middle east, then email your state senator and find a group of citizens that believe the same and focus your time on taking action not
watching the news and just worrying about it.

Rule 2: Limit T.V. and Internet as entertainment.

In 2006, USA Today published an article that stated the average
household in America has 2.73 Televisions in their homes with an
average of 2.55 people living in each American home. WOW! This
article also stated that the average television was on for 8 hours daily
and that the average amount of television watched per person daily
was 4 hours and 35 minutes. Here's the scary part, these numbers
are declining because of popularity of the Internet and video games.
It is no wonder that the obesity rate in children has sky rocketed in the
past 10 years, right along with the number of adults taking anti depres-
sants and other medications to help them calm their nerves or help
them sleep.

The truth is that this rule of thumb has been preached over and
over again, limiting yourself from T.V., Internet and Video games
should be as important as eating healthy. Most people are addicted to
all of these forms of stimuli because they have forgotten what else
there is to do in this world besides fixing your eyeballs to a screen that
unconsciously drains your energy level by dulling your scenes and
reality of life. Here are a few things that you can do to distance yourself.

a. Limit the amount of shows that you watch per week. Don't
   allow yourself to get caught up channel surfing and skipping
   from one show to the next until you are mentally drained.
   Choose one or two shows per day and stick to the plan.
   Technology can help you to do this. There are many types of

DVR's or even Internet sites that will allow you to cut the long commercials in between your favorite show while saving your precious time and brainpower. (I also recommend using the Mute Button on your Remote Control during commericals.) Remember though, plan your work and work your plan. Know what you are going to watch and then walk away and do something productive.

b. Plan things to do right after your T.V. show is finished. Go for a walk, get on a treadmill, read a book or meditate quietly for a while. These things will help your mind refresh itself before you begin or end your day.

c. Take the TV's out of the bedrooms, this will allow you to sleep better. I noticed years ago that older people with no family living in the house or single people living alone tend to always have TV's in their bedrooms. In correlation with this, most of these people had sleeping difficulties and got hooked on sleeping medications and so on. Many times all it would take was removing the T.V. out of the bedroom and giving them something relaxing to do before they lay down. Also don't allow your kids to have a T.V. in their room. Make them go outside or interact with a friend or relative. Many children today are becoming socially impaired because of this and lack normal communication skills that are necessary for life.

Rule 3: Take vacations from all technology.

This should be a new age biblical rule, if any. Get away and reconnect with your family, friends or people you don't even know. Don't take your mobile phone with you all the time everywhere you go. Don't check your personal email every hour on the hour. Don't text message a conversation if you can talk to a person in person. These rules imply sanity in the modern world today and should become a normal part of getting in tune with yourself and others.

a. Take a day or two out of the week to fast from T.V., Video Games and Internet. Moderation, again, is the key when it comes to technology. Set a day of the week and stick to it.

b. Plan a day and or time of day that the cell phone is actually turned off, out of sight and mind. Let everyone know this time and or day and give those people that may need to contact you in an emergency situation with an alternate route that doesn't involve stress for you

c. Go on a yearly vacation and leave your cell phone, work phone, emails and everything to do with technology behind you. Let it go and reconnect to real people and most importantly you.

Rule 4: *Find productive inspiration in technology as a tool.*

The real meaning of this rule is to use technology for what it's worth. Don't overuse these gifts of technology to bombard or numb your senses, but to guide and help you become more productive and efficient with time and money, therefore creating more time to work on personal and self relationships.

Use technology as a tool to connect you to motivational and educational tools that give you structure and inspire you and others in your daily life. Use technology to connect with your greater purposes in life and to unite with others that share the same beliefs and want to shift this awareness towards real results to better the world. Use technology to express yourself in thought, art, and knowledge or with any other positive influence that you can think of.

This is the reason that I created this book and created generationawareness.org, to allow all of us to make a difference and come together as one world generation. One generation that is ageless, colorless, cultureless, non-segregated, just an open source, nonjudgmental society sharing and inspiring each other with greater awareness and insight towards our mind, body and spirit. Our awareness must lead us to creating a shift in our collective thoughts as a species to be of service to one another by revisiting old truths that have been overlooked, misinterpreted or forgotten and developing new truths and new ways of consciousness that must come to pass in order to protect our earth, ourselves, our children and their futures.

Generationawareness.org provides you with all of the tools and exercises within this book that will assist you for a healthier lifestyle and provide you with the means to form positive daily habits in mind, body and spirit. You will become a powerful piece of the puzzle, a unique source of energy that will help to mold this collective vision that many are beginning to take part in all over the world.

It is my prayer, my belief, and my intention to perpetuate what many of us know as a critical mass of higher consciousness on a global level. This book and these concepts that have evolved can be used as a great source to stay linked and tapped in as a growing and consciously aware human being.

Remember that these life lessons and the greater knowledge and spiritual enlightenment that you acquire from all of this has nothing to do with being better, knowing more, having one up on the less fortunate, intelligent or less in tune people on this earth. But rather learning that we are all equal beings that share the same quest to better ourselves on this human journey and find our highest purpose of all, how to share, give, receive, acknowledge and experience unconditional love. All of this begins with you understanding and unconditionally loving yourself. So make sure to nurture yourself and everyone around you. Find and surround yourself with people that will not judge you but lift your spirit high so that you can be free, people that will accept you taking off the mask and showing your true spiritual face. Create healthy habits that equally promote a healthy mind, body and spirit. Free yourself and others from judgment, criticism and always learn from and practice forgiveness. Most importantly always remember that your inspiration is more powerful than you could ever imagine so never be afraid or hesitate to share it with others. Find your gifts and use them for as long as you live, moment-to-moment, day-to-day and throughout all of the years of your journey! Stand tall and stay humble by letting go of your ego and know that you are supported by millions and millions that feel the same. **Listen from your heart and live in spirit!**

To Be Continued...

Sincerely,
C.A. Human

Bibliography

William James, the father of American physiology, Pragmatist philosopher & psychologist (1842 - 1910) Page 8

Earl Nightingale, "Lead the Field", Nightingale Conant Publishing Page 37, 47, 49

Psychologist , Author, Motivational Speaker, Zig Ziglar, "How to be A Winner" Page 21, 47

Napoleon Hill , "Think and grow rich" Page 34, 46, 47

Anthony Robbins "Awaken the Giant within" page 34, 35

Psychologist & Author William McDougall (1871– 1938). Death Bed studies 39

Lia Scallon, "The Sounds of Sirius", http://www.soundsofsirius.com/artic_healpower.htm , , Organization SOS, Last viewed July, 2009, Page 48

Stewart Dawes & Dr. Valerie Hunt, "The Science of Human Vibration", http://www.freshmag.com.au/science.html Fresh Magazine, Sydney, Au. Last viewed July of 2009. Page 48

Public Broadcast Services Inc. "Timeline: Life and Death of Electric Car" http://www.pbs.org/now/shows/223/electric-car-timeline.html Jumpstart Productions, Last viewed July, 2009 page 56

WATER

Environmental Protection Agency. "Online Training in Watershed Management", http://www.epa.gov/watertrain/cwa/ , EPA, Last updated November 17th, 2008, Last viewed July, 2009 Page 62 to 63

Environmental Protection Agency, "Clean Water Act (CWA)", http://www.epa.gov/oecaagct/lcwa.html , EPA, Last updated June

18th 2009, Last viewed July 2009 Page 62 to 63

http://www.lcv.org/images/client/pdfs/2004_cand_profiles_.pdf, page 62, 63 http://100777.com/node/1639,

Author, Larry West, About.com Environmental Issues, "Why is Chlorine Added to Tap Water?", http://environment.about.com/od/earthtalkcolumns/a/chlorine.htm, About.com a part of New York Times Company, Last viewed July, 2009. Page 62, 63

Wikipedia.org, "Trihalomethanes", http://en.wikipedia.org/wiki/Trihalomethanes , Last updated June 18th of 2009, Last viewed July, 2009. Pages 63

NUTRITION

Authors, Dr. T. Colin Campbell & Thomas M. Campbell II, "The China Study", BenBella Books Publishers, Pages 85 to 86.

Worldhealth.net, "1 in 3 Americans are Overweight or Obese", http://www.worldhealth.net/news/1_in_3_americans_are_overweight_or_obese, Tarsus Group plc. Last viewed July, 2009. Page 66

American Heart Association, "Over Weight and Obesity Statistics, Updated 2008" http://www.americanheart.org/downloadable/heart/1197994908531FS16OVR08.pdf, AHA inc. Last viewed July, 2009. Pages 66

International Food Information Council, "Overweight, Obesity & Weight Management", http://www.ific.org/nutrition/obesity/index.cfm IFIC.org, Last viewed July 2009 Pages 66

NewTreatments.org, "Food Combining", http://www.newtreatments.org/FoodInfo/ga/458/Food%20combining:%20Don't%20mix%20carbs%20with%20proteins%20or%20fats , Last viewed July, 2009. Pages 70 to 71

Health & Beyond online, Author Dr. Herbert M. Shelton, "Nine rules for proper food combining", http://www.chetday.com/fcprins.html , Last viewed July, 2009. Pages 70 to 71

Dr. Herbert Shelton, Food Combining Made Easy, Copyright Publication **Date**: June 1940. **Publisher**: Willow Publishing , **Page 70, 71**

http://www.dmanisi.org.ge/ImportanceofDmanisi.html , "Cradle of the first Europeans", Last viewed July, 2009 Pages 78, 79, 80

National Geographic, April 2005 edition, Author John Fichman, Title: Dmansi Find, page 78, 79, 80

http://www.milksucks.com/osteo.asp, page 81, 82

Author, Pete Hardin, "…because the FDA says it's safe?" http://www.themilkweed.com/Feature_07_Sep.pdf , Last viewed July, 2009 Page 81, 82

Author Mitch Cohen, http://articles.mercola.com/sites/articles/archive/2001/08/25/milk-part-three.aspx , Dr. Joseph Mercola Website, Last viewed July, 2009 Pages 81, 82

Authors Sheldon Rampton & John Stauber, "Monsantos and Fox: Partners in Censorship", http://www.primitivism.com/monsanto.htm , Last viewed July, 2009 Page 81, 82

Author, Paul Goettlich, "Conduits of Life", http://www.mindfully.org/Food/Why-Eat-Organic-Food.htm, Page 81

*** http://www.gracelinks.org/, page 81

Author, Donna Feldman MS, RD. "The Glycemic Index or GI Diet", http://www.thedietchannel.com/the-glycemic-index-diet , Last viewed July 2009. Page 87, 88

Wikipedia.org, http://en.wikipedia.org/wiki/Glycemic_index#Criticism , Last updated and viewed on July 12th, 2009 page 87, 88

Author Shane Ellison, "Skeletons in the FDA's Closet", http://www.newswithviews.com/Ellison/sharne5.htm , Last viewed July, 2009. Pages 100, 101

Author Shane Ellison, "Lipitor A Closer Look", http://www.newswithviews.com/Ellison/sharne6.htm , Last viewed July, 2009.Pages 100, 101

Duane Graveline MD MPH, "A Critical Review of Statins", http://www. spacedoc.net/statins_a_critical_review.htm ,Last viewed July, 2009. Pages 100, 101

"Seniors", http://www.bravehealth.com/seniors.htm , Last viewed July, 2009. Page 105

National Institute of Arthritis and Musculoskeletal and skin disease, "Living with Arthritis" http://www.niams.nih.gov/Health_Info/Arthritis/default.asp ,Last viewed July, 2009. page 105, 106

"Ottawa Panel Evidence-Based Clinical Practice Guidelines for Therapeutic Exercises in the Management of Rheumatoid Arthritis in Adults" http://www.ptjournal.org/cgi/reprint/84/10/934.pdf , Journal of the American Physical Therapy Association, Last viewed July, 2009. Pages 117, 118

Outwitting Insomnia, author: Ellen Mohr Catalon, Publisher; New Harbinger Pubns Inc Copyright; November 1990 Pages 230, 231

http://www.sleepfoundation.org, Last viewed July, 2009. Pages 230, 231

Author Elisabeth Scott M.S. "Sleep Benefits: Power Napping for Increased Productivity, Stress Relief & Health" http://stress.about.com/od/lowstresslifestyle/a/powernap.htm, Pages 229 to 231

Author, Judy Rigby, "The Importance of Touch", http://www.chisuk.org.uk/articles/result.php?key=63 , Last viewed July, 2009. page 232, 233

"Physcogenic Diseases in Infancy", Distributed by New York University Film Library, Copyright 1952, Produced by, Rene A. Spitz M.D. page 232, 233

Dr. Tiffany Fields Touch Research Institute, http://www6.miami.edu/touch-research/, Last viewed July, 2009. Pages 233, 234

Chakra Breathing; Helmut G. Sieczka: translated from the German and edited by Jalaja Bonheim, copyright Life Rhythm 1994, page 245, 246

Getting in the Gap; Author, Dr. Wayne Dyer: Published by Hay House Inc., Copyright 2003; page 265

USA TODAY NEWSPAPER, "Average Home has more TV's than People", http://www.usatoday.com/life/television/news/2006-09-21-homes-tv_x.htm, Last viewed July, 2009. page 284

Visit **GenerationAwareness.org** today to reference several related Books, CD's, Workshops, Seminars and more. I look forward to visiting with you soon!

LaVergne, TN USA
20 May 2010
183385LV00004B/1/P

9 781608 441631